CULTURE & CONTEXT
IN HUMAN BEHAVIOR CHANGE

Joseph L. DeVitis & Linda Irwin-DeVitis
GENERAL EDITORS

Vol. 27

PETER LANG
New York • Washington, D.C./Baltimore • Bern
Frankfurt am Main • Berlin • Brussels • Vienna • Oxford

CULTURE & CONTEXT IN HUMAN BEHAVIOR CHANGE

Theory, Research, and Applications

CLIFFORD R. O'DONNELL & LOIS A. YAMAUCHI
EDITORS

PETER LANG
New York • Washington, D.C./Baltimore • Bern
Frankfurt am Main • Berlin • Brussels • Vienna • Oxford

Library of Congress Cataloging-in-Publication Data

Culture and context in human behavior change: theory, research, and applications /
edited by Clifford R. O'Donnell, Lois A. Yamauchi.
p. cm. — (Adolescent cultures, school, and society; v. 27)
Includes bibliographical references and indexes.
1. Change (Psychology). 2. Social psychology. 3. Environmental psychology.
I. O'Donnell, Clifford R. II. Yamauchi, Lois A.
III. Series: Adolescent cultures, school & society; v. 27
BF637.C4C85   302—dc22   2004018153
ISBN 0-8204-6902-5
ISSN 1091-1464

Bibliographic information published by **Die Deutsche Bibliothek**.
Die Deutsche Bibliothek lists this publication in the "Deutsche
Nationalbibliografie"; detailed bibliographic data is available
on the Internet at http://dnb.ddb.de/.

Cover design by Joni Holst

The paper in this book meets the guidelines for permanence and durability
of the Committee on Production Guidelines for Book Longevity
of the Council of Library Resources.

© 2005 Peter Lang Publishing, Inc., New York
275 Seventh Avenue, 28th Floor, New York, NY 10001
www.peterlangusa.com

All rights reserved.
Reprint or reproduction, even partially, in all forms such as microfilm,
xerography, microfiche, microcard, and offset strictly prohibited.

Printed in the United States of America

This volume is dedicated, with much aloha and appreciation, to the person whose work continues to inspire us all:

Roland G. Tharp

Contents

Acknowledgments ix

Section I: Introduction

Chapter 1. Considering the Context of Behavior Change:
A Volume in Honor of Roland G. Tharp 3
LOIS A. YAMAUCHI AND CLIFFORD R. O'DONNELL

Section II: Psychology and Behavior Change
EDITOR: CLIFFORD R. O'DONNELL

Chapter 2. Behavior Therapy: Regulation by Self, by Others, and
by the Physical World. 13
IAN M. EVANS

Chapter 3. Child Development and Changing Behavior
in Diverse Societies: An Activity Settings Approach 41
ASHLEY E. MAYNARD

Chapter 4. Community: The Ties That Bind 63
RICHARD N. ROBERTS

Chapter 5. Juvenile Delinquency: Peers, Mentors, and
Activity Settings 85
CLIFFORD R. O'DONNELL

Section III: Education and Teacher Development
EDITOR: LOIS A. YAMAUCHI

Chapter 6. Culture Matters: Research and Development
of Culturally Relevant Instruction 103
LOIS A. YAMAUCHI

Chapter 7. The Contribution of Settings to School Improvement
and School Change: A Case Study 127
WILLIAM M. SAUNDERS AND CLAUDE N. GOLDENBERG

Chapter 8. Extending Instructional Conversation 151
GORDON WELLS AND MARI HANEDA

Chapter 9. School Reform and the Education of Culturally
and Linguistically Diverse Students 179
AMANDA DATNOW, SAMUEL C. STRINGFIELD,
AND MARISA CASTELLANO

Section IV. Conclusion
EDITORS: LOIS A. YAMAUCHI AND CLIFFORD R. O'DONNELL

Chapter 10. Behavior Change in the Natural Environment:
Everyday Activity Settings as a Workshop of Change. . . . 207
RONALD GALLIMORE

Chapter 11. Man of Knowledge and Conviction:
Biographical Tribute to Roland Tharp 233
LISA TSOI HOSHMAND

Contributors 257

Author Index 259

Subject Index 269

Acknowledgments

This volume was a collective effort, made possible by many people. We thank our chapter authors for their important contributions and help in shaping the completed work. We are especially grateful to Ronald Gallimore for his concluding chapter, initial idea for the book, and recruitment of us as the editors.

Mark Nakamura and Tasha Wyatt were also important to this volume. Mark prepared the camera-ready copy and Tasha prepared the indices. Their pride in their work, thoughtful suggestions, and cheerful dispositions made working with them truly pleasurable, and we extend a warm mahalo.

Finally, we are grateful to Barbara McKenna for assisting us in acquiring the photo of Roland Tharp, Ashley Maynard for the cover photo of the Mayan children, for technical assistance provided by Valerie Dutdut and, as always, warm support from Barbara O'Donnell and Tracy Trevorrow.

Clifford R. O'Donnell
Lois A. Yamauchi

Section I
Introduction

CHAPTER 1

Considering the Context of Behavior Change: A Volume in Honor of Roland G. Tharp

Lois A. Yamauchi
Clifford R. O'Donnell

This volume was inspired by the work of Professor Roland G. Tharp, who is known and appreciated for theory and research over 40 years on changing behavior in family therapy, behavior therapy and modification, community interventions, teacher development, and educational interventions designed to reduce the achievement gap in disadvantaged communities. Throughout his career, Tharp's primary interest has been the development of principles of behavior change and the testing of their validity in realistic applications and settings. The purpose of this book is to examine current theory, research, and applications in initiating and maintaining behavior change across many of the fields in which Tharp has worked. These topics are important both for individual well-being and program effectiveness.

Although the chapters in this volume represent a diversity of domains, they are united by a focus on the social and cultural context. Early approaches to behavior change focused on individual psychotherapy and psychological interventions. More recently, conceptions and approaches have broadened to incorporate the role of contexts. In juvenile delinquency, there has been a shift from a search for the "magic bullet" to "correct" the character of delinquents to a growing understanding of the influence of family, school, neighborhood, and peer contexts on the development and prevention of delinquent behavior (Howell, 2003). The field of community psychology has been defined by the importance of context. Context is the unit of analysis, the basis for theory, and the guiding principle for methodology and program development (Revenson et al., 2002).

In fields traditionally focused on individual change, such as behavior therapy, there is increasing attention to the influence of context (Evans, this volume). Developmental psychology previously focused on how children's thinking changed when they experimented with the material world and tried to make sense of what they found (Piaget, 1975). While these ideas continue to be important, developmental scholars now emphasize understanding the skills and knowledge valued by a child's community and the role of parents, teachers, peers, and other significant people in children's learning and development (Maynard, this volume; Rogoff, 2003; Wood, 1988).

In education, there has also been a shift from a consideration of the learner in isolation to a focus on the social context of teaching and learning (Tharp & Gallimore, 1988; Wood, 1988). Such a perspective acknowledges that students' prior experiences, both in and out of school, influence academic outcomes (Tharp, Estrada, Dalton, & Yamauchi, 2000). Effective instruction involves the creation of school settings that facilitate learning, including the integration of students' prior knowledge with new information presented.

A focus on the context of schooling is reflected in current educational research. Teachers are also viewed as learners, whose behaviors are influenced by the social and cultural context (Tharp & Gallimore, 1988). Attention is paid to the professional development settings designed to change teachers' behaviors, as well as to the role of educational policy on classroom and school level outcomes.

Our evolving understanding of behavior change as situated in social and cultural contexts can be found scattered across many fields and publication outlets, obscuring the emergence of common principles and findings. This volume brings together an interdisciplinary perspective on initiating and maintaining behavior change. The chapters reflect various behavioral and social disciplines, including education and developmental, clinical, and community psychology. The authors summarize what is known about changing human behavior, identify new research challenges, and highlight Tharp's influence on advances in their fields.

Evans focuses on self-regulation of behavior as Tharp's contribution to behavior therapy, and places this within behavior therapy's theory of change. In doing so, Evans integrates the different types of behavior therapy using a set of universal principles. He begins by describing the foundation of behavior therapy, classical and instrumental conditioning, continues to discuss the relationship of cognition and affect, and concludes with the influence of and implications for self-regulated behavior.

In integrating the different behavior therapies into a unified theory of change, Evans notes Tharp's important role in recognizing that behavior therapy exists within "complex spheres of social influence" (p. 16) that are provided by culture. Within this context, classical and instrumental conditioning become "models of behavioral responsiveness to situational regularities" (p. 36). Evans concludes that as behavior therapy addresses problems created by experiences in the environment, it is not enough to only attend to individual behaviors. Effective therapy must also address the social context of those behaviors, placing the person within his or her culture.

From her perspective as a developmental psychologist, Maynard presents the increasingly important role of culture in human behavior change. As she notes, "changing behavior is at the heart of developmental psychology" (p. 56). Further, "knowing about the cultural context enhances the understanding of processes of change" (p. 41). Maynard uses activity setting theory, to which Tharp has made valuable contributions, to explicate the influence of culture on behavior change. She begins by examining how Tharp and his colleagues analyzed the activity settings of Native Hawaiian and Navajo children to design classroom educational practices to be more compatible with their cultures and, thereby, improve academic achievement.

Using Tharp's work with Native Hawaiian and Navajo children as a template, Maynard shows (a) how the analysis of activity settings can be used to bridge cultures between parents and teachers for the benefit of Latino students, (b) how changes in the schooling of mothers and siblings can affect child-rearing and sibling-interaction, and (c) how the effects of socioeconomic changes can be better understood. She concludes with an analysis of how the influence of culture is shifting the activity settings of research and how these behavior changes will transform developmental psychology.

Roberts describes his personal, intellectual, and professional development, beginning as a graduate student in Tharp's seminar, to illustrate the values, methods, and defining characteristics of community psychology. Using his own research programs as examples, Roberts distills six principles for community action research and provides guidance for the implementation of these principles. In addition, he exemplifies a process that is essential to the advancement of the field: the creation of a community of learners—colleagues who engage in joint productive activity, develop "ties that bind," and create new knowledge in the process.

Roberts' first experience in a community of learners was with Tharp and colleagues engaged in the study of cognition in younger children. Later, influenced by Tharp and through the creation of his own community of learners, Roberts came to understand that cognition is a community process, "not a function of isolated development, but rather that of interdependent framing of issues, ideas, and ways of being that were created in the cauldron of meaningful activity with others" (p. 65). He recognized that it was the development of intersubjectivity, or shared understanding, that leads to new knowledge.

Tharp's work on the integration of cultural practices in education for Hawaiian students was an early model for Roberts' own community action research projects. Roberts reviews these projects, noting both the mistakes and the successes. He relates the values and methods of these activities to those aspired to in community psychology for families, communities, and service support systems that are now exemplars for action research in community psychology.

O'Donnell traces the current emphasis on mentoring in delinquency prevention back to Tharp's use of natural mentors in his Arizona program in the late 1960s. He shows how this program led to current research on the importance of social networks, including the key role of peer networks, in the facilitation or inhibition of delinquency (Tharp, 2003). O'Donnell presents the implications of this research for the future of delinquency prevention, including the need for major changes in assessment, program design and, ultimately, the juvenile justice system itself.

Yamauchi reviews research on culturally relevant instruction, pedagogy that is compatible with the values and expectations of students' cultural backgrounds. Highlighting Tharp's contributions to this field, she presents his research at the Kamehameha Early Education Program (KEEP) as a model for designing and implementing culturally relevant instruction. She uses Tharp's work as a backdrop to describe four cultural dimensions that make a difference in classrooms (Tharp et al., 2000). She also discusses three current issues in this area: (a) insider-outsider researcher tensions, (b) stereotyping and simplification, and (c) how to address the needs of heterogeneous classrooms. Her chapter provides evidence that culture does matter in classrooms and schools, a position long held by Tharp, but unacknowledged by many when he first began his research on this topic 30 years ago.

Saunders and Goldenberg apply concepts developed by Tharp to analyze how one school improved student performance (i.e., changed student behavior) through the establishment of settings designed to change teachers' instruction. They studied the effects of teacher professional development at Pine, an urban elementary school serving a diverse group of students, many of whom were English language learners and a majority of whom qualified for free or reduced lunch. Academic achievement at Pine increased steadily over the five years of their study, rising from the 27th to the 60th percentile rank and surpassing district averages.

Saunders and Goldenberg analyze changes in faculty meetings and other settings at Pine that contributed to teachers' improved instruction and student achievement. They emphasize how Tharp's research on behavioral and organizational change influenced their own work: *"Rousing Minds to Life* (Tharp & Gallimore, 1988) directed our attention towards the fundamental challenge of creating schools that are vibrant and productive learning contexts for both teachers and students" (p. 128). Tharp's research on activity settings analysis and intervention is also reflected in the authors' focus on how behavior change is initiated and maintained by a network of settings.

Datnow, Stringfield, and Castellano investigate the extent to which comprehensive school reform (CSR) models address the needs of culturally and linguistically diverse students. They present results of a four-year case study of 13 schools serving multilingual and multicultural student populations and also implementing a CSR model. The work integrates "two of the most rapidly developing areas in school improvement research: (a) identifying practices that improve education for culturally and linguistically diverse students, and (b) examining the implementation and outcomes of [CSR] models" (p. 180). Inspiration for this study came directly from Tharp, who encouraged the authors to extend their research on CSR to focus on educational practice for diverse students.

Applying the research of Tharp and others, Datnow et al. identify the ways in which popular CSR models help and hinder efforts to promote the cultural identities of students in schools and the ways in which educators' perceptions about student diversity interacts with their ideas about school reform. This work is important because, although current educational policy has increased adoption of CSR models in many schools, most models do not explicitly provide guidance for implementation in different linguistic and cultural contexts.

Wells and Haneda provide a comprehensive discussion of the instructional conversation, a pedagogical method that incorporates both conversational and instructional elements. They note that although many had criticized transmission-oriented classroom discourse, it was not until Tharp and Gallimore (1988) "coined the term 'instructional conversation' (IC) and provided an explicit model of what an IC entails that the significance of this rather general recommendation became the focus of systematic practice and research" (p. 151).

The goal of Wells and Haneda's chapter is to extend our understanding of IC, both in terms of theory and application. The authors review the theoretical foundations of IC and make linkages between it and other theoretical perspectives from psychology, education, and linguistics. Their points are highlighted by examples of ICs in a wide range of classrooms and subject areas, including a third grade multilingual social studies class and a graduate seminar in education.

Gallimore synthesizes the previous chapters of this volume and distills common elements of behavior change across multiple disciplines. He cites Tharp's contributions to these general principles; for example, identifying Tharp and Wetzel's (1969) book *Behavior Modification in the Natural Environment* as a landmark in directing attention to consideration of the social context:

> Their book presented and illustrated a behavior change paradigm sharply contrasted to prevailing practice: The "natural environment" for Tharp and Wetzel included two components: (a) Interactions within existing social relationships, and (b) the settings, in which those relationships were situated (p. 207).

Gallimore elaborates on socially situated settings and their role in behavior change. He traces the historical and theoretical foundations of using the natural environment as the context of intervention. Drawing on examples from previous chapters and from Tharp's work in many domains, Gallimore outlines characteristics of settings important for change, discusses why change is so difficult, and suggests future research challenges.

Culture and Context in Human Behavior Change: Theory, Research, and Applications is an interdisciplinary volume that covers the fields of clinical, developmental, and community psychology, delinquency prevention, and education. In all of these areas, Roland Tharp has made significant contributions and has helped us to see that there are universal principles that operate in all spheres of human activity. It is impressive that Tharp has influenced so many researchers, students, teachers, families, and communities. As his life and work has inspired so many, we conclude this volume with Hoshmand's biographical chapter on Tharp. Her account provides insights into how he was able to make so many important contributions to such seemingly diverse fields. This accomplishment becomes even more amazing when we consider his award-winning achievements in poetry and film direction, also described in this short biography. Hoshmand concludes with a career summary and listing of Tharp's awards and publications, a resource that invites further exploration and is filled with the promise of continuing to rouse our minds to life.

References

Howell, J. C. (2003). *Preventing and reducing juvenile delinquency: A comprehensive framework.* Thousand Oaks, CA: Sage.

Piaget, J. (1975). *Equilibration of cognitive structures.* Chicago: University of Chicago Press.

Revenson, T. A., D'Augelli, A. R., French, S. E., Hughes, D. L., Livert, D., Seidman, E., Shinn, M., & Yoshikawa, H. (Eds.) (2002). *A quarter century of community psychology: Readings from the American Journal of Community Psychology.* New York: Academic/Plenum.

Rogoff, B. (2003). *The cultural nature of human development.* New York: Oxford University Press.

Tharp, R. G. (2003). Juvenile delinquency: Culture and community, person and society, theory and research. In C. R. O'Donnell (Ed.), *Culture, peers, and delinquency* (pp. 1–11). New York: Haworth Press.

Tharp, R. G., Estrada, P., Dalton, S. S., & Yamauchi, L. A. (2000). *Teaching transformed: Achieving excellence, fairness, inclusion, and harmony.* Boulder, CO: Westview.

Tharp, R., & Gallimore, R. (1988). *Rousing minds to life: Teaching, learning, and schooling in social context.* Cambridge: Cambridge University Press.

Tharp, R. G., & Wetzel, R. (1969). *Behavior modification in the natural environment.* New York: Academic Press.

Wood, D. (1988). *How children think and learn: The social contexts of cognitive development.* Oxford, UK: Blackwell.

SECTION II

Psychology and Behavior Change

Clifford R. O'Donnell

Editor

CHAPTER 2

Behavior Therapy: Regulation by Self, by Others, and by the Physical World

Ian M. Evans

Behavior therapy, derived from principles of conditioning and learning, is indisputably the most successful method of clinical intervention yet developed. It is successful not only by becoming a dominant professional school, but more importantly by virtue of its beneficial results across a wide range of human problems. Although the field has now eroded into different areas—applied behavior analysis on one pole and cognitive-behavior therapy on the other—the cracks and fault lines are mostly on the surface. Beneath them lies a substratum of behavior regulation principles that has proved stable enough to support a variety of new influences, some indistinguishable from the original, others layered more permeably on top of the old. To this foundation of theory, principle, and application, Roland Tharp has made a significant contribution by showing that the design of situations of interpersonal influence for the alteration of maladaptive behavior (psychotherapy) can include structuring one's own repertoire to improve the ability to self-regulate. The purpose of this essay is to place his contribution in contemporary perspective, articulating in the process behavior therapy's theory of change.

Autonomy and Control

Across many editions of a popular text, Watson and Tharp (e.g., 1977) laid out a map of principles encompassing self-directed change that would allow individuals to gain greater control over their own lives. Self-modification was an enigmatic concept at the time, with the presumed primacy of external manipulation and control of behavior by others having long been a philosophical flashpoint for behavior therapy (Evans, 1997). The original conflict was best captured in the debate between Carl Rogers and B. F. Skinner (1956), the geopolitical *zeitgeist* for which had been the preservation of individual freedoms in democracies, as opposed to state regulation apparently inherent in communist dictatorships. Literary works such as *Brave New World* and *1984* conveyed profound warnings against bureaucratic control. In the old Soviet Union political dissent could result in psychiatric hospitalization. Thomas Szasz argued that *all* psychiatric intervention was no more than social oppression, a viewpoint reinforced in movies like "One Flew Over the Cuckoo's Nest" and "A Clockwork Orange."

Against this backdrop, Rogers championed personal choice and self-determination; therapy should promote freedom and self-actualization. Skinner countered that the laws of behavior revealed free-will to be illusory. Human behavior is determined. Only by understanding the principles could one hope to win even partial release from negative control by others (Skinner, 1974). While many critics remained unconvinced, radical behaviorists felt the case had been made and continued using unfortunate terms like behavioral "engineering." Regrettably, restricting patients' access to basic comforts so that these could be used as rewards for "appropriate" behavior became an acceptable practice, as did the use of contingent electric shock and other aversive procedures.

The Natural Social Environment

Tharp and Wetzel's (1969) community-based program in Arizona was the first systematic work in behavior therapy to address the reality that interventions did not have to be delivered by trained therapists. In fact it was even better to teach behavior change skills to those people in the client's life who were the most authoritative, either through their access to meaningful rewards or simply because previous social learning histories had given them influence. This realization was soon translated to procedures whereby teachers, parents, even peers, could be targeted as the individuals whose modified behavior would in turn influence the designated client. The concept was not entirely new. Some of the earliest demonstrations of behavior analysis had revealed the influence exercised by nurses in residential psychiatric settings (e.g., Ayllon & Michael, 1959). These staff, however, were still professionals, in positions of power. The significance of Tharp's work was to show it was the individuals in the *natural* environment who exerted so much influence. More telling, theoretically, was the realization that if certain people can differentially effect change, then the special relationship between therapist and client must be important to behavior therapy outcomes (Wilson, Hannon, & Evans, 1968).

Reciprocal Interpersonal Influences

Understanding control in the context of relationships was particularly important for marital therapy, one of Tharp's earliest interests. The fundamentals of intimate relationships—love, communication, mutual support—had not been easily captured within a behavioral framework. The earliest versions of behavioral marital therapy had come from Stuart's (1969) model that marriage involved the reciprocal exchange of rewards. Treatment meant training couples to reinforce each other on a *quid pro quo* basis. The concept of reciprocal influence was not unrecognized in radical behaviorism, whose advocates had always enjoyed the classic cartoon of two rats lounging in a Skinner box, one saying to the other "Boy, have I got this guy conditioned! Every time I press this lever he drops in a pellet of food." Humans, however, can estimate accumulated costs and benefits. So Weiss (Weiss & Heyman, 1997) proposed instead that in successful relationships the numerous small items of help and affection accrue, much like a savings account builds credit. From this reorientation behavioral marital therapy shifted towards improving communication and negotiating skills.

But this was still a deficit orientation, with the process of change being the acquisition of new skills for managing conflict. All conflict requires by definition that someone be dissatisfied and demanding change that is not acceptable to another party. So another way to manage conflict is to increase acceptance of the original source of dissatisfaction. In the integrated model developed by Jacobson (Jacobson & Christensen, 1996), acceptance became the cornerstone of behavioral intervention. Logically, clinical problems of any kind—being socially determined—require that there be a complainant, someone distressed by the behavior, including the individual exhibiting it. Baer (1982) recognized that the ultimate definition of *any* clinical improvement is that the level of complaint has been reduced. All treatment outcomes that are judged successful, therefore, derive solely from lowering the level of the source of the complaint or from raising the threshold (tolerance) of the complainant.

Culture and Control

If social mores determine the acceptability of intervention strategies, and relevant social groups decide on the acceptability of a behavior and the meaningfulness of its degree of change (the "social validity" of an outcome—Wolf, 1978), then it is clear that culture is going to have a major role to play in how control gets defined and exercised. What cultural understanding does is to help us see the individual in the context of a highly influential social environment. Individualistic cultures, such as Anglo-European societies, take for granted the central importance of the individual—and his or her "perfect rights." In collectivist cultures, however, the needs of the extended family or tribal community may take precedence. Behavior therapy had quickly recognized social group influences, in contrast to intra-individual schools of therapy. In this sense, modern cognitive therapy, with its causal focus on maladaptive thoughts and dysfunctional attitudes, is incompatible with behavior therapy. Nevertheless, the implication of culture for understanding the targeted complaint as a group-constructed phenomenon heavily influenced by the environment has not been fully appreciated even in behavior therapy.

Few have explained this myopia better than Winkler's (1986) analysis of whether good quality of life is a right or a duty. He argued that there are spheres of influence over human behavior, in which personal responsibility may be one, but proximal environmental influence is another, and distal influences (such as the effects of advertising or the accessibility of certain commodities) represent a third. In the case of obesity, for example, there are individual influences such as eating irrespective of hunger and exercising too little, environmental influences such as the easy availability of fast food, and societal influences, such as the deceptive advertising of high calorie foods as "97% fat free." Despite acknowledging these, the field of behavior therapy, according to Winkler, emphasizes the duty of the individual to modify an unhealthy lifestyle, and neglects the need to modify macro-level influences.

To investigate this bias, McFadden and I (1998) surveyed the behavioral literature on the treatment of obesity and smoking. Our question was whether there was any appreciation shown, from the treatment targets selected or from the individual-to-cultural level of the intervention, of the extent to which behavioral excesses were viewed as at least partially a consequence of environmental influences rather than personal inadequacies. Basically, there was no such evidence. So, by targeting supposedly deficit self-control in clients, is the therapist blaming the victim by holding the individual personally responsible for behavior that has been strongly influenced by societal conditions? Assuming these sources include historical injustices, colonization, and exploitative immigration policies, indigenous collectivist societies suffer the double jeopardy that arises from disadvantageous social policies on the one hand and individually focused clinical interventions on the other.

In summary, then, behavior therapy exists within complex spheres of social influence, including the unacknowledged contingencies of the natural environment, reciprocal influences of intimate relationships in which acceptance is the opposite of control, and culturally defined acceptable practices. Many interesting questions as to how behavior therapy facilitates change arise from these insights. To examine them it is first necessary to describe the hypothesized mechanisms of change that underlie behavior therapy, with its roots embedded in elemental conditioning and learning principles.

Underlying Mechanisms of Change

Classical Conditioning

An organism's survival is dependent upon its ability to anticipate future events. If environmental events occur in predictable patterns, any organism will, without specific voluntary awareness, show a permanent adaptation in behavior that we label learning. The simplest example is a temporal relationship between two discrete stimuli such that the occurrence of the second (unconditioned stimulus, UCS) is dependent on the occurrence of the first (conditioned stimulus, CS). This contingency, known as classical or Pavlovian conditioning, results in a change in behavior: a reaction somewhat similar to that previously evoked only by the second stimulus (unconditioned response, UCR) will now be evoked by the first (conditioned response, CR). One of the most profound insights of behaviorism was the possibility that this lawful way in which organisms respond to physical relationships could account for the acquisition of emotional responses to previously neutral circumstances (e.g., phobias).

Even more interesting for treatment was the application of another of Pavlov's discoveries, extinction. If the event that has become a CS now occurs frequently in the absence of the original UCS, the acquired response becomes increasingly less likely to occur and eventually will disappear ("extinguish"). Herein lies the rationale of many behavior therapy techniques such as systematic desensitization, flooding, and implosion, all of which rely on the same basic element of repeated exposure to a feared but objectively harmless CS in the absence of the truly painful UCS (Levis & Malloy, 1982). Creating alternative, safe experiences is still today the primary procedure of many strategies designed to reduce pathological affect (i.e., feelings not commensurate with the true level of threat). Behavior therapy helps people change by arranging conditions that will reverse the consequences of prior learning.

There are certain newer understandings of classical conditioning that aid in the translation of basic phenomena to the intricacy of the clinical situation. (a) Not all stimuli serve as potential CSs for all UCSs; they have to be attended to and they have to be relevant. For example, nausea is more likely to be strongly conditioned to the taste of a substance that has caused vomiting than its visual appearance (Davey, 1992). (b) Simple pairing of two stimuli may be insufficient to produce conditioning—the CS must explicitly "predict" the UCS. Inhibitory conditioning is therefore also possible, such that a stimulus predicts when an aversive event will *not* occur, thus becoming a "safety signal" (Rescorla, 1988).

(c) Although not intended by an experimenter (or therapist), and unrecognized by the participant (or client), *contextual* cues readily become part of the stimulus complex to which a new response is conditioned (Bouton, 1988). All real life stimuli are compounds of many elements that will have a particular valence according to previous experiences, which may then block or overshadow conditioning to novel elements in the compound. (d) With humans, words and images can be used as conditioned stimuli, and these are rarely entirely neutral at the outset. The evaluative connotation of words derive from the same associative processes as classical conditioning, as may preferences and attitudes in general (Staats, 1996).

Conditioning can occur without awareness—in other words a human can be conditioned without being able to describe the contingency between the CS and the UCS. Of course, if told of the relationship, the individual will readily behave as though having directly experienced the contingency, the enormous value of symbolic communication being that events do not have to be experienced to be anticipated. The opposite process is much less influential, however, which is an important point for clinical practice. Once affective responses have been acquired through experience, verbal information, such as the UCS will no longer occur, does not reliably change evaluative responses (Unger, Evans, Rourke, & Levis, 2003)—what is sometimes called affective perseverance (Sherman & Kim, 2002).

Instrumental (Operant) Conditioning

Skinner had the prescience to distinguish between circumstances where the sequence of events is not influenced by the individual's behavior (as described above), and those in which the individual's actions operate upon the environment to alter it in some predictable way. Survival also requires that if the change is positive, the action be repeated when similar contexts occur, and if the result is negative, the likelihood of repeating the behavior be reduced. The problem for theory is to define "positive" and "negative" in the above law. One tradition has been to think in hedonistic or evolutionary terms, such as satisfying a basic need (e.g., thirst), or reducing a secondary drive state (e.g., the need to feel powerful). Skinnerians, however, prefer to define "positive" operationally as that which increases the probability of the behavior producing it; hence the term *reinforcement* (strengthening) being preferred to *reward* (something valued).

The idea that a behavior can sometimes be reinforced by an event that is not apparently pleasant or beneficial, is a fundamental heuristic for clinical behavior change. To understand the function of a behavior one needs to analyze the variables that, when manipulated, alter its frequency. The critical issue for a clinician is that any behavior considered pathological could have a wide variety of functions. A major purpose of behavioral assessment is to hypothesize and then test what the possible unique functions are that maintain behaviors such as fire setting in an adolescent, aggression in an autistic child, or pain behavior in an adult. An essential feature of behavior therapy is the recognition that apparently purposeless acts always serve a function; in the above examples this might be reducing intolerable feelings, such as powerlessness, loneliness, or anger.

If the positive consequence of an action strengthens it, a negative consequence does not seem to weaken it. Instead, the individual will desist as long as the possibility of punishment exists, and if the action has also been serving a positive function, select and engage in an alternative, equally functional response. So in practice, interfering with one behavior may simply increase the frequency of another—these unintended consequences are not always desirable (Voeltz & Evans, 1982). It is helpful to think of reinforcement and punishment contingencies as motivational variables that allow the organism to expend energy efficiently on the actions that produce adaptive outcomes and not to waste it on unsatisfactory or harmful ones. That the influence of contingencies on behavior can be analyzed more like the economic distribution of resources (costs and benefits) has become generally accepted in operant theory.

Just as classical conditioning principles are much more complex than they appear, so research on contingency management reveals many complexities of clinical relevance. (a) If a behavior is intrinsically reinforcing, such as the enjoyment of reading a book, imposing an artificial external reward contingency can have unfortunate results: When the external contingency is removed, the frequency of the behavior may drop below its previous level (Kohn, 1993). (b) Well-studied relationships between the operant *rate* and the schedule of reinforcement are generally uninteresting in practical contexts, since almost none of our behavior, except for factory work, involves performing the same action over and over again. Our everyday activities are organized into routines that have a predictable beginning, and end when the function of the routine has been fulfilled (Brown, Evans, Weed, & Owen, 1987). (c) Behavior that has been only intermittently reinforced (partial reinforcement) is more resistant to extinction. This helps explain why some real-world behaviors persist despite apparent lack of reinforcement. The principle has also been used to suggest ways in which desirable behaviors might be maintained once formal treatment conditions have ended. However, it is far more useful to promote behaviors that will be reinforced in clients' natural social environments. (d) Behavioral repertoires are complex, and responses are invariably inter-related. High probability (preferred) behaviors can serve as reinforcement for lower probability ones. (e) There are individual differences in tendencies to seek rewards rather than avoid punishments. A child might study hard in order to be successful and enjoy parental approval, or study equally hard in order to avoid failure and criticism. There are also individual differences in ability to select an activity that will earn a large reward sometime in the future, versus one that results in a much smaller reward immediately. (f) Behavior can be what Skinner called "rule governed." Depending on one's history of consistently being reinforced when promised, individuals will comply with a verbally stated contingency ("if you do this I will give you that") without having to undergo laborious shaping procedures by reinforcing successive approximations. (g) Social consequences such as praise or criticism are not intrinsic to the action in the way that physical consequences are, and so social communities can and do shape an endless diversity of behavior. For skills that are social and therefore arbitrary, reinforcement and feedback are essentially the same thing.

There are interactions among behaviors within individuals and also between them. (a) Within individual repertoires, the acquisition of one behavior or skill (e.g., eye-hand motor coordination) makes another possible (e.g., doing surgery). Human learning is cumulative and hierarchical, and differences in the more basic behavioral repertoires, especially deficits caused by limited learning opportunities, account for many individual differences in response to ostensibly the same situation (Staats, 1996). (b) Interaction between individuals can be illustrated by the fact that some people's behaviors are aversive to others. Behaviors that lead to a reduction in an aversive event will be reinforced. Think how many parents have been negatively reinforced when their harsh response—like smacking a child—has resulted in a brief cessation of the annoying behavior that precipitated it. Thus the parent's yelling or smacking is reinforced by the termination of the child's misbehavior, but this will be short-lived. The parental outburst may simply have interrupted the child briefly. For if the function of the child's annoying behavior had been to elicit a reaction of some kind from the parent (even negative attention is still attention), then it will have been successful and thus reinforced. This vicious cycle was called the coercive trap by Patterson (1982).

It can be seen that many of the complexities around reinforcement contingencies for changing behavior are related to the fact that the reinforcing event is never neutral. It may have emotional properties; the nature of the contingency might be analyzed by the person, not always correctly; and current reinforcement conditions appraised relative to past experiences. There is likely to be interaction between classical and instrumental conditioning, and behaviors themselves will interact. This has been most thoroughly analyzed in the context of learning paradigms in which emotion serves as part of the controlling circumstances for behavior. These are considered next.

Affect Interacts with Behavior

This subheading is not an oxymoron. Of course emotion *is* behavior. However a fundamental principle that has permeated behavior therapy is that the visceral, autonomic nervous system responses that are the physiological expression of affective arousal have a powerful influence over approach and avoidance actions.

Active Avoidance Paradigm

The best expression of this concept was the elegant two-factor theory developed by Mowrer (1939) and Miller (1948) to explain avoidance behavior. The active avoidance paradigm in the laboratory is one in which there is a classical contingency between a warning signal (CS) and an aversive event such as an electric shock (UCS). After the shock comes on there is some arrangement to permit escape, such as jumping over a low barrier to a safer compartment. With repetition of these conditions the latency between the onset of the warning tone and the escape response becomes shorter, until eventually the animal responds to the warning tone sufficiently fast that the shock is avoided entirely. The apparent paradox is that the animal will continue for many trials to avoid a shock that is no longer present. When the contingency was one of escape, the reinforcement for jumping over the barrier was the ending of the shock and thus the termination of pain. But when the shock is being regularly avoided before it even comes on, what is the reinforcement? The Mowrer-Miller theory was that anxiety becomes classically conditioned to the tone (factor one), thus making it aversive. Once the avoidance response occurs the tone and the anxiety end, so it is reduction in acquired anxiety (relief) that reinforces the avoidance (factor two).

Why does the anxiety conditioned to the warning tone not extinguish? The suggested answer to this is that the active avoidance response occurs so quickly the tone ends very rapidly too, thus there really are no prolonged extinction trials as such. To test this theory one might want to prevent the avoidance and the escape behavior (for example, by raising the barrier quite high) while presenting the tone repeatedly in a typical extinction procedure. Anxiety should then extinguish, so that later, when the barrier is lowered the animal will make no attempt to avoid. This is roughly what happens.

The parallel with clinical phenomena is not obvious until one recognizes that it is the avoidance of anxiety that seems to characterize many clinical syndromes. Through traumatic conditioning, or possibly some other more vicarious source, anxiety has become conditioned to stimuli that are not intrinsically harmful. Getting away from those stimuli reduces anxiety, and by then eliminating exposure to the feared situation anxiety is prevented from extinguishing. As anxiety-provoking stimuli in real life are complex and sequential, escape will occur to early elements of the stimulus sequence (even if being rehearsed cognitively), so that later elements are never confronted, thus conserving anxiety (Levis & Malloy, 1982). If images (sensory memories) elicit negative emotion, then it is equally plausible that individuals will attempt to avoid recreating a traumatic event in imagination, so that actively not thinking about something, or "putting it out of your mind" by distraction, is a form of avoidance that will conserve anxiety.

Overt behavior reinforced by anxiety (tension) reduction can be seen in syndromes like alcoholism or obsessive compulsive disorder (the compulsive act reduces the obsessive anxiety and prevents the individual from experiencing that the feared events do not occur). Another example might be bulimia, in which binging serves the function of reducing negative affect such as feelings of rejection, but then raises anxiety (of becoming overweight). Purging, although repugnant, reduces the even more unpleasant anxiety, and so purging is reinforced. Treatment would thus involve three crucial elements: (a) teaching other ways of coping with the original interpersonal stress; (b) reducing anxiety about being overweight; and (c) extinguishing the anxiety-based urge by preventing purging until the anxiety declines. All current behavioral treatment protocols for bulimia contain these elements, although the emphases and the ways in which each component is to be achieved vary greatly.

Avoidance of Affect—Or of Catastrophe?

According to extinction principles, CRs will not decline if the UCS is still present. In trauma it is thought that the UCR of fear/pain elicited by a terrifying experience is itself highly aversive. Conditioned fear is also aversive, and by being another visceral response of the autonomic nervous system it is experienced in a similar way to the original UCR. Thus, in some situations it is possible that a conditioned anxiety response is sufficiently unpleasant to reactivate the fear conditioning by the experience of the CR being like the consequence of experiencing the UCS. Eysenck (1968) was the first to propose this "incubation" idea and it has been elaborated in many forms since then, sometimes simplified as "fear of fear." To give an example, if someone who fears flying goes on a totally uneventful flight but has prolonged anxiety the entire trip, their experience at the end of the trip would be that flying is aversive and something to be avoided. Most memories of the event will be unpleasant ones. There is evidence that if general anxiety is elicited this will act as a prime, making recall of unpleasant sensations and images more likely, as will the individual's discourse (verbal descriptions to others about the experience). Images are internal behaviors with stimulus properties that easily substitute for real-life experiences.

If we further propose that people differ in the degree to which they find autonomic arousal aversive, then one could imagine that there will be some people, likely to show up as clients, who have anxiety sensitivity. They will work hard to reduce or avoid *any* negative feelings. In syndromes such as panic disorder, however, Salkovskis (1996) has argued the feelings are based on a cognitive process, the belief that a catastrophe is imminent, such as fainting in public, or having a heart attack. The individual then engages in safety-seeking behaviors, such as sitting, seeking out uncrowded places, or not exercising. These actions are then followed by feelings of relief, not because anxiety has been reduced, but because the anticipated catastrophe has been averted. If we return to the simple avoidance paradigm, this interpretation is similar to proposing that the individual fears that the UCS is still present. The safety-seeking behaviors are still avoidance, but with the relief coming not so much from anxiety reduction as from the non-occurrence of the (anticipated) UCS.

The interesting issue from the point of view of perspectives on change is whether these and other subtly different, so-called cognitive reinterpretation result in a different therapeutic strategy. As one might expect, the general treatment Salkovskis recommends is to encourage the client to test their hypothesis that if the safety seeking behavior is not performed, disaster will occur. The individual is encouraged not to avoid the feared situations, to experience the feeling of panic, and to refrain from the safety-seeking behavior. This presupposes that steps are taken to ensure the client does not actually faint or have a heart attack. Because of our ability to anticipate risk, we do not need to have experienced harm to feel threatened by improbable but plausible events. For example, someone who has read about the threat of deep-vein thrombosis in long plane flights might engage in safety-seeking behaviors, including taking aspirin, wearing elastic stockings, drinking lots of water, and moving around the plane. These actions can be considered causally related to the threat beliefs and it is anxiety that increases both vigilance and selective attention to any slight sensations in the legs. The pattern is likely to persist, since these particular safety-seeking behaviors are harmless and low cost, anxiety is regulated, and the individual feels in control because active preventative measures are being taken.

This example reveals an interesting contradiction in behavior therapy's model of change. If the threat were real, all the features of the above pattern, especially feeling in control of a situation, would be judged by clinicians as evidence of good coping skills. Teaching people how to cope with genuinely stressful situations has become a major clinical strategy. The emphasis can either be on managing the emotion, or on managing the problem (emotion-focused versus problem-focused coping). And individuals differ in their prior tendency to adopt one or other of these coping styles. Both seem to rely on the degree to which self-talk, re-appraisal of the meaning of events, and other conscious mental acts can be assumed to alter the reality of experience. Cognition has a role in changing affect.

Cognition and Affect

Although models like that of Salkovskis can be conceptualized within a conditioning paradigm, it is easier and maybe more understandable to clients, to talk about beliefs and other cognitive processes. But some scholars insist that cognitive mechanisms are causal rather than merely convenient metaphors. In the 1970s, influential theorists in behavior therapy, especially Rachman (1997), began to argue that studies of the actual origin of clinical anxiety disorders rarely showed evidence of specific traumatic events that looked anything like classical conditioning. An increasing number of theorists asserted that it was cognitive processes which caused negative emotion, such as the anticipation of threat, or uncertainty about one's ability to deal with it—low self-efficacy beliefs (Bandura, 1977).

The cognitive model of depression proposed by Beck put more weight on how styles of thought, such as automatic thoughts and irrational beliefs influenced mood. Such intrapsychical postulates were very different from contingency explanations like learned helplessness: If an animal is first exposed to inescapable shock, it will later learn adaptive avoidance behavior much more slowly. Jacobson, Martell, and Dimidjian (2001) analyzed depressed behaviors as serving an avoidance function. Their behavioral activation treatment consists in: (a) encourages small active tasks that are likely to lead to natural reinforcement; (b) re-establishing regular routines; and (c) changing clients' environments rather than their thinking. Another life contingency that might produce the inactivity characteristic of depression is one in which the availability of reinforcement is too low in proportion to the effortfulness of the task.

Cognitive theories have become alternatives to these associationistic and contextual theories, but instead of being able to incorporate and build on the laws of basic conditioning and the matching of behavior to environmental demands, they replaced them, leaving in the process many unanswered questions. The largest explanatory problem is that if an organism responds, say, with anxiety to a non-harmful stimulus because it perceives a threat, question arise as to the origin of the expectation. Why should some clients come to believe they are failures? Cognitive "explanations" merely push the causal mechanisms further back into hypothetical processes, such as memory retrieval.

The Hot Versus Cool Metaphor

Many of the cognitivists' criticisms of behavior theory were specious. Behavioral research clearly has demonstrated that words and images and thoughts are important behaviors with stimulus properties that regulate other behaviors (Staats, 1996). Because humans have evolved an elaborate symbolic and communicative system, we are not dependent only upon direct experience. In evolution, feelings that mobilized action needed to be simple, reflexive, and fast, whereas knowledge of the social and physical world required planning and reflection. These might be thought of as constituting two separate systems, albeit often interconnected. If there can be knowledge about feelings separate from feelings about feelings, then it is helpful to describe differences metaphorically, as a hot, affective system and a cool, cognitive system (Metcalf & Mischel, 1999).

Two recent principles about the way emotion is organized support a systemic model of this kind. One of these is that all negative emotions seem to be interlinked. Fear, depression, and shame are certainly separable feeling states, but share common characteristics—they are unpleasant and they motivate, as has been explained, narrowing behaviors of prevention and inactivity. Joy, love, and hope are all pleasant and they motivate promotion-focused behaviors, all linked in an appetitive, activating system that broadens people's creative and exploratory behaviors (Fredrickson, 2001). The second principle that suggests a systemic model is that positive emotion and negative emotion can and do co-exist. There is evidence from multiple sources that, although one positive feeling will increase others of a similar valence, positive feelings do not necessarily counteract negative feelings (Cacioppo & Gardner, 1999). There is much practical clinical value in thinking of emotion as a hot system made up of subsystems of positive and negative affect, rather than as a series of discrete responses. One implication is that activating one positive feeling will automatically enhance others (a sense of well-being), and that facilitating a positive feeling can be done for a client who is otherwise experiencing many negative ones. Another useful implication is that thinking of all negative affect as a system helps explain the obvious phenomenon that if a client is experiencing stress and discomfort from one source, such as problem at work, then other relatively minor annoyances, such as a petty marital disagreement, evoke much greater negative affect than warranted.

Motivation to Change

Thus far I have been considering how clinically relevant behavior is regulated, which should then illuminate the mechanisms available to the behavior therapist to facilitate change. It is obvious, however, that clients—like the light bulb in the old joke—must have some motivation to change, whether they are explicitly in behavior therapy or simply trying to manage their own lives. In some ways the *mechanisms* of change and the *motivation* to do so are really very separate topics, however in clinical contexts they are always interlinked.

Stopping Behavior: "Willpower" and Habit

Habits are hard to break because by definition they are relatively autonomous (occur without much executive effort), are cued by highly accessible stimuli, and are strengthened by repetition—Thorndike's Law of Exercise. It is almost a parody of behavior therapy that as a clinical method it contains a variety of useful principles for breaking habits, from relatively innocuous behaviors such as hair-pulling and nail biting, to more complex ones such as smoking, drinking, and gambling. Self-regulation of such behaviors involves the stated goal not to engage in the response, followed by the inhibition or voluntary cessation of the early components of the response pattern, despite there being a felt urge to perform the action. Any self-driven program to change a habit that depends only on the strength of the initial goal to stop ("willpower") is likely to fail, either because the behavior is elicited by interoceptive cues with minimal awareness, or because the urge elicited by external cues is strong and its reduction is pleasurable.

Given this, there are some straightforward techniques that can be taught to clients. A simple one, described early in the history of behavior therapy by Guthrie, involves generating the eliciting cue and carefully performing in its presence some other response, physically incompatible with the undesired habit. If the behavior to be stopped is one that obtains a desirable but forbidden object (expensive clothes for someone who shoplifts), the ability to inhibit the proscribed behavior is compromised if the desired object is physically present or vividly imagined. Cravings in the presence of the desired object are not easily explained in reinforcement terms. Instead it seems the object, or its imaginal representation, elicits strong positive emotional responses, components of the "hot" system. If these urges are thought of as conditioned affective responses, it might be possible to reduce them by exposure (an extinction effect). Intuitively, people have learned that to resist temptation requires avoiding the cues of the desired object. But according to theory, exposing oneself to these cues while inhibiting the approach behavior should reduce the affect experienced as an urge. If the client has enough control over the consummatory behavior to inhibit it while exposing themselves to the cue, this procedure can be entirely self-directed; if not, then the therapist has to design some way of regulating the habit while exposing the client to the cues. This is now a standard part of treatment for such addictive behaviors as smoking or drinking alcohol (Rohsenow et al., 2001).

Even if being managed in a therapeutic program, resisting life's temptations has to be implemented by the client, which can be enhanced by ensuring the client fully understands and accepts the principles behind therapeutic suggestions. Here, naïve theories about the nature of undesirable behavior can play a negative role. For example a person who has internalized the lay-person's myth that alcoholism is a disease and alcohol itself triggers further drinking, will be more likely, after a one-drink lapse, to abandon efforts at control and continue drinking. Marlatt developed a program to counter this abstinence violation effect by teaching people they can exercise restraint, even if they have had a drink or broken a diet (Marlatt & George, 1984). His model of *relapse prevention* involves additional elements that have made it potentially applicable to any other behavior problem the client is trying to stop. For example, a convicted pedophile could reduce his likelihood of re-offending by recognizing the importance of avoiding contexts (such as living next to a kindergarten) that contain many cues likely to elicit an urge. Avoidance behaviors must be implemented deliberately when desire to perform the act is low, so part of the overall relapse prevention strategy is also to recognize conditions that place the individual at risk, such as using drugs, feeling rejected, or having opportunity (being alone). An effective maintenance plan, therefore, will have built into it behaviors designed to avoid these environmental or emotional situations.

Initiating Behavior: Resolutions

Motivation to carry out necessary but unpleasant or unrewarding tasks is a second critical feature of self-regulation. As opposed to the previous category, where one is trying to stop oneself from engaging in a behavior, the need for self-motivation is in order to carry out important tasks, such as completing homework, or going off to a gym to exercise. There are various theories as to why it is difficult to do these things when we have stated that we really desire to do so. One widely cited concept is that verbally stated intentions and actual behavior rarely coincide, so that clients need to be trained to ensure that saying and doing are more closely aligned. The problem is that intentions are typically formulated and stated in one set of circumstances (you have just read an article on skin cancer and you resolve to use sunscreen) and enacted in a completely different context (at the beach you notice how well-tanned everyone is looking and you want to look the same). Another frequently cited model was put forward by Prochaska and DiClemente (1982). Essentially their position asserts that if someone says he or she wants to do something, but does not actually do it, he or she was not really committed to doing it in the first place. This lack of commitment is confirmed by the individual failing to engage in any behaviors that would facilitate major change (reading the homework instructions, or joining a gym). Clients are judged to be in different "stages" of change based on their willingness to perform change-facilitating behaviors.

In behavior theory, however, this model is considered tautological, since any activity that is truly preparatory for the intended action is a component of the desired behavior and may be just as difficult to perform as any other component. In addition to Winkler's observations regarding ecological influences, some individuals lack knowledge of the early components of a task that will make performance of the full routine more probable. Some clients also have hidden barriers to change in the form of conflicting emotional needs. A simplified example might be lack of exercise contributing to being overweight, which allows an insecure person to feel unattractive to others. Taking action to improve physical appearance might then facilitate anxiety-provoking dating or other social overtures. A yet more common problem is procrastination—failing to initiate even the earliest components of a task. Some tasks have external deadlines, such as renewing your car registration, and some have self-imposed deadlines, such as getting your car serviced. Having or setting deadlines generally increases task performance (Ariely & Wertenbroch, 2002). But if looming deadlines of either type cause anxiety, an individual's "coping style" for managing anxiety may simply be further avoidance.

In summary, avoiding tasks and succumbing to temptation are but two sides of the same behavioral circumstance. Procrastinators fill their time with other important or more enjoyable tasks, and addicts engage in excess behavior instead of more socially fulfilling activities. This has long been known in the operant laboratory: Extinction of one response always means an increase in the frequency of other, usually unmeasured, responses. Setting goals to do one thing inevitably requires abandoning intentions to do something else, and vice versa. Effective behavior therapy requires an understanding of the function both of the behavioral event of interest and its alternatives. Physically incompatible activities that serve similar emotional functions or that can achieve comparable goals are the most likely to achieve a reduction in the target behavior (Voeltz & Evans, 1982).

Motivation and Goal Setting

While rarely a formal component that is evaluated in treatment outcome research, behavior therapists will often ask clients to specify their goals for therapy in behavioral terms. The rationale for this, apart from encouraging the client to focus more precisely on what therapy is trying to accomplish and thus provide a client-centered yardstick for measuring success, is that achieving smaller, more attainable goals reinforces general efforts at change. Because success, thus defined, encourages change, self-monitoring of behavior has long been a reactive, self-regulatory strategy (Nelson, 1977). Whether achieving a goal actually generates feelings of success depends on attributions regarding the outcome (was it entirely due to your own efforts?), the degree of effort that had to be exerted to achieve the outcome, and the degree to which setting a personal standard of outcome is not compromised by a tendency to make invidious comparisons with others' achievements (Eccles & Wigfield, 2002).

Where behavior theory deviates most significantly from cognitive theories of motivation is that the latter present a picture of individuals planfully pursuing rationally selected goals. Goal setting as a cool, pulling mechanism is contradicted by the recognition that actions are context specific. Intentions are more likely to be successful if they specify what to do when a specific context arises. Therapy that focuses on how to react in a given circumstance, will, as suggested with such topics as behavioral activation and relapse prevention, be more successful than focusing on general goals. Self-acceptance may arise from focusing more on the process of new learning and change and less on making comparisons with others. Behavior therapy moves clients towards autonomy by helping them to structure goals and intentions for which there is a reduction in social comparison as the standard of success.

Self-Regulation and Autonomy

Regulation of behavior basically means producing one behavior, B, in order to decrease or increase the probability of another behavior, A. Self-regulation means that Behavior B and Behavior A are in the same individual repertoire. Autonomy means that Behavior B and Behavior A are both chosen by the individual. Self-management of affect adheres to the same operational definitions, but usually requires that Response B influences the stimuli that would normally trigger the emotion, Response A, for the simple reason that the autonomic responses of emotion are often not under voluntary control. "Stop crying," "don't get mad," are not as easily complied with—even when said to oneself—as "eat this ice cream," or "take a deep breath." Examples of overt, voluntary behaviors that alter affect by changing cues include distraction, moving away from frustrating situations (anger management), or concentrating on an erotic fantasy (enhancing sexual arousal). The latter example reminds us that emotional arousal seems to draw attention to bodily sensations and away from the task at hand, and this is particularly likely to interfere with complex performance, such as taking a test or playing an instrument. Thus, concentrating on the essential requirements of the task is another voluntary emotion-regulation method. An additional tactic is to self-induce responses known to counteract ("reciprocally inhibit") autonomic arousal, such as relaxing muscles, meditation, and controlling breathing, or, slightly less adaptive, drinking and smoking. In particular, clients can use the connotative properties of words to counteract the external cues evoking the emotion, such as talking to oneself in a reassuring way ("planes are engineered to withstand great strain").

Although most people implicitly know and use these strategies, those who are less good at doing so are more likely to become clients and thus have to be taught them. The therapist is still reliant on the individual deliberately implementing or rehearsing the strategies in the naturally occurring situations where they are needed. Occasionally in the clinic it is possible to re-create everyday situations in imagination and to rely on the safe therapeutic relationship to both induce calm and to direct muscular relaxation. This is what happens in systematic desensitization, the goal of which is classical extinction, but the procedure can be adapted as one of self-regulation. In the ideal form of self-directed change the individual must use these techniques to control emotion at the time of the event and before being overwhelmed by it. What is sometimes loosely called a coping strategy (Rohsenow et al., 2001) in the treatment of addictive behavior, actually involves teaching the client to say and think certain thoughts in the presence of the cue that elicits positive affect (the sight and smell of one's favorite alcoholic beverage). These self-statements might be such things as stating the negative consequences of drinking—the words and images should aid resistance (not consuming the drink) or avoidance (pushing the glass away, corking the bottle).

Emotion Regulation

A key feature of the above methods is that they use a variety of internally directed activities (physical, verbal, and imaginal) *voluntarily* to regulate affect. Behaviorists interpret self-instruction as using words as stimuli (Staats, 1996). In this sense the phenomenon resembles what cognitive scientists call controlled processing—performing complex skills in which the individual has to consciously focus on the task, often using internal dialogue. After a period of time, however, these same complex tasks become more automatic. A similar sort of process occurs with respect to emotion, in that during development children learn to regulate emotion and emotional expression, eventually using automatic rather than controlled processing.

Certain types of environmental opportunities and social experiences foster the development of internalized regulation of emotion without either the child or the social agents (peers, parents, teachers) being aware of them having this function. When a mother soothes an upset, crying child by holding and rocking, she is not reinforcing crying but creating conditions whereby the emotional system can return to equilibrium more rapidly, now and in the future. There are probably multitudes of different contexts whereby this can happen. One is imaginal play that allows children to experience a whole range of emotions, including fear, in contexts that are not genuinely threatening (Galyer & Evans, 2001). It is argued that adaptive emotion regulation can be defined functionally—one needs enough emotional arousal to be able to sustain an activity, but not so much that the individual is overwhelmed and the activity disrupted.

Unfortunately, the mechanisms whereby the affective system becomes well-regulated are not fully understood. As a result, behavioral interventions for those syndromes that appear to be characterized by poor emotion regulation, such as borderline personality disorder, depend on new *social* emotive experiences. For example, in Linehan's (1993) "dialectical" behavior therapy, a key component is emotion-regulation training by using a carefully constructed relationship with the therapist. Just a generally positive rapport seems to be inadequate, since the client with this syndrome experiences conflict between positive and negative emotions elicited in intimate relationships. The special therapeutic relationship that Linehan advocates is one grounded in consistently high levels of acceptance of the client, as opposed to premature limit-setting. Imposing limits always reduces client autonomy to some extent. In another context I have argued that setting limits without first having high levels of client acceptance creates coercive conditions, especially when the therapists are less qualified care staff who often demand that behavior conforms to arbitrary agency or household rules (Evans, 1999).

Emotion Accepted

The socially devalued behaviors of people who are disadvantaged, particularly the challenging behavior of people with mental retardation, are easily judged as something to be decreased rather than being recognized as a valid form of communication or emotional expression. In fact, a common therapeutic quandary, encapsulated by Linehan's term *dialectic*, is that by offering to be an agent of change, a therapist is also tacitly confirming that the client's behaviors or experiences are undesirable and need to be altered. What if the therapist were to propose that the client's behavior and feelings should be affirmed as they are, which for the client would mean accepting unpleasant feelings? Because clients often report fear of fear, or depression about their depression, perhaps what defines being a client is experiencing distress about one's distress? Some people are particularly averse to feeling any extreme emotion, and what they avoid are emotional experiences.

Many implications of this logic have recently been described in behavior therapy. A concept like experiential avoidance is used to understand the endless precautions against further discomfort taken by clients suffering chronic pain. Such clients exhibit patterns of protectiveness, including inactivity, that resemble very closely in function the safety-seeking behaviors already described. An extension of this concept that is growing in prominence is the approach developed by Hayes and colleagues that they call "acceptance and commitment therapy", or ACT (Hayes, Strosahl, & Wilson, 1999). Simplifying greatly, they propose it is not negative feelings that are the clients' problems, but their struggle to be rid of these feelings. ACT therefore focuses on alternative actions. the "mindful" experiencing of feelings, acceptance of thoughts rather than trying to counter them with rational argument, and doing new things based on the kind of life the client values rather than struggling to change old habits. Models such as ACT may be less about new mechanisms of change and more about shifting the targets for change away from clients' negative social comparisons and towards greater self-determination.

Self-Determination

There are many clinical situations where the task of the therapy is to assist the client gain greater autonomy. As explained above, this could be freedom from the unwanted influence of anxiety or depression, or freedom from the controlling influence of parental or cultural mores, standards of deportment, and role expectation—such as women as traditional homemakers. More commonly, however, the focus of behavior therapy is reducing the dependence of the individual on the actions of others, especially when these restrict personal choice in some way.

Because autonomy and independence are strongly culturally driven values, increased self-determination is only a desirable goal in relative terms. For people with mental retardation who are often devalued, however, normalization has finally come to be considered best clinical practice. This implies that the level of autonomy that should be achieved by a person with a disability can be gauged by comparison to similarly aged, nondisabled individuals in the culture. People with mental retardation are often served in supported accommodation and supervised by caregivers who have considerable control over daily resources, and certainly decisions about how to manage the patterns and rules of the home. Small wonder that conflict may arise in such contexts, usually in the form of aggressive and so-called "challenging" behavior on the part of the clients, with punitive consequences from the staff (Evans & Berryman, 1998).

There is now considerable evidence that teaching direct care staff to allow self-determination in clients reduces challenging behaviors. Sometimes this happens less as a change in the client's behavior and more as a reinterpretation of its meaning—another form of acceptance. This was nicely illustrated in one of the cases reported by Evans and Berryman (1998), in which the behavior of concern to the staff was stealing food from the kitchen. In the course of teaching the staff the principles of self-determination, we pointed out that because the group home and the food really belonged to all clients, helping oneself to a snack was actually a desirable, independent living skill. Later, when obtaining reports on outcomes, staff were asked for feedback on whether the problem of stealing food was improving. At this point the staff looked slightly mystified, saying: "Stealing food? That's no problem. He can get himself a meal whenever he likes." The staff had re-classified the behavior of helping oneself to food as being in the personal domain, not a violation of an arbitrary convention. In a similar vein, Evans and Meyer (2001) reported facilitating normal friendships for a teenager with Rett syndrome (which is characterized by severe motor and cognitive deficits). A group of this teen's peers accepted her limited skill level by expecting no more from her in terms of interactions than she was able to deliver—an example being that her total absence of verbal communication was described by one of her friends as her being "very good at keeping secrets." An early, unquestioned assumption of behavior therapy had been that it was necessary for clients to change in order to be accepted. Now it is recognized that social contexts can be made more accommodating.

Conclusion

What then is behavior therapy and what is its theory of change? Essentially behavior therapy is based on the fundamental tenet that problems which come to clinical attention are caused by environmental experiences that have resulted in learning by the individual that is faulty (excessive or deficient), dysregulated, or no longer serving its original function. Thus the task of the therapist is to arrange exposure to and engagement with new experiences that will eliminate old habits, teach alternative behaviors, or impart more flexible, adaptive skills that can be used to confront new social situations and environmental circumstances. Some social networks fail to support learning, and difficulties can also arise when social environments are over-controlling. So therapy must equally consist in making the social climate more facilitating of change or more accepting. The target for behavior therapy should never be the individual behavior alone, but the person in cultural context.

How the behavior therapist arranges these new learning opportunities can be extremely varied, which is why the search for the one correct, validated treatment protocol is a futile one. Because humans have an elaborate symbol system to represent the physical environment, to interpret the things that happen to them, and even to describe and understand their own feelings, verbal thought processes will have a major role in how a particular experience actually changes a person. A therapist can rely heavily on the communicative, social, and emotive opportunities arising from the interpersonal interaction with the client (the therapeutic "relationship"). But in doing so it will be especially important to access the "hot" motivational system to provide affective cues for learning, or meaningful reinforcement for the client's initial, hesitant approach to new experiences. Behavior therapy in this mode will have to devise ways to ensure that learning is sufficiently durable that it will continue in new social contexts.

To complicate matters, people only become clients in the first place if they experience distress with the circumstances of their lives. This unhappiness with current status might arise from many sources, including their own perceptions that life could be more meaningful, from frustrating domination by others, from other people putting pressure on them to change, or from the demands imposed by new circumstances, such as having children, a new job, or a loss of previous supports. The derivation of a client's motivation to change will play a substantial role in the sorts of experiences the therapist can design in order to create new learning. If motivation is high but still realistic, then more difficult and challenging experiences can be designed. If the individual is conflicted, strategies that produce yet more discomfort for the client are likely to be avoided through sabotaging therapy, failing to implement suggestions, and other forms of resistance to the discomfort of change, such as dropping out of treatment.

In many clinical contexts, therefore, the difficulty in producing change is not because motivation is weak, but because predictable forces sustain the undesirable behavior in some way, and the alternatives are so distressing that it is difficult to initiate even the first steps towards change. Behavior therapists, therefore, do not attribute lack of change to lack of commitment, but try to understand the complex contingencies that might be maintaining behavior—some of them social and cultural, as explained, but often they are internal, such as the regulation of an overt behavior by an affective response. Overt behavior that is motivated by avoidance of negative affect, especially anxiety and despair, will require carefully crafted new learning experiences to change to a promotion focus. This is largely why self-directed change can be so difficult. As Watson and Tharp realized, there is not much, in principle, that stops individuals from arranging for themselves the same sorts of new learning experiences as will be arranged by a therapist. However, many behaviors considered inappropriate by one's social group are serving the function of regulating affect but in a way that is difficult for the individual to appreciate.

Questions of the external control of behavior become especially salient when the person's lack of insight into their difficulty and their difficulty are one and the same. If clients are depressed because they hold rigid overgeneralizations about the world, that is their problem. A therapist can assess the way in which these beliefs might be preventing change but will then have to decide whether they are cause or effect, whether it is possible to contrive experiences that would change them directly, or whether there are accessible learning conditions that will change behavior in such a way that changes in beliefs will follow. Ironically, then, the therapist who knows the principles of learning and how experience and context shape behavior, can implement strategies that require no client understanding or even agreement. In this sense behavior therapy has the potential to be highly manipulative. While behavior therapists have long advocated the value of teaching the principles that are being used to foster change, influencing clients without their awareness in order to help them become more autonomous raises a fundamental paradox. Particularly in the area of severe disabilities, behavioral principles have proved sadly susceptible to applications, like aversive contingencies, that increase external control rather than improve choice.

Because scholarly behavior therapists mostly research one type of disorder only, they end up describing regulatory mechanisms in syndrome-specific terms. The behavioral protocols for panic, alcoholism, eating disorders, childhood aggression, and marital problems all have different languages around them. Only if one can step back and look at the common mechanisms of change does it become obvious that in every case we are talking about a relatively small number of universal principles. People change themselves by changing their environments; they differ in their opportunities and ability to do so, and in the responsiveness of their environments to change, for reasons the therapist needs to analyze. In early editions of *Self-directed Behavior,* Watson and Tharp relied heavily on the heuristic offered by understanding contingencies and how cues regulate behavior. In later editions there was an added focus on affect, interpersonal processes, and social support. Traditional classical and operant conditioning principles do not alone provide sufficient explanation for a science of behavior change. As models of behavioral responsiveness to situational regularities, however, they continue to serve as valuable building blocks to the appreciation of response interactions within individual repertoires and how differences in these personality repertoires then alter the learning experiences afforded by similar physical and social environments.

References

Ariely, D., & Wertenbroch, K. (2002). Procrastination, deadlines, and performance: Self-control by precommitment. *Psychological Science, 13,* 219–224.

Ayllon, T., & Michael, J. (1959). The psychiatric nurse as a behavioral engineer. *Journal of the Experimental Analysis of Behavior, 2,* 323–334.

Baer, D. M. (1982). The imposition of structure on behavior and the demolition of behavioral structures. In D. J. Bernstein (Ed.), *Response structure and organization: 1981 Nebraska symposium on motivation* (pp. 217–254). Lincoln: University of Nebraska Press.

Bandura, A. (1977). Self-efficacy: Toward a unifying theory of behavior change. *Psychological Review, 84,* 191–215.

Bouton, M. E. (1988). Context and ambiguity in the extinction of emotional learning: Implications for exposure therapy. *Behaviour Research & Therapy, 26,* 137–149.

Brown, F., Evans, I. M., Weed, K. A., & Owen, V. (1987). Delineating functional competencies: A component model. *Journal of the Association for Persons with Severe Handicaps, 12,* 117–124.

Cacioppo, J. T., & Gardner, W. L. (1999). Emotion. *Annual Review of Psychology, 50,* 191–214.

Davey, G. C. L. (1992). Classical conditioning and the acquisition of human fears and phobias: A review and synthesis of the literature. *Advances in Behaviour Research and Therapy, 14,* 29–66.

Eccles, J. S., & Wigfield, A. (2002). Motivational beliefs, values, and goals. *Annual Review of Psychology, 53,* 109–132.

Evans, I. M. (1997). The effect of values on scientific and clinical judgment in behavior therapy. *Behavior Therapy, 28,* 483–493.

Evans, I. M. (1999). Staff development, caring, and community. In J. R. Scotti & L. H. Meyer (Eds.), *Behavioral intervention: Principles, models, and practices* (pp. 413–431). Baltimore: Paul H. Brookes.

Evans, I. M., & Berryman, J. S. (1998). Supervising support staff in naturalistic behavioural interventions: Process and outcome. *New Zealand Journal of Psychology, 27(2),* 10–21.

Evans, I. M., & Meyer, L. H. (2001). Having friends and Rett syndrome: How social relationships create meaningful contexts for limited skills. *Disability & Rehabilitation, 23,* 167–176.

Eysenck, H. J. (1968). A theory of the incubation of anxiety/fear responses. *Behaviour Research & Therapy, 6,* 309–321.

Fredrickson, B. L. (2001). The role of positive emotions in positive psychology: The broaden-and-build theory of positive emotions. *American Psychologist, 56,* 218–226.

Galyer, K. T., & Evans, I. M. (2001). Pretend play and the development of emotion regulation in preschool children. *Early Child Development and Care, 166,* 93–108.

Hayes, S. C., Strosahl, K. D., & Wilson, K. G. (1999). *Acceptance and commitment therapy: An experiential approach to behaviour change.* New York: Guilford.

Jacobson, N. S., & Christensen, A. (1996). *Integrative couple therapy: Promoting acceptance and change.* New York: W. W. Norton.

Jacobson, N. S., Martell, C. R., & Dimidjian, S. (2001). Behavioral activation treatment for depression: Returning to contextual roots. *Clinical Psychology: Science and Practice, 8,* 255–270.

Kohn, A. (1993). *Punished by rewards.* Boston: Houghton Mifflin.

Levis, D. J., & Malloy, P. F. (1982). Research in infrahuman and human conditioning. In G. T. Wilson & C. M. Franks (Eds.), *Contemporary behavior therapy: Conceptual and empirical foundations* (pp. 65–118). New York: Guilford.

Linehan, M. M. (1993). *Cognitive-behavioral treatment of borderline personality disorder.* New York: Guilford.

Marlatt, G. A., & George, W. H. (1984). Relapse prevention: Introduction and overview of the model. *British Journal of Addiction, 79,* 261–273.

McFadden, A. S., & Evans, I. M. (1998). Behavioral health care: Have Winkler's admonitions regarding rights and duties been heeded? *The Behavior Therapist, 21,* 69–72.

Metcalf, J., & Mischel, W. (1999). A hot/cool-system analysis of delay of gratification: Dynamics of willpower. *Psychological Review, 106,* 3–19.

Miller, N. E. (1948). Studies of fear as an acquirable drive: I. Fear as motivation and fear-reduction as reinforcement in the learning of new responses. *Journal of Experimental Psychology, 38,* 89–101.

Mowrer, O. H. (1939). A stimulus-response analysis of anxiety and its role as a reinforcing agent. *Psychological Review, 46,* 553–564.

Nelson, R. O. (1977). Assessment and therapeutic functions of self-monitoring. In M. Hersen, R. M. Eisler, & P. M. Miller (Eds.), *Progress in behavior modification,* Vol. 5 (pp. 263–308). New York: Academic Press.

Patterson, G. R. (1982). *Coercive family process: A social learning approach,* Vol. 3. Eugene, OR: Castalia.

Prochaska, J. O., & Di Clemente, C. C. (1982). Transtheoretical therapy: Toward a more integrative model of change. *Psychotherapy: Theory, Research and Practice, 19,* 276–288.

Rachman, S. (1997). The evolution of cognitive behaviour therapy. In D. M. Clark & C. G. Fairburn (Eds.), *Science and practice of cognitive behaviour therapy* (pp. 3–26). Oxford: Oxford University Press.

Rescorla, R. A., (1988). Pavlovian conditioning: It's not what you think it is. *American Psychologist, 43,* 151–160.

Rogers, C. R., & Skinner, B. F. (1956). Some issues concerning the control of human behavior: A symposium. *Science, 124,* 1057–1066.

Rohsenow, D. J., Monti, P. M., Rubonis, A. V., Gulliver, S. B., Colby, S. M., Binkoff, J. A., & Abrams, S. B. (2001). Cue exposure with coping skills training and communication skills training for alcohol dependence: 6- and 12-month outcomes. *Addiction, 96,* 1161–1174.

Salkovskis, P. M. (1996). Avoidance behaviour is motivated by threat beliefs: A possible resolution of the cognitive-behaviour debate. In P. M. Salkovskis (Ed.), *Trends in cognitive and behavioural therapies* (pp. 25–41). Chichester, UK: Wiley.

Sherman, D. K., & Kim, H. S. (2002). Affective perseverance: The resistance of affect to cognitive invalidation. *Personality and Social Psychology Bulletin, 28,* 224–237.

Skinner, B. F. (1974). *About behaviorism.* New York: Knopf.

Staats, A. W. (1996). *Behavior and personality: Psychological behaviorism.* New York: Springer.

Stuart, R. B. (1969). Operant-interpersonal treatment for marital discord. *Journal of Consulting and Clinical Psychology, 33,* 675–682.

Tharp, R. G., & Wetzel, R. J. (1969). *Behavior modification in the natural environment.* New York: Academic Press.

Unger, W., Evans, I. M., Rourke, P., & Levis, D. J. (2003). The S-S construct of expectancy versus the S-R construct of fear: Which motivates the acquisition of avoidance behaviour? *The Journal of General Psychology, 130,* 131–147.

Voeltz, L. M., & Evans, I. M. (1982). The assessment of behavioral interrelationships in child behavior therapy. *Behavioral Assessment, 4,* 131–165.

Watson, D. L., & Tharp, R. G. (1977). *Self-directed behavior: Self-modification for personal adjustment* (2nd ed.). Monterey, CA: Brooks/Cole.

Weiss, R. L., & Heyman, R. E. (1997). A clinical-research overview of couple interactions. In W. K. Halford & H. Markman (Eds.), *The clinical handbook of marriage and couples interventions* (pp. 13–41). Brisbane, Australia: Wiley.

Wilson, G. T., Hannon, A. E., & Evans, I. M. (1968). Behavior therapy and the therapist-patient relationship. *Journal of Consulting and Clinical Psychology, 32,* 103–109.

Winkler, R. C. (1986). Rights and duty: The need for a social model. In N. J. King & A. Remenyi (Eds.), *Health care: A behavioral approach* (pp. 265–277). New York: Grune & Stratton.

Wolf, M. M. (1978). Social validity: The case for subjective measurement, or how applied behavior analysis is finding its heart. *Journal of Applied Behavior Analysis, 11,* 203–214.

CHAPTER 3

Child Development and Changing Behavior in Diverse Societies: An Activity Settings Approach

Ashley E. Maynard

While research on culture and development has been going on for decades, current trends such as globalization and immigration have contributed to the urgency to understand the complexity of the world's cultures and what it means to grow up in a specific cultural place. Researchers who study child development and culture are also concerned with what it means to emigrate from, or to have ancestors from, different cultural places (e.g., Greenfield & Cocking, 1994). In general, developmental psychology is concerned with *what* changes over time and with what stays the same. Developmental researchers also have the goal of identifying the mechanisms of those changes, the *how* and *why* behind the changes themselves. At the heart of the study of culture and development is the idea that knowing about the cultural context enhances the understanding of processes of change. Many researchers who study culture and development are aware that cultural contexts are not constant, and analysis is required to understand changes in the contexts themselves.

Over the past several decades, an increasing number of researchers have turned their attention to the interplay of culture and development, with particular attention to a variety of contexts (Cole, 1996; Cole, Gay, Glick, & Sharp, 1971; Cole & Scribner, 1977; Dasen, 1977; Greenfield & Bruner, 1966; Greenfield, Reich, & Olver, 1966; Rogoff, 1990, 2003; Vygotsky, 1978; Weisner, 1998; Whiting & Edwards, 1988; Whiting & Whiting, 1975). By going to the field, these researchers have challenged the conventional assumption that objectivity is attainable and is best achieved through controlled laboratory experiments (Greenfield, 1997a, 1997b). Researchers who take seriously the role of culture in child development have turned to a variety of methods to explore the contexts of development in order to understand developmental processes, rather than focusing simply on variables under question (Greenfield, 1997b).

An important theory of culture and development holds that development is a process of the child's changing participation in cultural activities (Rogoff, 1990;

Rogoff, Baker-Sennett, Lacasa, & Goldsmith, 1995). As children mature, they can contribute to activities in new ways. Children do not simply "ape" activities they see others perform (Hirschfeld, 2002), they take in information from the environment through schemas and respond in intelligent and creative ways (Piaget, 1952), sometimes changing activities as they go (Greenfield, Maynard, & Childs, 2003).

The thesis of this chapter is that an understanding of culture and development is best achieved through analysis of the activity settings in which children participate. An activity settings approach analyzes aspects of the contexts surrounding development leading the researcher to a greater understanding of the meanings of cultural practices for the development of individuals (Gallimore, Weisner, & Goldenberg, 1993). In this chapter, an introduction to activity settings analysis sets the stage for discussion of previously published work and for predictions about the changing nature of developmental psychology as an activity setting in and of itself. The focus for the chapter is on several domains where activity settings have changed as a result of successful interventions or a major socioeconomic shift, such as an increase in schooling or in commercial activity. In each case, analytical description illustrates how changes in at least one aspect of the activity setting engendered changes in other aspects. Developmental change, therefore, can be seen on an individual level and at a more systemic level in the activity setting.

Activity Settings Analysis

Focusing on the child in the context of culture naturally points to an interest in the activities in which the child finds himself. Weisner and Gallimore relate work from activity theory in the sociocultural school and ecocultural theory (Weisner & Gallimore, 1985) in their activity settings approach (Gallimore, Goldenberg, & Weisner, 1993; Weisner & Gallimore, 1985; Weisner, Matheson, & Bernheimer, 1995). The premise of Weisner and Gallimore's activity settings analysis is that the activities that make up the routines that comprise people's day-to-day lives provide opportunities for children to learn what is important in their culture and how to behave in culturally-appropriate, meaningful ways (Weisner, 1989). Tharp and Gallimore (1988) conceptualize activity settings as the critical spaces for learning, where the learning can range from academic material learned in formal education to weaving or tailoring in informal education processes. An activity settings approach is useful to understand child development (Farver, 1999) and cultural communities as well (O'Donnell, Tharp, & Wilson, 1993;

Tharp & Gallimore, 1988). Indeed, processes of development may be elucidated by an approach that examines children's activities and interactions *in situ*, such as activity settings analysis (Farver, 1999). Activity settings analysis provides a way to examine the contents and contexts of cultural activities, and to find out how they are meaningful to the participants.

The ecological and cultural context in which activity settings are embedded influences child development by shaping the objective conditions surrounding activities and the subjective meanings of activities to the participants (Gallimore et al., 1993). The meaning of activities for child development is a mix of features that can be assessed through ethnographic observations. These features include the *personnel* present, the *tasks* themselves, *scripts* for conduct, the *motives and emotional experiences* of actors in the tasks, and the *cultural values* being communicated in the activity (Gallimore et al., 1993; O'Donnell et al., 1993).

The *personnel* who are available to children may vary according to ecocultural factors such as the local economy and the particular social organization of a group of people. For example, if it is the custom for mothers and fathers to both work in the local fields, then infants are likely to be left home with sibling caretakers who will watch over them (Weisner, 1989). As another example, Israeli kibbutzim children must adapt themselves to multiple caregivers and to spending much of their time with other children (Sagi, van Ijzendoorn, Aviezer, Donnell, & Mayseless, 1994). In both of these examples, children might learn a lot about the care of children through actual participation in child care practices. In many communities in the United States, on the other hand, the mother is often considered the primary caretaker, and children may have fewer opportunities to learn to care for children during childhood (Weisner & Gallimore, 1977; Whiting & Edwards, 1988). The personnel available influence lessons children learn about child caretaking.

Data to be considered in an activity settings analysis also include the *tasks* or activities themselves. Learning to weave, infant care, learning to figure the area of triangle, doing household chores, or playing are examples of activities in which children might engage.

The *scripts* for conduct in the activity include the typical pattern of social interaction and the cultural norms for self-expression. For example, in Zinacantec Maya culture in the highlands of Chiapas, Mexico, as in many cultures, older people are given respect (Vogt, 1969). This is demonstrated in many ways, such as when a large group of people is gathered together and the older people present are the first ones offered chairs, food, and drinks, if any. The comfort of elders is attended to first. This is an implicit script that is acquired through socialization in childhood and is reinforced throughout life.

The *motives* or purpose for doing the task are another important factor in an activity settings analysis. Analysis of motives requires understanding the meaning of the activity for the people who are doing it and their motivations for doing it. People's motives for participating in an activity influence how they behave in the task or activity. Individuals present may have different motives, and their participation may reflect this variety.

Lastly, an activity settings analysis involves understanding the *cultural values*, goals, and beliefs of the people participating. Looking at a particular activity through the lens of the culture's goals or values helps the researcher to understand how any activity could help to build a culturally competent individual over time. The structure and organization of activities reflect an underlying cultural belief system, and this belief system becomes represented in the minds of the participants as they engage in, transmit, and transform cultural practices.

Coordinated Changes in Reading Aptitude and Activity Settings in Hawaiian and Navajo Classrooms

The Kamehameha Early Education Program (KEEP) (Tharp, 1982; Tharp, Jordan, Speidel, Au, Klein, Calkins, Sloat, & Gallimore, 1984) is a useful example to illustrate the activity settings approach. The overarching goal of KEEP was to teach kids to read (R. Gallimore, personal communication, October, 2001). Native Hawaiian children were having trouble learning to read, and they showed a low level of attention to teachers and classwork. Instead they favored a strong orientation to peers, something which the teachers found disruptive (Gallimore, Boggs, & Jordan, 1974; Tharp & Gallimore, 1976). The conventional assumption was that the children had some kind of deficit in learning. Instead of accepting this limited assessment, the research team conducted ethnographic studies of the children's routines at home and found that children spent a lot of time with siblings, with older siblings acting as caretakers and guides or teachers for their younger siblings (Gallimore et al., 1974). This information provided the central clue to improving reading among Native Hawaiian children: making the classroom activity settings more congruent with those of the home might help the children in their struggle to learn to read (Weisner, Gallimore, & Jordan, 1988). Indeed, the use of peer teaching in the classroom contributed to significant gains in scholastic achievement in the Native Hawaiian group who participated in the intervention (Gallimore et al., 1974; Gallimore, Tharp, & Speidel, 1978).

An activity settings analysis provides insights into *how* and *why* the researchers were able to effectively change the behavior of the children to produce better reading. While the nature of the *task*, teaching children to read, remained the same, there were several changes in the activity setting which made the task more effective. First, the responsibility of the teaching *personnel* shifted from resting solely on the teachers to incorporating both the teachers and the students themselves. By incorporating the students themselves as personnel, the *script* for the task changed: Now the students would be responsible for their own learning and for that of others in their peer groups. This change in the script likely changed the *motives* on the part of the students, who became engaged in the process of learning together. Lastly, the changes in the activity setting are also reflected in the researchers' understanding of the *cultural values* of the students; students who were accustomed to functioning as sibling caretakers at home and at spending time interacting with and aiding peers were now able to apply that value to the classroom. The students' cultural values were now valued by the classroom activity setting, and learning improved as a result.

Navajo KEEP

After the KEEP program's success as an adaptation of familiar cultural activity settings to the classroom, Tharp and his colleagues were ready to test the hypothesis that its effectiveness was a result of cultural adaptations by trying KEEP in a new setting, a Navajo community on the U. S. mainland (Tharp, 1994). Children there, like the Native Hawaiians, were having trouble learning to read. Tharp and his colleagues were ready to observe the children and make necessary adaptations to help them. The KEEP paradigm had to be adapted to fit into the Navajo context.

Tharp and his colleagues found some interesting differences between the home activity settings of the Navajo children and the Hawaiian children. For example, Navajo children were accustomed to work with same-sex personnel in tasks at home, and they expressed a cultural value of thinking about a story as a whole rather than hearing it in parts and analyzing one part at a time. The Navajo children were operating under a more holistic script for understanding their world. KEEP was adapted to this and other scripts with the use of ethnographic findings of various activity settings in the Navajo community.

Tharp's research in both the Native Hawaiian and the Navajo communities shows how the strengths of the children are employed best when there is some congruence between the cultural scripts practiced at home and those practiced at school. That is, an intervention designed to help children learn to read was made more effective by linking the activity settings with which children were most familiar, those at home, to the activity settings at school.

Teachers Change Classroom Practices as They Gain Cultural Knowledge

An activity settings approach allows for the understanding of the ways that changes in one's knowledge or assumptions can effect changes in the activity settings, and their subsequent outcomes. In an intervention study, called Bridging Cultures, designed to help Latino students better bridge the culture between home and school, Trumbull, Greenfield, Rothstein-Fisch, and Quiroz (2001) targeted seven Los Angeles area teachers with the goal of increasing the teachers' cultural knowledge. Specifically, the researchers wanted to help the teachers understand culture as a process, generally, and two cultural frames of reference, individualism and collectivism. The belief was that if teachers understood the patterns of communication and learning found in the students' homes, they could organize instruction to be more consistent with those patterns (Trumbull, Greenfield, Rothstein-Fisch, & Maynard, in press; cf. Au & Jordan, 1981).

Trumbull, et al. (in press) document the ways that a core group of seven Los Angeles area teachers came to understand cultural processes and values, and adapted their classroom practices as a result. The approach to the sessions was not prescriptive as to specific changes that teachers should make in the classroom, but rather provided a general introduction to culture as a frame of reference from which to generate changes. It is significant that the researchers did not try to tell the teachers what to do; from the perspective of university researchers it made more sense to let the teachers lead the way on classroom innovations, as the teachers themselves were the personnel most involved in the school situation. Teachers came to be included as personnel in the intervention process and in subsequent publication of data.

Classroom Outcomes

The outcomes were powerful. Teachers became more collectivistic in their approach to classroom management strategies and policies. Further, they related to parents and families with greater understanding and mutuality. These findings are evidenced by the changes teachers made in the relevant classroom activity settings. For example, whereas teachers had expected children to perform work independently before the intervention, after the intervention teachers employed children as personnel to help each other succeed in the classroom. This is similar to the personnel shifts made by Tharp and colleagues in the KEEP and Navajo KEEP interventions. Teachers also changed the tasks that children performed in the classroom and the scripts for completing the tasks; for example in one teacher's classroom the script for completing an assignment shifted from independent completion to joint composition of stories. Teachers learned that knowledge for social purposes was important in the home cultures of the students, whereas the typical classroom values factual knowledge for knowledge's sake. After the intervention, the script for getting information from students shifted from disregarding what teachers had previously thought of as "just stories," to incorporating those stories and asking for elaborations on particular points of fact to expand on children's stories. These changes in the personnel and the scripts for activities impacted the children's motives, as they appeared to be more interested in school. The changes in the teachers' values impacted the activity settings of the classroom; now that teachers saw the children's cultural frame of reference as a legitimate way of doing activities in school, that value was communicated to students in practice.

Changes in Parent-Teacher Conferences

The teachers in the intervention also made changes in the activity setting of parent-teacher conferences. Greenfield, Quiroz, and Raeff (2000) reported significant cultural conflict between parents and teachers concerning the divergent ways the two groups were thinking of children. For the parents, the teacher was the child's primary educator, responsible for teaching literacy and numeracy skills. Parents saw their job as moral educators, raising their children to be good citizens. Teachers became very frustrated by parents who would constantly ask, "How is my child behaving?" when they were trying to focus on the child's academic performance. Another issue was that teachers did not understand why parents brought their entire family to the conference nor did they understand why a parent would praise another child present after the teacher gave praise to the student in her classroom. Furthermore, teachers had a difficult time scheduling conferences with individual families.

After the Bridging Cultures intervention, teachers changed the activity setting of the parent conferences, again by incorporating more of a collectivistic frame of reference. For example, after the teachers understood that parents saw themselves as moral educators, they made sure to include that kind of information in the meetings. After the intervention, teachers understood why parents would bring their entire family to the meeting, and why they would praise another child present after the teacher gave praise to one child; from the collectivistic perspective, children and families are more comfortable doing activities together (and they may have lacked child care) and they are less comfortable with having individuals singled out. Teachers learned that Latino immigrant parents valued the teachers' ability to manage a larger group of people, and they began to invite more than one family to group conferences, thus decreasing the overall number of meetings they had to hold while at the same time raising their status in the eyes of parents.

As a result of changes in the teachers' understanding of the cultural values of the parents, the activity setting of parent-teacher conferences also changed in terms of the five features of activity settings analysis. Teachers came to understand that the personnel did not have to be restricted to the parents and the teachers alone, but that the personnel could include the other family members and even multiple families. The task of meeting with parents to discuss children's performance was enhanced by teachers' understanding of the parents' frame of reference. The script of the activity setting changed to accommodate the parents' desire to understand their children as citizens of the classroom and their desire to spread praise among all their children. The teachers' motives shifted from controlling the interaction and struggling with the parents over the topics of conversation to engaging the parents in a joint process of discussing each child's performance as a complete package of academic attainments as well as citizenship contributions. By understanding the cultural values of the participants in the activity setting and aligning two previously divergent sets of cultural values, the teachers made the experience more enjoyable and productive for all.

The Schooling of Mothers and Siblings Affects Activity Settings at Home

We have seen how changes in schooling have been found to induce changes in students' behaviors in the classroom, but do these changes go beyond the school day? While school is a taken for granted activity setting for children in the United States, many children throughout the world do not have the opportunity to attend school. Researchers have been able to study the impact of schooling in communities where some children attend school and others do not. The findings point to changes in home activity settings after experience with school. School changes students as personnel in future activity settings and it changes how tasks are scripted and motivated. Two sets of findings have emerged regarding the impact of schooling, that of maternal schooling and that of sibling schooling (in a context where there is a general absence of maternal schooling). Overall, there is a multiplier effect of schooling; mothers who go to school are more likely to send their children to school (UNICEF, 2003), and siblings who go to school for a longer period are more likely to have siblings who persist in the educational pathway (Hauser & Wong, 1989). The specific effects of mothers' schooling center around social-class mobility and better health care, where mothers who have been to school experience the possibility of different pathways to success and healthy living. The findings on the effects of sibling schooling are quite limited, but they reflect the fact that siblings who go to school make changes in home activity settings that have effects similar to the changes made by mothers, including a more didactic language style.

Maternal Schooling

There are important findings in the literature on maternal schooling that point to changes in activity settings as a result of schooling experience. Mothers who have been to school have been found to have fewer children (Cleland & Jejeebhoy, 1996; Tapia Uribe, LeVine, & LeVine, 1994), thus changing the personnel composition of their households. Mothers with greater schooling experience have also been found to change the scripts of activities. For example, Chavajay and Rogoff (2002) asked groups of Guatemalan Maya mothers and three related children to construct a three-dimensional puzzle and found that communication structures in groups of mothers and their children differed significantly in the mothers who had more schooling. The mothers with more schooling engaged their children in hierarchical interactions, dividing the labor among the group. Mothers with less schooling were involved in multiparty engagements, where everyone played an equal role. This change in the script reflects a change in the way that the mothers see themselves and their children as personnel.

Maternal schooling also changes the nature of the tasks of mothering and of maternal guidance. In a sample in Cuernavaca, Mexico, Richman, Miller, and LeVine (1992) found that mothers with more schooling were more likely to look at and talk to their infants and to feed them more often when they cried. Also in Mexico, Zukow (1984) found that mothers engaged their children in a more dialectic language interactive style, questioning children and interacting with them as equal participants in a dialog. Mothers who have been to school verbally stimulate their children more than mothers who have not (Tapia Uribe et al.,

1994; Von der Lippe, 1999), and engage in more decontexualized talk (Tapia Uribe et al., 1994). Decontextualized talk, about things that are not present in time or space, is a hallmark of formal education and of other institutions, including bureaucracies such as health clinics (LeVine, LeVine, & Schnell, 2001). Women who have been to school can communicate in this specialized speech register and are more likely to participate in settings where they can communicate competently. Thus women who have been to school are more likely to make use of health services, including family planning, because they are familiar with this academic register (LeVine et al., 2001). In other words, the important maternal task of caring for one's health and the health of one's children is affected by schooling experience.

Mothers with more schooling are likely to experience a shift in their motives and cultural values toward raising children who are creative and verbally stimulated so that they can grow up to have good occupations (von der Lippe, 1999). In a study of Zinacantec Maya families in Chiapas, Mexico, Greenfield and Maynard (1997) found a relationship between schooling and weaving, an activity related to commerce; mothers who had been to school were able to use paper patterns, designed for embroidery, in their weaving activities. The value of a technological skill, weaving, was increased by changes in commercial activity in the community, as women began to weave designs to sell to tourists. Those schooled mothers who could weave with paper patterns could innovate more than unschooled mothers who could not. Yet mothers who had more schooling also steered their daughters away from the traditional activity of weaving and toward more schooling. While the schooled mothers saw the value of selling more textiles themselves, they saw more value in their daughters' educational attainments so that they could engage in non-traditional activities. This example shows how the education of women can erode the importance of traditional cultural activities through its impact on the socialization process.

Sibling Schooling

While women's schooling is increasing around the world, in some communities girls are only beginning to be educated. Worldwide, there are currently 121 million children of school age who are not attending school, many of whom have parents who also did not attend school (UNICEF, 2003). This raises the question as to the effect of having a sibling who goes to school, even if one's mother has not. Working with Zinacantec families in Mexico, Maynard (2004) found that even a small amount of sibling schooling had an impact on children's interactions, whereas the limited schooling achieved by the mothers did not. Children who had been to school talked more to their younger siblings and were more likely to give explanations than children who had not been to school. Furthermore, children who had been to school were more likely to talk to their siblings from a distance, instructing them in tasks, than were children who had not been to school, who were more likely to remain within arm's reach of their siblings in case they were needed. The script of the sibling activity setting shifted away from a traditional value of quietness and observation with bodily closeness toward a more distant, verbal style reflective of the school pattern.

Weaving Apprenticeship Changes as a Result of a Socioeconomic Shift to Commercial Activity

Activity settings analysis tolerates the notion that communities are not static. A shift in values or available personnel can change the scripts for activities, or even the nature of tasks themselves. Economic, social, and demographic changes may bring new practices to communities or may engender an evolution of existing practices in order to adapt to a changing environment. Processes of development and socialization practices may also change over time as communities change or with immigration (Greenfield, 2000). For example, Greenfield and colleagues found that scripts for teaching girls to weave changed dramatically between 1970 and the 1990s (Greenfield, Maynard, & Childs, 2000, 2003). In 1970, the script for teaching girls to weave involved a highly scaffolded process where a teacher from the older generation was always near the learner (Childs & Greenfield, 1980). This script for cultural teaching is emphasized when resources are scarce and the cost of error is very high (Greenfield, 1984; Rogoff, 1990). Under this script, cultural conservation is emphasized (Greenfield & Lave, 1982). By the 1990s, the script for teaching girls to weave shifted to a more independent, trial-and-error learning process in which teachers were often from the same generation as the learner (Greenfield et al., 2000, 2003). This script emphasizes cultural innovation.

As the economy changed in Zinacantán, activity settings also changed. The personnel assigned to teach girls to weave shifted from the older generation to the younger generation. The script of learning to weave shifted to a more independent, trial-and-error process. The motivations to weave shifted from a predominant goal of clothing one's self and one's family to weaving more for others, especially the production of textiles to sell in the marketplace to tourists. This motivation may also have shifted the Zinacantecs' feelings and values about weaving: weaving that has always been thought of as women's work can now produce money. The task of weaving itself has thus changed in response to the market economy; indeed many girls are now maturing without knowing how to weave, working for wages instead. The activity setting of weaving changed to adapt to a changing world.

Developmental Psychology Changes as Researchers Understand Culture

Research endeavors are also subject to activity settings analysis. There are personnel, usually consisting of research faculty and the students they are training. The tasks to be accomplished are many, including the design of research studies, the navigation of the Institutional Review Board process, the procurement of funding, the training of students, the collection of data, data analysis and dissemination. There are typical scripts for each of these activities. The motivations for conducting research range from improving living and learning conditions for children and their families, to intellectual curiosity, to attaining tenure and professional advancement, among others. The beliefs and cultural values expressed in research are often taken for granted, implicitly guiding the practice of data collection and reporting.

Shifts in the Activity Setting of Research

Researchers who study culture in human development have made some important shifts in the activity setting of research. For example, the research personnel have come to include indigenous collaborators who can inform a study's methods and help to ensure ecological validity of the findings. Definitions of categories of personnel have also changed. For example, as researchers have come to understand cultural context better, they have moved toward an inclusion of more than nuclear family members in the concept of family (Parke & Buriel, 1998). Researchers must define what they mean by family, which can include single-parent families, blended families, and extended kin (Gauvain, 2001).

Those who study culture and development have taken on new methods in their investigations, thus changing the tasks to be completed. Along these lines, early cross-cultural psychologists who worked on development committed the fallacy of transferring a task developed in one culture to another culture, in hopes of maintaining methodological consistency and objectivity (Greenfield, 1997a).

More culturally minded developmental psychologists have learned to adapt the task of research to the cultural milieu. For example, Saxe and Moylan (1982) studied concrete operations in Oksapmin in Papua New Guinea through studying children's performance on a task designed with familiar cultural materials, string bags familiar to children. The researchers ask questions such as, "If a seven-year-old child were to weave a string bag to come up to the elbow of his father, where would it have to come up to on the child?" Obviously the bag would reach a point higher on the child's arm than on the arm of the father, and giving such an answer would indicate that the child had an understanding of concrete operations. The underlying psychology of conservation is present in various ways of measuring concrete operations, but children can only express their knowledge of conservation if that knowledge is tapped by tasks that make sense within a familiar cultural frame of reference.

Maynard and Greenfield (2003) similarly adapted a task to study cognitive development based on fieldwork experience with Zinacantec Maya people in Mexico. Instead of assuming that a child with conservation abilities would be able to demonstrate such skills on any apparatus, Maynard and Greenfield used the ethnographic observation that weaving tools were adapted to developmental capabilities of learners to inform a research design using indigenous tools to tap concrete operations. The findings indicated that parents were assigning the weaving tools at the children's appropriate stages of development, and that the children could exhibit the expected cognitive abilities at the expected developmental stages.

Researchers who study culture and development have taken on a variety of tasks as legitimate methods of data collection, in addition to the usual quantitative methods employed in psychological research. These include ethnographic field notes and ethnographic video collection, as well as other methods used in anthropology and ethology, such as interviews, the study of narrative, and naturalistic observation (Greenfield, 1997b).

A shift in values is evident in the increasing attempts to understand a variety of cultural beliefs and values present in many of the world's cultures. An appreciation for the world's diversity also translates into an increase in interest in ethnic minority groups in the United States. Early research involving children in minority groups operated under a "deficit model," where minority children were seen as having a deficit in terms of readiness for and aptitude in school. A more cultural approach aims to understand the backgrounds and frames of reference of all children, valuing a range of possible scripts that children may be familiar with and translating them to research literature. Activity settings analysis could be used by researchers to better understand their own motivations, beliefs, and values.

Activity settings analysis could also be used by researchers to understand the motivations, beliefs, and values of the participants of a potential study. Such an understanding could lead to new questions and methods for research better adapted to incorporate the participants' frame of reference. For example, Weisner (1996) reports a mother's comments about her child who was subjected to the Strange Situation procedure, designed to measure attachment quality of the mother-child relationship in American families. According to the Strange Situation paradigm, a secure attachment is indicated by the child's distress with separation from the caregiver, and the ability to be comforted upon the caregiver's return. Other reactions to the paradigm are considered to indicate insecure attachments, including a child who is undisturbed by the caregiver's departure and nonplussed at her return. The mother in Weisner's example saw her child behaving in a way that she herself thought was very adaptive and secure, but that the coders of the procedure labeled "insecure." The mother commented that the child was behaving just in the manner in which she had raised him. There was a mismatch between the views of the researcher and the values of the mother whose childrearing practices were in question. For the culturally minded researcher who wants to understand attachment, a preliminary investigation of what is valued in the infant-care relationship would be a guide toward more sensitive, appropriate, and valid methods. This would decrease the number of mismatches between the experience of the research subjects and the investigator.

As another example of a shift in values, work with Yucatec Maya families where children do not engage in elaborate pretend play and where play is not supported by parents (Gaskins, 1996; Gaskins & Göncü, 1992) challenges the widely held assumption that children in all cultures engage in pretend play and that pretend play is helpful, or even necessary, for development (Singer, 1995). As researchers stretch their belief systems to include other possible ways of knowing, conventional assumptions are challenged and the field of developmental psychology asks deeper questions about the nature of development, and about what is necessary or sufficient for development.

Predicted Changes in the Activity Setting of Research

Developmental psychology has changed significantly in recent years. For example, in the past, those interested in studying cognitive development focused on how children's thinking changed when they tested hypotheses through active experimentation in a world of objects (e.g., Piaget, 1952). Although these ideas continue to be important, many developmental researchers now emphasize the surrounding social milieu that supports the development of skills and knowledge valued by a child's community and the roles of significant others such as parents, peers, and siblings in supporting that development (e.g., Gauvain, 2001; Harwood, Miller, & Lucca Irizarry, 1995; Maynard, 2002; Rogoff, 1990). The momentum already achieved by researchers studying culture and development can be augmented by the following predicted changes:

1. *Researchers will learn to use a variety of methods and will often employ multiple methods in research.* A researcher armed with knowledge of multiple methods will be able to ask any question and then decide on the best method to answer the question. This will involve training in both qualitative methods, such as ethnography, and quantitative methods, such as experimental design (cf. Weisner, 1997).

    1a. *Training in human development will involve ethnographic fieldwork in another cultural place* (cf. Weisner, 1996, 1997). Understanding of activity settings and processes of development will be enhanced by exposure to other ways of being in the world.

2. *More descriptions of context will be included in research reports.* Research reports in journals and books will include descriptions of cultural context (cf. Harkness, 1992), including the real-world activities in which children participate. This will help others to interpret the findings and to design parallel studies to uncover common mechanisms or phenomena of development.

3. *More descriptive examples, including transcripts and other snapshots of behavior will be included in research reports.* This has already been asked of authors seeking to publish in journals such as *Child Development* and in seeking funds for research with grant proposals. Inclusion of such information will allow the reader to assess whether what has been measured is a valid reflection of reality (as expressed in the examples).

4. *Research on culture and development will continue to challenge conventional assumptions, thus enhancing our understanding of both.*

5. *There will be a new multidisciplinary journal looking specifically at culture and development.* The editorial board will be comprised of scholars from diverse disciplines such as psychology, anthropology, applied linguistics, education, and sociology. There currently exists no journal specifically focused on culture and child development, though there are several important journals looking at culture and psychology more generally.

6. *Textbooks will shift from putting cultural information in "boxes" aside from the text to making culture as a process a central focus of the discussion of development.* A new textbook with such a focus is already being prepared for publication by Greenfield, Keller, and Kagitscibaci, and other textbooks will likely adapt to new knowledge discovered in the study of culture and development.
7. *Give all of the above, the language of marginalization will become more and more scarce as multiple pathways of development are brought out into relief. A language of inclusion will develop to encompass the many possible cultural frames of reference and contexts that support the developing child.* The effects of these changes will include better learning environments and opportunities for all children, better access to health care, a reduction in racism (especially institutional racism), and better, more ecologically valid research designs and intervention projects.

Conclusions

In this chapter we have seen how sustainable change in individual development and in cultural practices is made possible at the level of activity (cf. Gallimore et al., 1993; O'Donnell & Tharp, 1990; O'Donnell et al., 1993). An activity settings approach is ideal for understanding child development in its cultural context. Activity settings analysis is flexible and adapts easily to changes in the cultural surround.

The study of changing behavior is at the heart of developmental psychology. As they develop, children change as personnel in activity settings, thus changing others' responses to them and the scripts that are enacted. As the cultures of the world change, activities are adopted across cultures, but they are adapted to the frame of reference of the personnel performing them (Cole, 1996). We have seen in this chapter how changes in schooling have helped children learn, how schooling has influenced changes in activity settings outside of school, and how socioeconomic changes at a distal level effected changes at the proximal level of weaving apprenticeship. Rather than using culture as an independent variable (Greenfield, 1997b), activity settings analysis provides a picture of development as a complete process where activity creates a person at the same time that the person is creating it.

Note

Special thanks to Darnell Cole and Su Yeong Kim for helpful comments on an earlier draft of this chapter.

References

Au, K., & Jordan, C. (1981). Teaching reading to Hawaiian children: Finding a culturally appropriate solution. In H. Trueba, G. Guthrie, & K. Au (Eds.), *Culture and the bilingual classroom* (pp. 139–152). Rowley, MA: Newbury House.

Chavajay, P., & Rogoff, B. (2002). Schooling and traditional collaborative social organization of problem solving by Mayan mothers and children. *Developmental Psychology, 38*, 55–66.

Childs, C. P., & Greenfield, P. M. (1980). Informal modes of learning and teaching: The case of Zinacanteco weaving. In N. Warren (Ed.), *Studies in cross-cultural psychology, Vol. 2* (pp. 269–316). London: Academic Press.

Cleland, J., & Jejeebhoy, S. (1996). Maternal schooling and fertility: Evidence from censuses and surveys. In R. Jeffery & A. M. Basu (Eds.), *Girls' schooling, women's autonomy and fertility change in South Asia* (pp. 72–106). Thousand Oaks, CA: Sage Publications.

Cole, M. (1996). *Cultural psychology: A once and future discipline.* Cambridge: Harvard University Press.

Cole, M., Gay, J., Glick, J., & Sharp, J. (1971). *The cultural context of learning and thinking: An exploration in experimental anthropology.* New York: Basic Books.

Cole, M., & Scribner, S. (1977). Cross-cultural studies of memory and cognition. In R. V. Kail, Jr., & J. W. Hagen (Eds.), *Perspectives on the development of memory and cognition.* Hillsdale, NJ: Erlbaum.

Dasen, P. R. (1977). Cross-cultural cognitive development: The cultural aspects of Piaget's theory. *Annals of the New York Academy of Sciences, 285*, 332–337.

Farver, J. A. M. (1999). Activity setting analysis: A model for examining the role of culture in development. In A. Göncü (Ed.), *Children's engagement in the world* (pp. 99–127). New York: Cambridge University Press.

Gallimore, R., Boggs, J. W., & Jordan, C. (1974). *Culture, behavior, and education: A study of Hawaiian-Americans.* Beverly Hills: Sage.

Gallimore, R., Goldenberg, C., & Weisner, T. S. (1993). The social construction and subjective reality of activity settings: Implications for community psychology. *American Journal of Community Psychology, 21*, 537–559.

Gallimore, R., Tharp, R. G., & Speidel, G. E. (1978). The relationship of sibling caretaking and attentiveness to a peer tutor. *American Educational Research Journal, 15*, 267–273.

Gaskins, S. (1996). How Mayan parental theories come into play. In S. Harkness & C. M. Super (Eds.), *Parents' cultural belief systems* (pp. 345–363). New York: Guilford Press.

Gaskins, S. (1999). Children's daily lives in a Mayan village: A case study of culturally constructed roles and activities. In A. Goncu (Ed.), *Children's engagement in the world: Sociocultural perspectives* (pp. 25–61). Cambridge: Cambridge University Press.

Gaskins, S. & Göncü, A. (1992). Cultural variation in play: A challenge to Piaget and Vygotsky. *The Quarterly Newsletter of the Laboratory of Comparative Human Cognition, 14,* 31–35.

Gauvain, M. (2001). *The social context of cognitive development.* New York: Guilford Press.

Greenfield, P. M. (1984). A theory of the teacher in the learning activities of everyday life. In B. Rogoff & J. Lave (Eds.), *Everyday cognition: Its development in social context* (pp. 117–138). Cambridge, MA: Harvard University Press.

Greenfield, P. M. (1997a). You can't take it with you: Why ability assessments don't cross cultures. *American Psychologist, 52,* 1115–1124.

Greenfield, P. M. (1997b). Culture as process: Empirical methods for cultural psychology. In J. W. Berry, Y. Poortinga, & J. Pandey (Eds.), *Handbook of cross-cultural psychology: Vol. 1. Theory and method* (pp. 301–346). Boston: Allyn & Bacon.

Greenfield, P. M. (2000). Culture and universals: Integrating social and cognitive development. In L. P. Nucci, G. B. Saxe, & E. Turiel (Eds.), *Culture, thought, and development. The Jean Piaget Symposium Series* (pp. 231–277). Mahwah, NJ: Lawrence Erlbaum Associates.

Greenfield, P. M., & Bruner, J. S. (1966). Culture and cognitive growth. *International Journal of Psychology, 1,* 89–107.

Greenfield, P. M., & Cocking, R. R. (1994). *Cross-cultural roots of minority child development.* Hillsdale, NJ: Erlbaum.

Greenfield, P., & Lave, J. (1982). Cognitive aspects of informal education. In D. Wagner & H. Stevenson (Eds.), *Cultural perspectives on child development* (pp. 181–207). San Francisco: Freeman, 1982.

Greenfield, P. M., & Maynard, A. E. (1997, November). Women, girls, apprenticeship, and schooling: A longitudinal study of historical change among the Zinacantecan Maya. In I. Zambrano (Chair), *Women's Schooling in Maya Chiapas: Naming the Unnamed.* 96th Annual Meeting of the American Anthropological Association. Washington, DC.

Greenfield, P. M., Maynard, A. E., & Childs, C. P. (2000). History, Culture, Learning, and Development. *Cross-Cultural Research: The Journal of Comparative Social Science. Special Issue in Honor of Ruth Munroe, 34,* 351–74.

Greenfield, P. M., Maynard, A. E., & Childs, C. P. (2003). Historical change, cultural apprenticeship, and cognitive representation in Zinacantec Maya children. *Cognitive Development, 18,* 455–487.

Greenfield, P. M., Quiroz. B., & Raeff, C. (2000). Cross-cultural conflict and harmony in the social construction of the child, in S. Harkness, C. Raeff, & C. R. Super (Eds.), *The social construction of the child, New Directions in Child Development* (pp. 93–108). San Francisco: Jossey-Bass.

Greenfield, P. M., Reich, L. C., & Olver, R. R. (1966). On culture and equivalence—II. In J. S. Bruner, R. R. Olver, P. M. Greenfield (Eds.), *Studies in cognitive growth* (pp. 270–318). New York: Wiley.

Harkness, S. (1992). Cross-cultural research in child development: A sample of the state of the art. *Developmental Psychology, 28*, 622–625.

Harwood, R. L., Miller, J., & Lucca Irizarry, N. (1995). *Culture and attachment: Perceptions of the child in context*. New York: Guilford Press.

Hauser, R. M., & Wong, R. S.-K. (1989). Sibling resemblance and intersibling effects in educational attainment. *Sociology of Education, 62*, 149–171.

Hirschfeld, L. A. (2002). Why don't anthropologists like children? *American Anthropologist, 104*, 611–627.

Keller, H. (2003). Socialization for competence: Cultural models of infancy. *Human Development, 46*, 288–311.

LeVine, R. A., LeVine, S. E., & Schnell, B. (2001). "Improve the women": Mass schooling, female literacy, and worldwide social change. *Harvard Educational Review, 71*, 1–50.

Maynard, A. E. (2002). Cultural teaching: The development of teaching skills in Zinacantec Maya sibling interactions. *Child Development, 73*, 969–82.

Maynard, A. E. (2004). Cultures of teaching in childhood: Formal schooling and Maya sibling teaching at home. *Cognitive Development, 19*(4): 517–536.

Maynard, A. E., & Greenfield, P. M. (2003). Implicit cognitive development in cultural tools and children: Lessons from Mayan Mexico. *Cognitive Development, 18*, 489–510.

O'Donnell, C. R., & Tharp, R. G. (1990). Community intervention guided by theoretical development. In A. S. Bellack, M. Hersen, & A. E. Kazdin (Eds.) *International handbook of behavior modification and therapy*. 2nd edition (pp. 251–266). New York: Plenum Press.

O'Donnell, C. R., Tharp, R. G., & Wilson, K. (1993). Activity settings as the unit of analysis: A theoretical basis for community intervention and development. *American Journal of Community Psychology, 21*, 501–520.

Parke, R. D., & Buriel, R. (1998). Socialization in the family: Ethnic and ecological perspectives. In W. Damon (Series Ed.) & N. Eisenberg (Vol. Ed.), *Handbook of child psychology: Vol. 3. Social, emotional, and personality development* (pp. 463–552). New York: Wiley.

Piaget, J. (1952). *The origins of intelligence in children*. New York: International Universities Press.

Richman, A. L., Miller, P. M., & LeVine, R. A. (1992). Cultural and educational variations in maternal responsiveness. *Developmental Psychology, 28*, 614–621.

Rogoff, B. (1990). *Apprenticeship in thinking.* New York: Oxford University Press.

Rogoff, B. (2003). *The cultural nature of human development.* New York: Oxford University Press.

Rogoff, B., Baker-Sennett, J., Lacasa, P., & Goldsmith, D. (1995). Development through participation in sociocultural activity. *New Directions for Child Development, 67*, 45–65.

Sagi, A., van Ijzendoorn, M. H., Aviezer, O., Donnell, F., & Mayseless, O. (1994). Sleeping out of home in a kibbutz communal arrangement: It makes a difference for mother-infant attachment. *Child Development, 65*, 992–1004.

Saxe, G. B., & Moylan, T. (1982). The development of measurement operations among the Oksapmin of Papua New Guinea. *Child Development, 53*, 1242–1248.

Singer, J. L. (1995). Imaginative play in childhood: A precursor of subjunctive thought, daydreaming, and adult pretending games. In A. D. Pellegrini (Ed.) *The future of play theory: A multidisciplinary inquiry into the contributions of Brian Sutton-Smith* (pp. 187–219). Albany, NY: SUNY Press.

Tapia Uribe, M. F., LeVine, R. A., & LeVine. S. E. (1994). Maternal behavior in a Mexican community: The changing environments of children. In P. M. Greenfield & R. R. Cocking (Eds.) *Cross-cultural roots of minority child development* (pp. 41–54). Hillsdale, NJ: Lawrence Erlbaum Associates, Inc.

Tharp, R. (1982). The effective instruction of comprehension: Results and description of the Kamehameha Early Education Program. *Reading Research Quarterly, 17*, 503–527.

Tharp, R. G. (1994). Intergroup differences among Native Americans in socialization and child cognition: An ethnogenetic analysis. In P. M. Greenfield & R. R. Cocking (Eds.), *Cross-cultural roots of minority child development* (pp. 87–105). Hillsdale, NJ: Lawrence Erlbaum Associates.

Tharp, R., & Gallimore, R. (1976). *The uses and limits of social reinforcement and industriousness for learning to read (Technical Report Number 60).* Honolulu: Kamehameha Early Education Project, The Kamehameha Schools/Prince Bernice Pauahi Bishop Estate.

Tharp, R., & Gallimore, R. (1988). *Rousing minds to life: Teaching, learning, and schooling in social context.* Cambridge: Cambridge University Press.

Tharp, R. G., Jordan, C., Speidel, G. E., Au, K. H., Klein, T. W., Calkins, R. P., Sloat, K. C. M., & Gallimore, R. (1984). Product and process in applied developmental research: Education and the children of a minority. In M. E. Lamb, A. L., Brown, & B. Rogoff (Eds), *Advances in developmental psychology, Vol. III* (pp. 91–141). Hillsdale, NJ: Lawrence Erlbaum & Associates, Inc.

Trumbull, E., Greenfield, P. M., Rothstein-Fisch, C., & Quiroz, B. (2001). *Bridging cultures between home and school: A guide for teachers.* Mahwah, NJ: Lawrence Erlbaum Associates.

Trumbull, E., Greenfield, P. M., Rothstein-Fisch, C., & Maynard, A. E. (in press). Altering the Discourse of Schooling: How Teachers Bridge Cultures in Latino Immigrant Education. To appear in *Bridging Cultures in Latino Immigrant Education*. New York: Russell Sage.

UNICEF. (2003). *The state of the world's children 2004*. New York: Author.

Vogt, E. Z. (1969). *Zinacantan: A Maya community in the highlands of Chiapas*. Cambridge, MA: Harvard University Press.

Von der Lippe, A. L. (1999). The impact of maternal schooling and occupation on child-rearing attitudes and behaviours in low-income neighborhoods in Cairo, Egypt. *International Journal of Behavioural Development, 23*, 703–729.

Vygotsky, L. S. (1978). *Mind in society: The development of higher psychological processes*. (Eds. and Trans. by M. Cole, V. John-Steiner, S. Scribner, & E. Souberman). Cambridge, MA: Harvard University Press.

Weisner, T. S. (1989). Cultural and universal aspects of social support for children: Evidence from the Abaluyia of Kenya. In D. Belle (Ed.), *Children's social networks and social supports* (pp. 70–90). New York: John Wiley & Sons.

Weisner, T. S. (1996). Why ethnography should be the most important method in the study of human development. In R. Jessor, A. Colby, & R. A. Shweder (Eds.), *Ethnography and human development: Context and meaning in social inquiry* (pp. 305–326). Chicago: University of Chicago Press.

Weisner, T. S. (1997). The ecocultural project of human development: Why ethnography and its findings matter. *Ethos, 25*(2): 177–190.

Weisner, T. S. (1998). Human development, well-being, and the cultural project of development. In D. Sharma & K. Fischer (Eds.), *Socio-emotional development across cultures. New directions in child development, No. 81* (pp. 69–85). San Francisco: Jossey-Bass.

Weisner, T. S., & Gallimore, R. (1977). My brother's keeper: Child and sibling caretaking. *Current Anthropology, 18* (2), 169–190.

Weisner, T. S., & Gallimore, R. (1985, December). *The convergence of ecocultural and activity theory*. Paper presented at the Annual Meeting of the American Anthropological Association, Washington, DC.

Weisner, T. S., & Gallimore, R., & Jordan, C. (1988). Unpackaging cultural effects on classroom learning: Native Hawaiian peer assistance and child-generated activity. *Anthropology & Education Quarterly, 19*, 327–87.

Weisner, T. S., Matheson, C., & Bernheimer, L. (1995). American cultural models of early influence and parent recognition of developmental delays: Is earlier always better than later? In S. Harkness & C. Super (Eds.), *Parents' cultural belief systems: Their origins, expressions, and consequences* (pp. 496–531). New York: Guilford.

Whiting, B. B., & Edwards, C. P. (1988). *Children of different worlds: The formation of social behavior*. Cambridge, MA: Harvard University Press.

Whiting, B. B., & Whiting, J. M. (1975). *Children of six cultures: A psycho-cultural analysis.* Cambridge, MA: Harvard University Press.

Zukow, P. G. (1984). Folk theories of comprehension and caregiver practices in a rural-born population in Central Mexico. *The Quarterly Newsletter of the Laboratory of Comparative Human Cognition, 6,* 62–67.

CHAPTER 4

Community:
The Ties That Bind

Richard N. Roberts

Introduction

The year was 1975—a seminar room on the first floor of Gartley Hall. As second year clinical psychology students at the University of Hawai'i, we were taking our first course from Dr. Roland Tharp in Child Behavioral Clinical Assessment. Early in the semester Roland mentioned that he was "thinking of starting a set of studies on cognition with younger children. If any one is interested, come and talk to me." I did; and as they say, that was the beginning of an enduring relationship with a mentor, colleague, and friend who understood and created a "community of learners" long before this so-often-used phrase was in our lexicon. It was also at a time when some of the better known behavioral applied psychologists were on the clinical faculty of the Psychology Department of the University of Hawai'i. Cognition? Was that legal?

The work that engaged us over the course of the next several years occurred at the time Vygotsky was being rediscovered in U.S psychology/child development. *Thought and language* (Vygotsky, 1962) served as the jumping off point for many of our discussions and my early research endeavors. *Mind and society* (Vygotsky, 1978) followed a bit later. "Wow, now we were into some real meaty stuff." Roland intuitively understood the zone of proximal development and assisted us as we pushed our emerging understanding of these concepts in relation to our work and ourselves. It was the best place for me to be as a graduate student as we grappled with these constructs in a clinical program known at that time as a hot bed of behavior modification. It was a true Marxian dialectic. How could we integrate these two models and come to some higher order synthesis?

The challenge of integrating constructs that on the surface appear to be contradictory is perhaps one of the prime movers of science as described by Kuhn (1962) and more recently by Rappaport (1981). In praising these apparent paradoxes, Rappaport argued that it was one sided (and bad science) to become focused on one side of a dialectical problem while ignoring the other. He quoted McGrath (1978, p. 36), who concluded that *"most of the social issues of our time are fundamentally of this form: a basic opposition of two or more 'valid'* (that is morally correct) *principles"* and that *"most social issues of this form have at least two 'decent' solutions* (i.e., morally justifiable) *sides to them (often more than two)"* [italics in original].

In this chapter, this theme of connecting the "understood" with more uncomfortable but ultimately more intellectually satisfying paradigms for investigating and affecting human behavior will be explored as the science of community psychology has come of age (Revenson et al., 2002).

Roland's learning nest was the Kamehameha Early Education Project (KEEP). As a learning community, KEEP was a cauldron of ideas that exemplified this need to explore all of the opposing hypotheses and points of view in understanding the data as they emerged. It has been described elsewhere in much detail (Tharp, Estrada, Dalton, & Yamauchi, 2000; Tharp & Gallimore, 1988). It was a social experiment to transform the educational experiences of Hawaiian children by understanding and using their strengths, learning styles, and interactional patterns both with adults and other children as learning tools in the social construction of the educational experience. It was funded by a visionary group of Trustees of the Bernice Puahi Bishop Estate at the Kamehameha Schools. As a beginning graduate student it was a gold mine of ideas and relationships. Hours on the observation deck of the elementary school watching native Hawaiian kindergarteners and first graders using private speech to internalize that which had been interactive speech moments before, eventually led to my dissertation and first set of studies with respect to private speech and its relationship to early reading skills (Roberts, 1981; Roberts & Tharp, 1980). It also became the first of many lessons on the need to take scientific tools to the community to affect outcomes for children and families.

These research issues were foreign to my naïve language in talking about them and, as Senge (1994, p. xiv) has suggested, "Change is hard—it can only be done in a community of learners." As I joined into the stream, taking part in this learning community in the late 1970s, it created the paradigm that has since framed my professional life. What Roland helped create with us served us well. The mental models I now work with in the community-developmental psychology/systems development/health psychology/program evaluation paradigm were shaped and refined in this dialectic.

As my career grew and interests matured, the need to make research relevant to the everyday issues of families and communities became a more pressing issue for me. Working with my own graduate students in my first academic position was fulfilling. Together we created a community of learners where we were able to explore the application of Vygotskian theory to a range of school and clinical problems. I began to develop mental models of how I thought, realizing that the locus of my thinking did not occur "in here"—but somewhere within the social space of the interactions I was having with other people—independent of whether that other person or persons was physically present or not. That is, my perceptions, understanding, and will to action were not a function of isolated development, but rather that of interdependent framing of issues, ideas, and ways of being that were created in the cauldron of meaningful activity with others.

At the same time we were doing this work, the applied science of psychology was also going through a parallel evolution/revolution in confronting many of the same dialectic issues. The emerging emphasis on themes of relevance, larger units of analysis, interactional issues of shared power and decision making and the application of community and neo-Vygotskian perspectives in addressing human issues have been well documented in the recent volume on the first 25 years of community psychology as a field. As described by Yoshikawa and Shinn (2002),

> The issues identified by the participants in the Swampscott Conference in 1965 remain central to community psychology today. Facilitating change, fostering empowerment, promoting competence, and preventing dysfunction are still challenges, although we may have more examples to guide our efforts. (p. 44)

The emergence of the community research and action paradigm has expanded our understanding of social system structures and functions, emphasized diversity of populations, broadened the focus of interventions from individuals to social systems, and developed innovative methods for assessing contextual change.

Here at the Early Intervention Research Institute (EIRI), in our work with families, communities, and service/support systems, we have reduced many of these issues into six principles that guide our research, evaluation, and systems change activities. Interventions with families, including evaluation activities, work best when they are:

1. Responsive to family (community) challenges, priorities and strengths;
2. Developed in partnership with constituents;
3. Respectful for cultural norms and practices;
4. Psychologically and physically accessible to families;
5. Affordable to families and society; and
6. Coordinated with families and across service systems (Roberts, 1999).

Such a list may seem mundane at this point and obvious to anyone working in applied settings. Yet, they are not used routinely or holistically in the development or implementation of programs designed to assist families in addressing issues in raising children with complex needs in their local communities. Nor are these precepts used regularly to conduct research and evaluation on programs. For me, these principles emerged through learning opportunities stemming from projects that were large-scale, systems-change activities. In short, a "do with" rather than a "do to" paradigm is the underlying construct (Heron & Reason, 2001). In the examples to follow, the need for this "do with" mentality was learned often through some rather painful experiences—ones that became very powerful learning tools for the next time. These two examples include:

1. Prekindergarten Education Program (PREP)—an inclusive prenatal-to-age five proactive educational program for Native Hawaiian children and their families; and
2. Opening Doors into Rural Communities (ODRC)—the development of methodology for systems-change activities within early intervention programs for children ages zero to three in four rural communities across the U.S.

Each of these activities was a funded program (Federal, state, private) for which I was responsible in leading a team to affect change on a social problem using an evidence-based model of intervention.

Prekindergarten Education Program

In a search for a more applied context in which to practice this craft, at Roland's invitation I left the academic setting to return to Hawai'i in 1983 in order to begin a research and demonstration project parallel to KEEP that became known as PREP (Prekindergarten Education Program) for native Hawaiian children and their families prenatal to age five. It was in this context that community (both as a concept and as the context of intervention) became real to me (Roberts, 1988). However, I still had much to learn about the power of collaboration as a research methodology and an agent for change.

The research and demonstration activity associated with PREP is detailed elsewhere (e.g., Roberts, 1988). Its base proposition, similar to KEEP, was that Native Hawaiian children are like all children in that they grow up within a particular eco-cultural niche in nurturing environments that prepare them for life (Weisner, Gallimore, & Jordan, 1993). They enter school with a range of skills, language abilities, and attitudes formed by the experiences available to them within these eco-cultural settings. Though there is not a uniform Hawaiian experience in growing up (see D'Amoto as cited in Roberts, 1993b), there are archetypes that are the best predictors of the influences active in Hawaiian families and communities.

The goal of PREP was to develop, implement, and replicate a culturally competent educational system for young Hawaiian children and their families. To do so, it had to first understand the current childrearing practices and then to shape early education programs in ways that would enhance child development without damaging important ecological and cultural foundations of the communities and families with whom we were working. From the beginning, its intention was to create educational opportunities consistent with these archetypes and the families' value systems. We were not out to fix something that was broken. As I have written elsewhere,

> PREP differed significantly from its predecessor (KEEP) in that KEEP's mandate was to demonstrate ways to fix a broken educational system at the elementary school level. In contrast, PREP's task was to create proactive, culturally affirming, education opportunities for young Hawaiian children and their families in settings where there were relatively few, if any, formal community-based services. (Roberts, 1993a, p. 275)

The Settings

Program development was guided by constructs that included the following.

1. The program's primary focus would be educational. It had to recognize and address the educational, health, and social service needs of families from an educational perspective.
2. The program would be proactive and inclusive. Communities became the units for developing new educational opportunities rather than a particularly at-risk subset of the ethnic Hawaiian population (Heath & Plett, 1986).
3. The program had to be acceptable to Hawaiian community leaders and to have strong face validity with respect to their concerns about new programs coming into the community.
4. The program had to provide a natural progression of educational experiences for families beginning with the prenatal period and continuing until the child entered kindergarten. Given the mobility of Hawaiian families, the program had to be designed in such a way that parents could elect to participate in the entire program or could be involved in components and still find it meaningful for themselves and their child.

5. The program was to mirror the gradually expanding social networks of young children. First, the program was to focus on the parents and the extended family members in helping them to ensure a healthy, full-term infant. This was followed by an emphasis on providing educational opportunities for the child and the family within an increasing circle of social contacts as the child became introduced to the community. These experiences were to become more school-like as the child neared the age in which formal schooling would take place.

The prenatal-to-age five set of programs that met these needs became the setting for the PREP program. Families could enter the program at any of three points. The home-visiting program was designed for parents expecting a child through the first two years of life. Kupulani, or Growing Heavenward, first emphasized issues of health of the mother and the developing child. After the birth, a relatively standardized curriculum was followed with some individual family variation (Hosaka, 1983; Peet, 1986; Roberts, 1988).

Between the ages of two and three, children could attend the Traveling Preschool, which consisted of a van loaded with activities that pulled up to a local park, church, beach, or community center two mornings a week with a teacher and a hope that it did not rain that day. Parents, extended family members, or the babysitter and the children helped the teacher set up the learning centers on grass mats around the confined area. The two-hour period was filled with opportunities for children to interact within five to six learning centers set up each day. There was time for parent visits while the children had snacks. Visits from the bookmobile, librarian, public health nurse, and so on, were common. Informal parent-support networks formed. The emphasis on materials used in the settings was one of inexpensive toys and incidental learning. There was less emphasis on making parents teachers of their children than on providing fun, easy, culturally competent experiences for families around a semi-school-like setting. It was much less structured than a school but more structured than just going to visit friends.

At the age of four, children were eligible for the formal four-year-old preschool. Initially, the preschools were established and the teachers were hired to begin a relatively standard preschool curriculum. Over time, the preschool classrooms began to emphasize language and pre-literacy experiences with instruction and interaction that drew on the strengths of Hawaiian children. Several models of parent and extended family involvement were tried, with varying degrees of success.

As this entire programmatic effort was being created, the research and the evaluation efforts were also being developed. The tension between program development and research to inform that development process was a problem not unique to this setting. The problems in creating an interface between research and educational practice extend well beyond this project to the larger educational system in this country (Roberts, 1993a). Others, such as Cuban (1990), Keough (1990), and Tharp and Gallimore (1988) have pointed out the difficulties in wedding these two seemingly orthogonal enterprises.

Principles in Action

The distinct programs that constituted PREP were a combination of creating new ones, as well as consulting and cooperating with existing efforts already underway that served Hawaiian children and their families. Though the specific education programs within PREP were essentially new, it was not as though they were created in a vacuum devoid of educational and social service programs available for Hawaiian families. Rather, it was that the existing programs were too few, not integrated into a prenatal-to-age five framework, and not necessarily based on research findings with respect to the needs, desires, and concerns of Hawaiian families. Thus, research and evaluation had to be insinuated into a ongoing network of social and educational programs, some of which were already available, though in short supply and not sufficient to meet the demand. The status of the Kamehameha Schools/Bishop Estate (KS/BE) within the Hawaiian community was also a central feature of the developmental process. Hawaiian families both revered KS/BE and were angered by it. At the time of their inception, PREP programs were some of the first child development outreach efforts into communities initiated by KS/BE. Though this has since changed, the activities of the school were largely confined to the campus. At the time, its sister program (KEEP) was just beginning to move outreach efforts from the laboratory school to the Department of Education (DOE) schools with the intention of changing the educational system in the communities across the state. Therefore, this represented a major departure from earlier efforts. Here, research and the program development activities would occur simultaneously in the communities in a much less controlled environment (Roberts, 1993a, 1993b).

Though there are many facets of this endeavor that could be discussed, I would like to focus here on the methods of inquiry that were used to develop the research base for the program because of its consequences for the outcomes of the effort. The research team that was pulled together to begin the effort was a multidisciplinary group representing education, early childhood development, anthropology, psychology, and evaluation. As a multidisciplinary team, it was a highly competent, rich, and diverse group. Yet from the perspective of some of the lessons we have learned in other projects since PREP, it was incomplete and perhaps ill constituted to meet its objectives.

An examination of why this is the case is based on the transactional theoretical framework for community intervention and development presented by O'Donnell, Tharp, and Wilson (1993). This framework recasts community interventions from a static behavioral model of cause and effect to one in which meaning plays a central mediating role. Active participation by a variety of constituents (including the change agent) is seen as critical in community systems development and change. O'Donnell and Tharp (1990) suggested, "Interaction is the heart of an activity setting. Organized activity cannot impact on community development in the absence of human interaction" (p. 255). O'Donnell et al. (1993) further explicated the theory of community intervention by stating:

> The activity setting was selected as the basic unit of analysis for community intervention and development because it unifies subjective experience, behavior, and external features into a common phenomenon. It is the basis of the social process common to the participants. This social process develops individual and group cognition, and structures of meaning. Therefore, the activity setting is the unit by which community and culture are propagated. (p. 504)

As will be described below, the activity settings that were created in the research/program development teams were missing voices critical to the tasks. Roberts (1993c), in a critique of PREP, suggested that it was first necessary to create activity settings where administrators, program planners, and researchers could forge a common purpose for the program. The dynamic tension between research efforts and program development efforts was evident almost immediately. Though the long-term goals of the staff representing the research and the program sides of development were the same, the more immediate goals and the activities needed to meet them were not. Program staff needed a curriculum. Research staff needed time to observe, develop studies, and test ideas. The resolution of these issues had to come through purposefully creating joint productive activities that began to address the needs of the constituents involved (families, researchers, program staff). Over time models of how to do this were developed and tested leading to more productive learning environments for both staff and families.

Another tension that emerged involved debate about the core goal of the program. It is an enduring debate that underlies much of the work with minority groups and is discussed by French and D'Augelli (2002). Rappaport (1981) further stated that "Respecting and fostering minority culture, preparing children for the majority culture, integration of minority and majority, and strengthening local neighborhoods...are equally compelling values with *opposite* poles. It is by nature a dialectical problem and requires many divergent solutions" (p. 5). These issues continued to be debated throughout the life of PREP.

Perhaps a more fundamental issue that might have provided answers to many of these issues stood in the way of this working more smoothly. In later work we have embraced the concept of participatory action research (PAR) as the most appropriate methodology for systems-change activities. Though the research teams that worked together within PREP were composed of researchers and educational practitioners, they were missing a third leg of the triangle, which has served us well in other efforts. This includes representation for the constituents benefiting from the services themselves. With respect to the principles articulated earlier, PREP research and program development honored many of the components of PAR but did not include constituents in a meaningful way in the process itself. Family members were *sources of information* through interviews, evaluations, and observation, but were not *active participants* in the activity settings in which decisions were made about the programs that would be available for them and their children through the PREP program. Reflecting back on the quote from O'Donnell and Tharp (1990, p. 255), the intersubjectivity developed through the interactions of program staff and researchers was qualitatively different from the intersubjectivity that would be developed through a group representing researchers, program staff, and family members. Though all of the researchers and program staff were routinely talking with families in a variety of ways, the family voice in the process of program development was always filtered through this screen. Parents were present to the degree that they had influenced the intersubjectivity of the researchers and practitioners with whom they talked. More will be discussed about the consequences of this method of inquiry later in the chapter after one other large-scale system change example is described.

Opening Doors Into Rural Communities

Perhaps the closest we have come to honoring the six principles listed earlier can be seen in the series of program/systems change activities we have developed through grants from the U.S. Maternal and Child Health Bureau called Opening Doors. In our first Opening Doors Project (Project #MCJ–495091–01) we simply studied and asked questions of early intervention programs and families who used their services in a number of communities across the country. The second project, Opening Doors into Rural Communities (ODRC; Project #5H02MC00047), built on the lessons learned in the first and involved systems-change methodologies (Roberts, Akers, & Behl, 2002). Its goal was to assist communities and states in their efforts to integrate individual services into a more comprehensive, coordinated, early intervention system for young children with special health care needs (CSHCN) and their families. A PAR model included parents, community providers, and state policymakers in project development and enhanced the validity and sustainability of this effort. In concert with the staff at EIRI, the communities helped develop and validate a series of replicable procedures designed to: (a) guide communities and states in examining local service integration issues, and (b) provide a framework for systems change at both levels. Our third version of Opening Doors is now developing universal application procedures for families using multiple services.

At the start of the ODRC project, both the federal Government Performance and Results Act (GPRA) and Healthy People 2010 served as an impetus to establish measurable performance outcomes for state and community programs for CSHCN and their families. Healthy People 2010 objective 16.23 states, "All states will have a community-based system of care for children with special health needs and their families." Four target communities in Maine, Idaho, and Missouri were selected and volunteered to work with staff at the Early Intervention Research Insititute (EIRI) over the course of several years in this effort. Each of the four communities developed or enhanced existing local task forces composed of family representatives, direct service providers, and administrators. Local task forces in each community met regularly, and membership on each task force was relatively stable in most communities. A staff person from EIRI was included in the task force as the evaluator/moderator.

During our initial meetings with the four communities, each community's task force selected a service integration strategy based on their consensus using the results of their needs assessment as a guide. Examples included: coordinating early intervention and comprehensive mental health programs with medical and pediatric practices[1] so that families would receive consistent information and support as well as streamlining application and eligibility procedures across agencies to decrease duplication of information parents had to provide and overall paperwork.

Procedures for developing and implementing an action plan were based on the premise that the process must be interactive, collaborative, and self-guided.

ODRC staff worked in partnership with the four community task forces to: (a) develop an action plan to implement proposed strategies and planned changes at community levels; (b) identify key persons and agencies to work toward accomplishing the action plan and determining the indicators to measure their accomplishments; (c) achieve consensus through key stakeholders to work toward identified changes; and (d) implement the proposed strategies.

Participant Involvement

The success of any service integration effort depends on the investment and inclusion of key stakeholders. Parent involvement in the project went beyond simple participation on advisory boards to being involved in the development, implementation, evaluation, and dissemination of the project. Parents served as key members of the task forces and provided critical input as customers of community services, assisted in the interpretation of evaluation findings, directed the focus of community systems change activities, evaluated effectiveness of the action plans and products, and disseminated the consortium accomplishments via parent organizations as well as co-presenting at conferences. The project also involved private and public community service providers who gave insights into service integration at the family and community level—complementing parental input. The involvement of community and state policymakers was essential because of their knowledge of state and local policies.

Components of the Evaluation Process

Evaluation served as a cornerstone of the project. Rather than viewing evaluation as a summative tool to document the effects of the project at its end, we used a model of evaluation emphasizing several different ways it could, and was used to further the goals of the project along the way. Six major components of the ODRC Evaluation model will be discussed:

1. PAR as the paradigm for systems change. ODRC staff assisted the four consortium communities to develop a framework for using the PAR model to reorganize their services by building their partnerships between families, service providers, and researchers. As a way of conducting applied research and program development, PAR ensures that the voices of all constituent groups are heard since each group may view a given issue through a different lens. Melding these perspectives makes this process unique. A learning community creates the opportunity for team members to work toward a common understanding of their challenges and how they can use resources at hand to seek workable solutions within their own community (Fetterman, 1996; Innocenti & Roberts, 1999; Reason & Bradbury, 2001; Senge, 1994). Examples of these principles in action include: (a) parents of children with disabilities were hired as consultants in developing the ODRC Parent Phone Survey; (b) task force members shared the results data they collected with larger interagency councils; (c) task force members reviewed and edited the ODRC Community Self-Assessment during its development to ensure that the survey would be feasible and a meaningful guide for communities; and (d) participants reviewed summaries from focus groups and interviews

2. An action plan with specified objectives to guide the development and implementation of the work plan. The PAR process helps the team set specific objectives toward their long-term goal(s). Each community chose one service integration strategy and further refined it with respect to their own situation and community needs. These strategies were translated into the objectives that became the basis for the community's action plan to guide their activities. The process drove the PAR meetings by emphasizing strategies that would help them accomplish their action plan. In the role of evaluator, ODRC staff helped each team to stay on track and assisted them in the use of a series of research tools to help in community assessment.

3. Research tools developed to provide a snapshot of the community at any one time to supply data to the team for decision-making. With community input and assistance, the ODRC team developed four tools to assist communities in establishing a baseline to document the range of current services and supports available to families.

Measure 1: Community service mapping. Each community's map began at the center with a child with special health needs and their family. In addition to typical private and public agencies, other sources of formal and informal supports such as churches, consumers, and civic groups were considered and then shared with the larger community task force for additions and corrections.

Measure 2: Community self-assessment (CSA). A subcommittee on each task force completed drafts of the CSA initially. Upon re-administration of the CSA during Year Four, changes on the performance outcomes were noted and reflected upon.

Measure 3: Parent satisfaction phone survey. The survey collected information about the services families receive, and determined parent satisfaction with the appropriateness, affordability, accessibility, effectiveness, coordination, and family centeredness of the services received. The phone survey was conducted by two parents of children with disabilities who were hired and trained by ODRC staff.

Measure 4. Service integration matrix. Using data collected on Measures 1, 2, and 3, ODRC staff facilitated the completion of the service integration matrix by the subcommittee followed by a large task force meeting to prepare a final version. The matrix was adapted from a similar version developed by Konrad (1996). It consisted of seven vertical dimensions, such as partners/stakeholders or community task force governance/authority; and five variables on the horizontal axis to describe the degree of service integration. These ranged from "no communication" to "information sharing" to "integration/formalized relationships." Using a consensus-building process, the task for each PAR team considered each item on the vertical axis and depicted the degree of integration on the horizontal axis. For example, a community PAR team might rate its degree of integration on "Shared goals and mission" as being at the "information sharing/communication" level based on its perception that agencies shared information on their goals but had made limited efforts to collaborate on goals or a mission statement.

It was used for each task force to begin to examine how the services were organized in their community. At first, it was challenging for team members because they were not accustomed to thinking about the relationships among agencies in this way. Over time, the benefits of using the matrix became clearer. It facilitated discussions about how the task force should work together strategically toward a common goal and to determine the degree of integration necessary for achieving the outcome they desired. In the beginning, teams tended to assume that more integration was always better than less. Community members also tended to assume that the most desirable outcome was to create a fully integrated system using more formal relationships with one another than they were currently using. Most communities assumed that they had a more integrated system than they were able to document using more objective definitions included in the matrix support materials.

Each of the above tools was administered to establish a baseline and again at follow-up at the end of the 18-month intervention period.

4. Development of state community partnerships. As we have noted in earlier publications (Roberts, Akers, & Behl, 1996; Roberts, Behl, & Akers, 1996, Roberts & Magrab, 1999; Roberts & Wasik, 1994), community initiatives are enhanced by state-level support, though that support is not critical for them to develop and implement systems-change initiatives. It was much easier for communities to adjust to the constraints of state policy to meet their local objectives than to try to change the policy in order to be able to accomplish a specific goal. State programs were able to support community initiatives when they did not conflict with specific state mandates.

5. Systems integration as a means to an end rather than an end in itself. The process used by communities to reach their goals included assessing how well agencies worked together to achieve their strategy, but systems integration issues remained secondary. As noted previously, we found that agencies assumed they would have to achieve much more formalized methods of integration than what eventually was required for their objectives to be met.

At the end of the project, the movement from the first rating to the last with respect to actual integrative efforts generally involved less formal means of integration than teams first suggested would be the ideal.

6. Infusion of the CQI model. Though communities adopted a CQI model to some degree, they did not adopt it as their gold standard. Community members tended to be more pragmatic in their need to accomplish specific tasks. They used data as a confirmatory tool and were less likely to use the information in a proactive way. They tended to rely more on their intuitive sense of the community based on their experience as the operative data source.

As a measure of success of the community task force/PAR model, all four communities met their objectives in the agreed-upon time frame; all four community teams continue to operate with parent and professional partners working together several years later without the direct support of the ODRC staff. Two of the four communities were nominated for, and won the *National Communities Can Award*, a national recognition of communities working in an exemplary manner in providing integrated, family-centered, results-based services and supports for children with disabilities and their families.

Conclusions

So what does all of this tell us about community and the ties that bind them together? This chapter began with a discussion of a research and development program to benefit Native Hawaiian families with children from birth through age five. The process of systems development was a standard research and development approach in which families benefiting from the programs and individual teachers were key informants or subjects in studies. They served as the providers of information for others to understand and digest. Program research staff developed intersubjectivity with one another through conversations with teachers and each other about the meaning of the data. In doing so, they began the process of translating the information into curriculum to be tested and revised. Much was learned about contemporary Hawaiian family interaction in the process but with little time or capacity to institutionalize the lessons learned into programs benefiting the children and families from whom the information was gathered (Roberts, 1993b). Why was this the case? It was so because the decision makers were neither the community members nor the researchers or the program developers. From the beginning, the decision-making power was in the hands of the Trustees who were funding the project. As such, the destiny of the programs was not based on the data or the impact it had on the communities and families involved. Rather, it was based on the priorities of the funders and how any one program fit into the political and social agenda of that group. As the original Board of Trustees changed, the program was eventually dissolved and exists only in segments at this time for reasons that have nothing to do with the efficacy of the programs in affecting the educational progress of young Hawaiian children.

How then is this different from the experiences of the four communities in the ODRC project described in the last section of the chapter? These community collaboratives continue to be vibrant, using abridged versions of the evaluation and CQI strategies they learned as part of the original project. They continue to reinvent themselves each time they celebrate the success of one venture and move onto the next. They do it with little or no assistance from the ODRC staff. How is this possible and what lessons can be taken from their experiences that are in contrast to that of the PREP project in Hawai'i?

Though on the face of it the six principles listed in the beginning of this chapter would appear to be equally represented in each project, in fact, major differences underlie the models with respect to the intent of the project from the beginning. Above I wrote about a "do to/for" versus a "do with" mentality of program development and systems change. In the case of the PREP program, it was based on a "do to/for" approach. Though the research component honored the other principles admirably, it attended marginally if at all to the principle that programs should be developed in partnership with constituents. Other programmatic efforts that ran parallel to, and independent of the research strand were more participatory in that public and private community agencies serving Hawaiian children and their families worked collaboratively with the PREP staff in creating more collaboration and interagency support structures than were present before the program began. In this second situation, power was more equally shared with traditionally disenfranchised people than in the work of curriculum development. As such, the principles of empowerment evaluation were more real in the community collaboration setting than in our efforts at curriculum development. The intertwining of race and empowerment was a constant theme in Hawaiian activism in the 1980s, and the "do with" model of community interaction attended to this dynamic both more closely and more transparently than did the curriculum development efforts. This is not to say that the curriculum component was not respectful, for it was very much so. Rather, the intentional sharing of power was much more visible in the community work (cf., the discussion of race in action research by Bell, 2001; she has written about the power of PAR as a methodology for liberation of traditionally disempowered groups by placing the power of data in information in the hands of those who could use it most effectively to change their own circumstances).

The projects that followed PREP (particularly the ODRC Project) embraced a "do with" model from the beginning. As such, these later projects placed the power of change at the appropriate nexus—in the community, by the community, and with the community. Much has been written about models of evaluation and systems change that reflect these issues under the banner of empowerment evaluation (Fetterman, 1996), action research (Reason & Bradbury, 2001), participatory action research (Senge & Scharmer, 2001), learning communities (Senge, 1994), and so forth. The common themes among these various models involve both a philosophy of science and a set of values quite different from that seen in other, positivist forms of research and evaluation. Reason and Bradbury (p. 1) define action research as a

> participatory, democratic process concerned with developing practical knowing in the pursuit of worthwhile human purposes, grounded in a participatory worldview... bring(ing) together action and reflection, theory and practice, in participation with others, in pursuit of practical solutions to issues of pressing concern to people.

The understanding that "knowing comes from doing" is implicit in action research models. Knowledge is the product of the social construction of the interaction of people involved in a common situation or endeavor. From an epistemological perspective, participatory models grow out of a postmodernist view of science in which the concept of "truth or knowledge" is a socially constructed event. Knowledge in this framework sounds similar to the construct of intersubjectivity in Vygotskian theory described earlier and similar to what I was describing in the first part of this chapter as beginning to think "out there" in some interstitial space and not "in here." This is the type of knowledge, which is the product of intersubjectivity, which is the product of joint productive activity, and which is what we now see as the framework for PAR. As this knowledge becomes a purposeful activity within and across organizations, it becomes what Senge and Scharmer (2001) define as "community action research." They distinguish this from traditional action research in that it focuses on:

1. Fostering relationships and collaboration among diverse organizations and among consultants and researchers working with them;
2. Creating settings for collective reflection that enable people from different organizations to see themselves in one another; and
3. Leveraging progress in individual organizations through cross-institutional links so as to sustain transformative changes that otherwise would die out.

Those who are engaged in this process become a "community of learners." It is through this process of developing intersubjectivity that shared principles, knowledge, and the call to action can be formulated. Knowing is both the process and one of the products. The development of the awareness of intersubjectivity and the process that creates it "enables everyone to see how their efforts fit within the larger system" (Senge & Scharmer, 2001, p. 238). Implicitly the work of the ODRC communities mirrored and self-discovered (or stumbled on) the process Senge describes as the guiding features of the Society for Organizational Learning (SOL).

1. Establishing a shared statement of purpose and a shared set of guiding principles.
2. Developing infrastructures that support community building.
3. Undertaking collaborative projects that focus on key change issues and that create concrete contexts for further deepening common purpose and improving infrastructures.

As described by Wandersman (2003), the work of the Opening Doors into Rural Communities Project uses the constructs of community-centered models that " begin with the community and ask what it needs in terms of scientific information and capacity building to produce effective interventions" (p. 230). Green (2001 as cited in Wandersman, 2003) described the need as one in which:

1. Best practice is seen as process rather than as packaged interventions.
2. [It] emphasize(s) control by practitioner, patient, client, community or population.
3. [It] emphasizes local evaluation and self-monitoring.
4. Research [focuses] on the tailoring process and new technologies.

The values Wandersman ascribes to community science are very much in line with those used to drive ODRC—values linked, participatory, scientific, utilization, systems oriented, contextual, capacity building, longitudinal research and longer timelines, and capacity building.

In closing, Sarason (2003), in a recent article on the obligations of the moral scientific stance, describes a situation in which community interveners thought they knew a specific school culture sufficiently to develop interventions, but they turned out to be wrong. He suggests that research reports rarely tell the whole story (how does one do that in 15 pages?) and that the self becomes part of the story whether intentional or not. As I began this chapter, I did not intend to become part of the story and rarely write in the first person as I have done here. However, somehow this fits both because it was important to me to trace the evolution of my thinking over time and the seminal effect of the early interactions with Roland on that process.

Sarason (2003) asks the researcher a series of four questions for which the answers must be reported to understand the research he or she is describing.

(1) *"What tells the researcher he or she has what it takes to do this?"* I learned an important lesson from a Hawaiian father after one of the first parent meetings I held in 1983 while I was getting ready to begin the PREP program. On a beach outside the Nānākuli Elementary School on Leeward, O'ahu, I was talking with a father who was native Hawaiian. He said something that suggested to me that he was also an employee of Kamehameha Schools. I asked him about this and his answer was an important lesson with respect to Sarason's first question. His answer was, "No, and, if I was, the first thing I would do is fire you!" He was not mad at me. In fact, he did not know me. We continued the conversation after I picked up what was left of my ego from off the sand and told some jokes, and we left each other's company amicably. He was responding to the fact that a white guy of privilege was daring to start a program for low-income native Hawaiian children and their families. To him, I represented every missionary that ever stepped foot in Hawai'i who, in the words of Michener, "Came to do good and did well." Every time I think of this story, I say a private prayer of thanks to this man. He gave me a gift of understanding my place in that system. There were things I should do and other things I should not do because I was not the appropriate member of the team to do them. Others who held parent meetings after that time were from and of the culture. I had my role but it was not that.

(2) *Who is involved and how did they affect the process and how were they affected by it?* One of my most enjoyable experiences is to spend time with graduate students who have just come back from their first family visit in which they

went to the family's home and spent time with them going about their daily lives—bathing the kids, fixing dinner, going to the supermarket, or playing in the backyard. The uniform response is "wow, is that ever different from what we see and hear and are told by a father when he comes to see us in the clinic!"

Unless one is affected by an experience in a significant way, new knowledge has not been created. Thus, being objective and rational in the process and remaining aloof to the lesson of the activity is counterproductive to doing it. I was deeply affected by the Hawaiian father as I have been by both other parents I have interviewed and research team meetings I have attended over the years. If I feel I am not affected, then I have to question my involvement in the process. As Sarason (2003) so eloquently stated, "If we want, as we should, to be a scientific enterprise, we cannot afford to present our findings and ignore factors that may or may not—I would say will, affect those findings and how others will interpret them (p. 210). In our work in ODRC, we were purposeful in creating situations where multiple people in different roles interacted around the same topic/data with the explicit understanding that "everyone is right from their own perspective" as the rule for the meeting. "Our task is to find the higher order 'right' which combines all of the individual ones." We wanted people to be involved and to affect the process and be affected by it.

(3) *What did you have to do to get to this point of beginning the intervention/ implementation?* and (4) *Do the minimal conditions exist below which you should fold your tent and go elsewhere?* For me in my personal journey to get to this point in my research career, I had to do the work as best I knew how in Hawai'i as a graduate student, in New Jersey as an intern, in Greensboro as a new faculty member, in Hawai'i as a program director, and now in Utah as a Research Center Director and Professor once again—creating and participating in communities of learners that have interactively shaped thinking and roused minds to life. Though Sarason (2003) suggests that there are minimal standards leading to tent folding, personal and systemic goals could not have been met had we folded the tent prematurely in some of the earlier efforts I have described. I wonder if any of us could do what we do now without some of those earlier "sometimes painful" experiences that hone our professional edge and where the personal learning has a greater effect than that at the systemic level. Though the personal development can never be at the expense of the systemic level, both serve their purpose in moving the field forward.

As I said in the beginning in describing my graduate school days, each step has been the best place for me to be to get to this point—together with colleagues who are the ties that bind—collectively creating knowledge in a community of learners who now span the globe from Hawai'i to South Africa creating community where we find it and applying the lessons learned to the next time.

Note

1. The American Academy of Pediatrics (AAP, 2002) define the "medical home" as medical care provided to infants, children, and adolescents ideally that is accessible, continuous, comprehensive, family centered, coordinated, compassionate, and culturally effective. It should be delivered or directed by well-trained physicians who provide primary care and help to manage and facilitate essentially all aspects of pediatric care. The physician should be known to the child and family and should be able to develop a partnership of mutual responsibility and trust with them. (p. 184)

References

American Academy of Pediatrics. (2002). Policy statement: The medical home. *Pediatrics, 110*, 184–186.

Bell, E. E. (2001). Infusing race into the US discourse on action research. In P. Reason & H. Bradbury (Eds.), *Handbook of action research: Participative inquiry and practice* (pp. 48–58. Thousand Oaks, CA: Sage.

Cuban, L. (1990). Reforming again, again, and again. *Educational Researcher, 19*(1), 3–13.

Fetterman, D. M. (1996). Empowerment evaluation: An introduction to theory and practice. In D. M. Fetterman, S. J. Kaftarian, & A. Wandersman (Eds.), *Empowerment evaluation: Knowledge and tools for self-assessment and accountability*. Thousand Oaks, CA: Sage.

French. S. E., & D'Augelli, A. R. (2002). Diversity in community psychology. In T. A. Revenson, A. R. D'Augelli, S. E. French, D. L. Hughes, D. Livert, E., Seidman, M., Shinn, & H. Yoshikawa (Eds.), *A quarter century of community psychology: Readings from the American Journal of Community Psychology* (pp. 65–77). New York: Kluwer Academic/Plenum Publishers.

Heath, R. W., & Plett, J. D. (1986). *The identification of priority sites for parent-child services*. Honolulu: Kamehameha Schools/Bernice Pauahi Bishop Estate.

Heron, J., & Reason, P. (2001). The practice of co-operative inquiry: Research 'with' rather than 'on' people. In P. Reason & H. Bradbury (Eds.), *Handbook of action research: Participative inquiry and practice* (pp. 179–188). Thousand Oaks, CA: Sage.

Hosaka, C. J. (1983). *The quilt and T-shirt curriculum strand: A social-educational context* (Technical Report No. 110). Honolulu, HI: The Kamehameha Educational Research Institute.

Innocenti, M. S., & Roberts, R. N. (1999). Participatory realism: Defining the role of non-evaluator. In R. N. Roberts & P. R. Magrab (Eds.), *Where children live: Solutions for serving young children and their families* (pp. 133–172). Stamford, CT: Ablex.

Keough, B. K. (1990). Narrowing the gap between policy and practice. *Exceptional Children, 57*, 186–190.

Konrad, E. L. (1996). A multidimensional framework for conceptualizing human services integration initiatives. In J. M. Marquart & E. L. Konrad (Eds.), *New direction for evaluation: Evaluating initiatives to integrate human services* (pp. 5–19). San Francisco: Jossey-Bass.

Kuhn, T. S. (1962). *The structure of scientific revolutions*. Chicago: The University of Chicago Press.

McGrath, J. E. (1978). *Social science and social action: A retrospective look through the pages of the Journal of Social Issues*. Mimeograph, University of Illinois at Urbana-Champaign.

O'Donnell, C., & Tharp, R. (1990). Community intervention guided by theoretical development. In A. A. Bellack, M. Hersen, & A. E. Kazdin (Eds.), *International handbook of behavior modification and therapy* (2nd ed., pp. 251–266). New York: Plenum Press.

O'Donnell, C., Tharp, R., & Wilson, K. (1993). Activity settings as the unit of analysis: A theoretical basis for community intervention and development. *American Journal of Community Psychology, 21*, 501–520.

Peet, D. Y. (1986). The Kupulani prenatal/perinatal curriculum: Family-based pre-parenthood education. *Early Education Bulletin No. 16*. Honolulu, HI: Kamehameha Schools/Bernice Pauahi Bishop Estate.

Rappaport, J. (1981). In praise of paradox: A social policy of empowerment over prevention. *American Journal of Community Psychology, 9*(1), 1–25.

Reason, P., & Bradbury, H. (Eds.). (2001). *Handbook of action research: Participative inquiry and practice*. Thousand Oaks: Sage.

Revenson, T. A., D'Augelli, A. R., French, S. E., Hughes, D. L., Livert, D., Seidman, E., Shinn, M., & Yoshikawa, H. (Eds.). (2002). *A quarter century of community psychology: Readings from the American Journal of Community Psychology*. New York: Kluwer Academic/Plenum Publishers.

Roberts, R. N. (1981). Naturalistic assessment for classroom intervention: Speech and motor behavior as predictors of academic competence. *Behavioral Assessment, 3*, 15–30.

Roberts, R. N. (1988). Ka Ho 'Okipu Ana, Welcoming our baby. *Children Today, 17*, 6–11.

Roberts, R. N. (1993a). The family, the school, and the interface. In R. N. Roberts (Ed.), *Coming home to preschool: The socio-cultural context of early education* (pp. 275–289). Norwood, NJ: Ablex.

Roberts, R. N. (Ed.). (1993b). *Coming home to preschool: The socio-cultural context of early education*. Norwood, NJ: Ablex.

Roberts, R. N. (1993c). Early education as community intervention: Assisting an ethnic minority to be ready for school. *American Journal of Community Psychology, 21*, 521-535.

Roberts, R. N. (1999). Supporting families where children live: Community principles in action. In R. N. Roberts & P. R. Magrab (Eds.), *Where children live: Solutions for serving young children and their families* (pp. 31–72). Stamford, CT: Ablex.

Roberts, R. N., Akers, A. L., & Behl, D. D. (1996). Family-level service coordination within home visiting programs. *Topics in Early Childhood Special Education, 16,* 279–301.

Roberts, R. N., Akers, A. L., & Behl, D. D. (2002). *Opening doors into rural communities: Final report* (#6 H02MC00047). Early Intervention Research Insititute, Utah State University, Logan.

Roberts, R. N., Behl, D. D., & Akers, A. L. (1996). Community-level service integration within home visiting programs. *Topics in Early Childhood Special Education, 16,* 302–321.

Roberts, R. N., & Magrab, P. R. (Eds.). (1999). *Where children live: Solutions for serving young children and their families.* Stamford, CT: ABLEX.

Roberts, R. N., & Tharp, R. G. (1980). Naturalistic study of children's self-directed speech in academic problem-solving. *Cognitive Research and Therapy, 4,* 341–352.

Roberts, R. N., & Wasik, B. H. (1994). Home visiting options within Head Start: Current practice and future directions. *Early Childhood Research Quarterly, 9,* 311–325.

Sarason, S. B. (2003). The obligations of the moral-scientific stance. *American Journal of Community Psychology, 31*(3/4), 209–212.

Senge, P. M. (1994). *The fifth discipline: The art and practice of the learning organization.* New York: Doubleday.

Senge, P., & Scharmer, O. (2001). Community action research: Learning as a community of practitioners, consultants, and researchers. In P. Reason & H. Bradbury (Eds.), *Handbook of action research* (pp. 238–249). Great Britain: Cormwell, Trowbridge, Wiltshire.

Tharp, R. G., Estrada, P., Dalton, S. S., & Yamauchi, L. A. (2000). *Teaching transformed: Achieving excellence, fairness, inclusion and harmony.* Boulder, CO: Westview.

Tharp, R. G., & Gallimore, R. (1988). *Rousing minds to life.* Cambridge, UK: Cambridge University Press.

Vygotsky, L. S. (1962). *Thought and language.* Cambridge, MA: MIT Press.

Vygotsky, L. S. (1978). *Mind in society: The development of higher psychological processes.* (Eds. and Trans. by M. Cole, V. John-Steiner, S. Scribner, & E. Souberman). Cambridge, MA: Harvard University Press.

Wandersman, A. (2003). Community science: Bridging the gap between science and practice with community-centered models. *American Journal of Community Psychology, 31*(3/4), 227–242.

Weisner, T. S., Gallimore, R., & Jordan, C. (1993). Unpackaging cultural effects on classroom learning: Hawaiian peer assistance and child-generated activity. In R. N. Roberts (Ed.), *Coming home to preschool: The sociocultural context of early education* (Vol. 7, pp. 59–90). Norwood, NJ: Ablex.

Yoshikawa, H., & Shinn, M. (2002). Facilitating change: Where and how should community psychology intervene? In T. A. Revenson, A. R. D'Augelli, S. E. French, D. L. Hughes, D. Livert, E., Seidman, M., Shinn, & H. Yoshikawa (Eds.), *A quarter century of community psychology: Readings from the American Journal of Community Psychology* (pp. 33–49). New York: Kluwer Academic/Plenum Publishers.

CHAPTER 5

Juvenile Delinquency: Peers, Mentors, and Activity Settings

Clifford R. O'Donnell

The modern history of empirically based prevention and intervention programs for juvenile delinquency began with the use of behavior modification on street-corners (Burchard & Tyler, 1965), by probation officers (Thorne, Tharp, & Wetzel, 1967), and in a token economy for "pre-delinquent" boys called Achievement Place (Phillips, 1968). Although these applications were innovative and exciting, it was the classic work of Tharp and Wetzel (1969), in their book *Behavior Modification in the Natural Environment*, that provided the theoretical context and continues to influence the field today.

Tharp and Wetzel introduced a natural mentoring system called the triadic model, in which a consultant with intervention expertise supervises a natural mentor, called a mediator, who has regular contact with the youth. Each person in the chain reinforces the desirable behavior of the next person. The model uses the mentors or nonprofessionals in the everyday lives of youth to reduce delinquency and promote pro-social behavior.

The work of Tharp and Wetzel and the triadic model became the basis for a similar mentoring project called the Buddy System. However, instead of using natural mentors, the Buddy System paid adults in the community to be mentors (Fo & O'Donnell, 1974). Mentor training emphasized the importance of rapport, communication, and the development of warm, positive, and trusting relationships with their youth. Mentors were also trained and supervised by consultants in the use of contingency reinforcement to improve the behaviors for which each youth had been referred, such as truancy, fighting, classroom disruption, and poor academic achievement.

The results showed that contingency reinforcement was highly successful in improving these behaviors. However, the results on delinquency prevention, as measured by arrests three years after referral, were mixed. For the 335 youth who participated in the Buddy System, those who had been arrested for a major offense in the year before referral (N = 73) were less likely to be arrested than the 218 randomly-assigned control youth. In contrast, youth participants who had not been arrested (N = 262) were more likely than control youth to be arrested.

These results were interpreted as a peer network effect, i.e., some of those without prior arrests formed friendships with those already arrested (O'Donnell, Lydgate, & Fo, 1979).

Behavior Modification in the Natural Environment, in combination with the Buddy System, have influenced two developments in the field of delinquency: (a) the importance of peer networks in understanding how prevention programs may inadvertently do harm by facilitating delinquency, and (b) the use of mentoring in prevention programs. Interestingly, both developments are related by common theory. Each of these developments is discussed below in the context of activity setting theory.

Peer Networks

To facilitate the development of a theory to understand how youth programs may have harmful effects, studies on the influence of the environment on psychological problems were reviewed (O'Donnell, 1980). These studies showed how the physical environment affected social interaction, participation in settings, and the development of social networks. Social networks were found to have a powerful influence on many psychological problems (O'Donnell & Tharp, 1982).

The question then became whether social networks, especially peer networks, affected delinquency programs. An examination of many types of programs, from social service, to diversion from the juvenile justice system, to adult prison visits, to youth gang alternatives, indicated that peer networks could have a marked effect on the effectiveness of delinquency programs (O'Donnell, Manos, & Chesney-Lind, 1987). The effect was similar to that found in the Buddy System, i.e., friendships formed during the program among youth at-risk for delinquency could counter any positive program gains. All of the programs reviewed showed either no or negative program effects from participation. The result was clear: facilitation of friendships among at-risk youth, however inadvertent, countered positive program effects.

Social networks are created by participation in the activities of specific settings. Peer networks are no exception. At-risk youth living in the same neighborhoods, attending the same schools, and facing similar problems at home and school, are likely to know each other. Friendships among these youth form on the same basis as other relationships, i.e., propinquity, similarity, and free time lead to common activities (Kupersmidt, DeRosier, & Patterson, 1995). Participation in these activity settings contributes to the development of *intersubjectivity*, i.e., where these youth form common bonds through social interaction and the development of common experiences, emotions, and cognitions (O'Donnell & Tharp, 1990; O'Donnell, Tharp, & Wilson, 1993). Unfortunately, when there is a lack of responsible adult supervision in these activity settings, this greater intersubjectivity among at-risk youth may support delinquency (Schwendinger & Schwendinger, 1982; Steinberg, 1986; Wilson, 1980).

Peer networks, of course, are but one part of the larger social networks of adolescents. Family, school, and neighborhood networks are also important. These networks and their activity settings provide the context for adolescents and the key to understanding their behavior. However, peer networks have the greatest effect on delinquency because most adolescents are highly receptive to peer influence and are becoming more independent from their families (Cullingford & Morrison, 1997). The peer network effect is evident in a rich variety of studies. For example, most delinquent activity is committed in groups (Coie & Miller-Johnson, 2001; Emler, Reicher, & Ross, 1987; Erickson & Jensen, 1977; Gold, 1970; Warr, 1996; West & Farrington, 1973), high-risk adolescents reward peer deviant behavior (Dishion, McCord, & Poulin, 1999), and participation in activity settings with high-risk and delinquent peers is one of the best predictors of delinquency (Agnew, 1991; Arnold & Hughes, 1999; Lyon, Henggeler, & Hall, 1992; O'Donnell, 1992; O'Donnell et al., 1987; Patterson & Dishion, 1985; Patterson & Yoerger, 1997; Poole & Rigoli, 1979; Thornberry, Lizotte, Krohn, Farnworth, & Jang, 1994; White, Pandina, & LaGrange, 1987). Indeed, a synthesis of longitudinal research showed that the best predictors of serious and violent delinquency from ages 12–14 to ages 15–25 were involvement with antisocial peers and a lack of social ties (Lipsey & Derzon, 1998). Moreover, association with delinquent friends most often occurs prior to delinquent behavior (Elliott & Menard, 1996; Kennan, Loeber, Zhaang, Stouthamer-Loeber, & Van Kammen, 1995).

One form of the peer network is the youth gang. Youth gang members have a much higher rate of delinquency than delinquent non-gang members. Furthermore, this higher rate primarily occurs during, rather than before or after, membership in the gang (Thornberry, 1998). Gang activities facilitate delinquent behavior. This facilitation effect is an excellent example of the power and influence of networks on the activities of their members.

Families, schools, and neighborhoods directly affect the lives of youth in many ways. Conventionally, the socializing and supervision roles of the family have been considered the functions that help to prevent delinquency (Hoge, Andrews, & Leschied, 1994). Certainly families can, and most often do, directly affect the socialization of their children to promote pro-social behavior and control antisocial activities. By the adolescent years, however, the influence of the family typically diminishes and their effect on the risk for delinquency becomes primarily indirect by facilitating or inhibiting contact with at-risk peers. Facilitating contact occurs when family problems, such as alcohol, drug, psychotic, and criminal problems (Dembo, Williams, Wothke, Schmeidler, & Brown, 1992), lack of adult supervision (Schwendinger & Schwendinger, 1982; Steinberg, 1986; Wilson, 1980), and child abuse, neglect, and rejection (Maxfield & Widom, 1996; Scudder, Blount, Heide, & Silverman, 1993; Widom, 1989) increases the amount of time youth spend outside the home. Unsupervised free time spent outside of the home increases the potential association with, and influence of, delinquent peers (Patterson & Yoerger, 1997; Simons, Johnson, Beaman, Conger, & Whitbeck, 1996). Conversely, familial attachment can inhibit contact and decrease involvement with delinquent peers (Warr, 1993). Natural mentors, i.e., adults already known to youth and their families, may be equally effective. In a recent study, youth with natural mentors were less affected by the negative behavior of their peers. It was concluded, "natural mentors may encourage young people not to befriend peers who engage in problem behaviors" (Zimmerman, Bingenheimer, & Notaro, 2002, p. 238).

Similarly, academic problems and commitment to school have been considered directly related to delinquency (Herrenkohl, Hawkins, Chung, Hill, & Battin-Pearson, 2001; Maguin & Loeber, 1996; Thornberry, Lizotte, Krohn, Farnworth, & Jang, 1991). However, difficulty in school has indirect effects as students with serious academic problems, disciplinary referrals, or high truancy rates are more likely to have contact with other students with the same problems (Dishion, Patterson, & Kavanagh, 1992). As with families, school policies can affect delinquency by facilitating or inhibiting contact with at-risk peers, such as through academic tracking systems, detention, and suspension.

The same is true for neighborhoods, i.e., their characteristics affect delinquency indirectly by providing opportunities for delinquent behavior and contact with at-risk peers. These opportunities and contacts are offered in neighborhoods with easy access to firearms (O'Donnell, 1995), weak social ties, and few adult-supervised activities, and where peers are involved with drug abuse and sales, gangs, and criminal activities (Figueira-McDonough, 1993; Griffin, Scheier, Borvin, Diaz, & Miller, 1999; Gottfredson, McNeil, & Gottfredson, 1991; Sampson, Raudenbush, & Earls, 1997; Shannon, 1988).

Family, school, and neighborhood networks are interrelated within communities. Overall, low-risk families, schools, and neighborhoods, minimize contact with at-risk peers and high-risk families, schools, and neighborhoods, maximize such contact. The effect of problems in one type of network can be alleviated by the conditions of the other networks. For example, youths with family and school problems may be protected if they live in neighborhoods where there are activities supervised by responsible adults and low rates of crime and drug abuse (Dishion, Patterson, Stoolmiller, & Skinner, 1991; Poole & Rigoli, 1979). Likewise, youths who live in high-risk neighborhoods may be protected by attachment to family and school success.

This process, in which families, schools, and neighborhoods influence peer networks and thereby facilitate or inhibit delinquency forms the community-peer model of delinquency (O'Donnell, 2000, 2003). The community-peer model has several implications. Perhaps the most important is that delinquency prevention programs should increase their focus on the activity settings and networks, especially the peer networks, of participants. Information about families, schools, neighborhoods, and peers is needed. Currently, most programs focus on individual behavior change. In this model, individual behavior change occurs and is maintained through the context for participants: their activity settings and networks. Therefore, the effectiveness of delinquency prevention projects depends on their effect on settings and networks.

A second implication is that settings and networks must be assessed during and after participation in the program. Assessment during the program will provide information on effectiveness and impact. Relationships formed during the program may continue, so assessment after program participation is important to determine long-term effectiveness. Programs that fail to affect relationships with delinquent peers are unlikely to be effective and, worse yet, programs that facilitate friendships with delinquent peers are likely to do harm.

The third implication is that programs should consider how to reduce these potential harmful effects. There is a great need for, and currently a notable lack of, programs designed to alter association with high-risk peers (Tolan & Guerra, 1994). One possibility is to provide services individually to discourage contact among at-risk participants (Klein, 1971). Another is to promote pro-social relationships (Feldman, Caplinger, & Wodarski, 1983), although encouraging relationships between at-risk and pro-social youth is difficult because pro-social youth typically reject their antisocial or aggressive peers (Bierman, 1990). A number of thoughtful suggestions have been made recently to address these potential harmful effects. These suggestions include (a) developing adult-supervised activities for youth, (b) using cooperative learning techniques in the classroom to facilitate student relationships, (c) splitting up at-risk students by assigning them to different classes, (d) monitoring students to assess and, when necessary, intervene with peer networks, (e) promoting positive activities to enhance the social appeal of at-risk youth for pro-social students, and (f) working with peer group leaders to promote norms with positive values (Kupersmidt, Coie, & Howell, 2004).

In addition, the effect of school policies that promote contact and relationships among at-risk students, such as academic tracking, detention, and suspension need to be systematically assessed. When these policies are found to be harmful by facilitating antisocial peer networks, alternatives need to be developed. Eventually, our juvenile justice policies need to be reviewed. The community-peer model suggests that placing youth arrested for delinquent offenses in detention and correctional facilities not only doesn't "correct," but often does harm by increasing their likelihood of repeated offenses. Our expensive juvenile justice system, originally created to protect youth (Eddy & Gribskov, 1998), is long overdue for systematic evaluation and reconsideration.

Mentoring in Delinquency Prevention

Mentoring of youth goes back about 3,000 years to when Homer described Odysseus leaving his infant son, Telemachos, in the care of a companion named Mentor (Butler, 1900/1944). The oldest and largest youth mentoring organization in the United States, Big Brothers Big Sisters (BBBS), was founded in 1904 (Big Brothers Big Sisters, 2004). By historical standards, the triadic model and the Buddy System were late developments in the use of mentoring. However, they were the first mentoring projects to focus on improving specific behaviors to prevent delinquency (Fo & O'Donnell, 1974; Tharp & Wetzel, 1969). Since then, especially in the last 10 years, interest in mentoring to prevent delinquency has increased dramatically. The *Guide for Implementing the Comprehensive Strategy for Serious, Violent, and Chronic Juvenile Offenders*, published by the federal Office of Juvenile Justice and Delinquency Prevention (OJJDP) recommended the use of mentoring as a promising strategy to prevent delinquency (Howell, 1995). In 1996, OJJDP sponsored the Juvenile Mentoring Program (JUMP). Currently, there are over 200 JUMP projects for youth in the juvenile justice system, children of incarcerated parents, and youth at-risk for delinquency (Novotney, Mertinko, Lange, & Baker, 2000).

Many studies show that mentoring can be effective. Decreases in drug or alcohol use and hitting behavior, and improvements in school performance, attitudes, and peer and family relationships, have been reported (Curtis & Hanson-Schwoebel, 1999; Keating, Tomishima, Foster, & Alessandri, 2002; Taylor,

Lo Scuito, Fox, Hilbert, & Sonkowsky, 1999; Thompson & Kelly-Vance, 2001; Tierney, Grossman, & Resch, 1995; Van Patton, 1997). Other studies, however, show mixed or no results (Abbott, Meredith, Self-Kelly, & Davis, 1997; DuBois, Neville, Parra, & Pugh-Lilly, 2002; Jackson, 2002; Roberts, Liabo, Lucas, DuBois, & Sheldon, 2004; McPartland & Nettles, 1991; Royse, 1998).

A recent review of mentoring reported that several variables could increase effectiveness and help to resolve these inconsistent findings (Hayashi & O'Donnell, 2004). Perhaps the most important is an emphasis on a strong mentor-youth relationship. Mentoring is more effective when mentors are involved with youth for at least a year and youth have a positive perception of their mentors (DuBois, Holloway, Valentine, & Cooper, 2002; LoSciuto, Rajala, Townsend, & Taylor, 1996; Slicker & Palmer, 1993). The heart of mentoring is this relationship, and it is difficult to imagine an effective program without strong relationships. Indeed, a short-term, unsuccessful relationship may be harmful to youth (DuBois, Holloway et al., 2002; Rhodes, 2002). For this reason, youth with behavioral or emotional problems may not be appropriate for most mentoring programs, especially those with volunteer mentors who are not trained to address these problems (Grossman & Rhodes, 2002). Mentoring alone does not seem to improve these behaviors (DuBois, Holloway et al., 2002).

To facilitate strong mentor-youth relationships, programs need to develop appropriate recruitment of youths and mentors. It is important for programs to decide first on the youth it will serve, i.e., the age-group, gender, at-risk status, etc. (Hayashi & O'Donnell, 2004). Mentors with successful personal relationships or helping role experience, such as in teaching or social work, are more likely to be effective (DuBois, Holloway et al., 2002; Hayashi & O'Donnell, 2004; Rhodes, Grossman, & Resch, 2000).

Training for mentors should be ongoing and include information on cultural differences, such as the relevant history, values, and expected behaviors of the racial and ethnic groups of the participants. Possible generation differences between mentors and youth in music, style of dress, and interests are also important. Indeed, knowledge of youth culture should be included in all mentor training programs (Corsaro, 1985; Gottlieb & Ten Houten, 1966). Equally essential is ongoing support for mentors. Providing mentors with the opportunity to share their frustrations and successes, perhaps through a mentor support group, is valuable to maintain their commitment to the program.

Changes and corrections are an inevitable part of any program. To know when and how to do so, it is necessary to develop a system to monitor the activities and relationships of mentors and youth, as well as any parental involvement.

This system is best designed as part of an overall evaluation plan based on relevant data to assess ongoing program effectiveness.

All of these variables are important for mentoring programs, but additional variables may be especially important for mentoring youth who are at high risk for delinquency, have incarcerated parents, or are in the juvenile justice system. Children with an incarcerated parent "are six times more likely than other children to be incarcerated at some point in their lives" (Farley, 2004, p. 1). Although a BBBS study showed improvements with just good mentor-youth relationships (Tierney et al., 1995), programs for youth who are at-risk for engaging in illegal activities may be more effective if they focus on changing specific behaviors, after establishing strong relationships. In one program to divert youth from the juvenile justice system, focusing on training youths in specific skills was particularly important for its success (Blechman, Maurice, & Buecker, 2000).

The importance of matching mentors and participants across demographic characteristics such as ethnicity, race, or gender may depend on whether youth are at-risk for delinquency. Although perceived common interests may be of greater importance for youth overall (Ensher & Murphy, 1997), demographic characteristics may be more important for youth at-risk for delinquency. In the JUMP programs, boys were more likely to avoid drugs and gangs if they had male mentors. Overall, greater improvement was reported for youth paired with mentors of the same ethnicity or race. These mentors reported that they understood their youth better than did cross-pair mentors (Novotney et al., 2000). Regardless of race, ethnicity, or gender, all mentors in these programs should receive training on developing relationships with aggressive and antisocial youth.

In addition to the valuable database being developed in JUMP (Novotney et al., 2000), several programs have some evidence of success with these high-risk youth. For example, Amachi reported improvements in self-confidence and academic performance (Farley, 2004), and the Seattle Office of the Juvenile Rehabilitation Administration reported preliminary findings showing their mentoring group with a 34% lower felony recidivism rate (Washington State Institute for Public Policy, 2002). Developing successful programs for this high-risk group would have an important impact.

Finally, the importance of peer networks presented above is a potential source for this success. The effectiveness of mentoring high-risk youth would likely be increased by an assessment and focus on peer networks. The first step in this assessment process is for mentors to find out with whom their youth are spending time. After a trusting mentor-youth relationship is established, conversations about mentee activities and friends are likely to occur quite naturally.

Mentor visits and observations of these activities are also likely to be informative. If the assessment indicates that a peer network is supporting problem behavior, an intervention strategy needs to be developed in cooperation with the youth. Possibilities include arranging for supervision of these activities by responsible adults, perhaps by program mentors, involving the youth in different activity settings, and facilitating relationships with pro-social peers.

In conclusion, the contributions of Roland Tharp to the peer network and mentoring literature can not be over-emphasized. With his colleagues, he built on the theoretical contributions of Barker (1960, 1968), Bronfenbrenner (1979), Cole (1985), Leont'ev (1981), Rogoff (1982), Vygotsky (1978, 1981), and Whiting (1980) to advance cultural-historical-activity theory (CHAT) (Tharp, 2003) toward becoming a comprehensive theory of human behavior and experience (O'Donnell & Tharp, 1990; O'Donnell, Tharp, & Wilson, 1993; Tharp, Estrada, Dalton, & Yamauchi, 2000; Tharp & Gallimore, 1988).

Activity setting theory provides not only an understanding of peer networks, but also several means to intervene with them. Networks are formed in activity settings and activities occur in collaboration with network members. Activity settings and social networks are two sides of the same coin: "behavior and relationships form a cycle linked by activities in which who you know leads to who you are to who you know, until who you are is who you know" (O'Donnell & Tharp, 1990, p. 257). These are powerful concepts for the development of effective delinquency prevention. Mentoring also takes place in activity settings and activity setting theory has been used to explore its developmental and socio-historical foundations (Gallimore, Tharp, & John-Steiner, 1994). The contributions of Roland Tharp to delinquency prevention and mentoring are united by his contributions first to the triadic model and later to activity setting theory. For all his many contributions, we are indebted to him and thankful for the intellectual excitement he brings to his work, and thus to ours.

References

Abbott, D. A., Meredith, W. H., Self-Kelly, R., & Davis, E. (1997). The influence of a Big Brothers program on the adjustment of boys in single-parent families. *The Journal of Psychology, 131*, 143–157.

Agnew, R. (1991). The interactive effects of peer variables on delinquency. *Criminology, 29*, 47–72.

Arnold, M. E., & Hughes, J. N. (1999). First do no harm: Adverse effects of grouping deviant youth for skills training. *Journal of School Psychology, 37*, 99–115.

Barker, R. G. (1960). Ecology and motivation. In M. R. Jones (Ed.), *Nebraska symposium on motivation* (pp. 1–49). Lincoln: University of Nebraska.

Barker, R. G. (1968). *Ecological psychology.* Stanford, CA: Stanford University Press.

Bierman, K. (1990). Improving the peer relations of rejected children. In B. B. Lahey & A. E. Kazdin (Eds.), *Advances in clinical child psychology* (pp. 131–149). New York: Plenum Press.

Big Brothers Big Sisters (2004). Guide to effective programs for children and youth. Retrieved March 15, 2004 from www.childtrends.org/Lifecourse/programs/BigBrothersBigSisters.htm.

Blechman, E.A., Maurice, A., & Buecker, B. (2000). Can mentoring or skill training reduce recidivism? Observational study with propensity analysis. *Prevention Science, 1,* 139–155.

Bronfenbrenner, U. B. (1979). *The ecology of human development.* Cambridge: Harvard University Press.

Burchard, J., & Tyler, V. (1965). The modification of delinquent behavior through operant conditioning. *Behaviour Research and Therapy, 2,* 245–250.

Butler, S. (1900/1944). *The odyssey of Homer.* Roslyn, NY: Classics Club/Walter J. Black.

Coie, J. D., & Miller-Johnson, S. (2001). Peer factors and interventions. In R. Loeber & D. P. Farrington (Eds.), *Child delinquents: Development, intervention, and service needs* (pp. 191–209). Thousand Oaks, CA: Sage.

Cole, M. (1985). The zone of proximal development: Where culture and cognition create each other. In J. V. Wertsch, (Ed.), *Culture, communication, and cognition: Vygotskian perspectives* (pp. 146–161). Cambridge: Cambridge University Press.

Corsaro, W. A. (1985). *Friendship and peer culture in the early years.* Norwood, NJ: Ablox.

Cullingford, C., & Morrison, J. (1997). Peer group pressure within and outside school. *British Educational Research Journal, 23,* 61–80.

Curtis, T., & Hansen-Schwoebel, K. (1999). *Big Brothers Big Sisters school-based mentoring: Evaluation summary of five pilot programs.* Philadelphia: Big Brothers Big Sisters of America.

Dembo, R., Williams, L., Wothke, W., Schmeidler, J., & Brown, C. H. (1992). The role of family factors, physical abuse, and sexual victimization experiences in high-risk youths' alcohol and other drug use and delinquency: A longitudinal model. *Violence and Victims, 7,* 245–266.

Dishion, T. J., McCord, J., & Poulin, F. (1999). When interventions harm: Peer groups and problem behavior. *American Psychologist, 54,* 755–764.

Dishion, T. J., Patterson, G. R., & Kavanagh, K. A. (1992). An experimental test of the coercion model: Linking theory, measurement, and intervention. In J. McCord & R. Tremblay (Eds.) *Preventing antisocial behavior: Interventions from birth through adolescence* (pp. 253–282). New York: Guilford Press.

Dishon, T. J., Patterson, G. R., Stoolmiller, M., & Skinner, M. L. (1991). Family, school, and behavioral antecedents to early adolescent involvement with antisocial peers. *Developmental Psychology, 27,* 172–180.

DuBois, D. L., Holloway, B. E., Valentine, J. C, & Cooper, H. (2002). Effectiveness of mentoring programs for youth: a meta-analytic review. *American Journal of Community Psychology. 30,* 157–197.

DuBois, D. L., Neville, H. A., Parra, G. R., & Pugh-Lilly, A. O. (2002). Testing a new model of mentoring. In J. E. Rhodes (Ed.) *A critical view of youth mentoring: New directions for youth development #93* (pp. 21–57). San Francisco: Jossey-Bass.

Eddy J. M., & Gribskov, L. S., (1998). Juvenile justice and delinquency prevention in the United States: The influence of theories and traditions on policies and practices. In T. P. Gullotta, G. R. Adams, and R. Montemayor, (Eds.), *Delinquent violent youth: Theory and interventions* (pp. 12–52). Thousand Oaks, CA: Sage.

Elliott, D. S., & Menard, S. (1996). Delinquent friends and delinquent behavior: Temporal and developmental patterns. In J. D. Hawkins (Ed.), *Delinquency and crime: Current theories* (pp. 28–67). New York: Cambridge University Press.

Emler, N., Reicher, S., & Ross, A. (1987). The social context of delinquent conduct. *Journal of Child Psychology and Psychiatry, 28,* 99–109.

Ensher, E. A., & Murphy, S. E. (1997). Effects of race, gender and perceived similarity, and contact on mentor relationships. *Journal of Vocational Behavior, 50,* 460–481.

Erickson, M. L., & Jensen, G. F. (1977). Delinquency is still group behavior: Toward revitalizing the group premise in the sociology of deviance. *Journal of criminal law and criminology, 68,* 262–277.

Farley, C. (2004). Amachi in brief. Public/Private Ventures. Retrieved March 15, 2004 from www.ppv.org/ppv/publications/assets/167_publicaion.pdf

Feldman, R. A., Caplinger, T. E., & Wodarski, J. S. (1983). *The St. Louis conundrum: The effective treatment of antisocial youths.* Englewood Cliffs, NJ: Prentice-Hall.

Figueira-McDonough, J. (1993). Residence, dropping out, and delinquency rates. *Deviant Behavior: An Interdisciplinary Journal, 14,* 109–132.

Fo, W. S., & O'Donnell, C. R. (1974). The Buddy System: Relationship and contingency conditions in a community intervention program for youth with nonprofessionals as behavior change agents. *Journal of Consulting & Clinical Psychology, 42,* 163–169.

Gallimore, R., Tharp, R. G., & John-Steiner, V. (1994). The developmental and socio-historical foundations of mentoring. In C. Herrrington (Ed.). *Mentoring.* New York: Columbia University Institute for Urban Minority Education.

Gold, M. (1970). *Delinquent behavior in an American city.* Belmont, CA: Brooks/Cole.

Gottfredson, D. C., McNeil, R. J., III, & Gottfredson, G. D. (1991). Social area influences on delinquency: A multilevel analysis. *Journal of Research in Crime and Delinquency, 28,* 197–226.

Gottlieb, D. J., & Ten Houten, W. (1966). *The emergence of youth societies: A cross-cultural approach.* New York: Free Press.

Griffin, K, Scheier, L., Borvin, G. J., Diaz, T., & Miller, N. (1999). Interpersonal aggression in urban minority youth: Mediators of perceived neighborhood, peer, and parental influences. *Journal of Community Psychology, 27,* 281–298.

Grossman, J. B., & Rhodes , J. E. (2002). The test of time: Prediction and effects in duration in youth mentoring relationships. *American Journal of Community Psychology, 30,* 199–219.

Hayashi, Y., & O'Donnell, C. R. (2004). *A review of mentoring studies and websites: A report for The Melissa Institute for the Prevention and Treatment of Violence.* Miami: The Melissa Institute for the Prevention and Treatment of Violence.

Herrenkohl, T. L., Hawkins, J. D., Chung, I., Hill, K. G., & Battin-Pearson, S. (2001). School and community risk factors and delinquency. In R. Loeber & D. P. Farrington (Eds.), *Child delinquents: Development, intervention, and service needs* (pp. 211–246). Thousand Oaks, CA: Sage.

Hoge, D. R., Andrews, A. D., & Leschied, W. A. (1994). Tests of three hypotheses regarding the predictors of delinquency. *Journal of Abnormal Child Psychology, 22,* 547–559.

Howell, J. D. (Ed.) (1995). *Guide to implementing the comprehensive strategy for serious, violent, and chronic juvenile offenders.* Washington, DC: Office of Juvenile Justice and Delinquency Prevention.

Jackson, Y. (2002). Mentoring for delinquent children: An outcome study with young adolescent children. *Journal of Youth & Adolescence, 31,* 115–122.

Keating, L. M., Tomishima, M. A., Foster, S., & Alessandri, M. (2002).The effects of a mentoring program on at-risk youth. *Adolescence, 37,* 717–734.

Kennan, K., Loeber, R., Zhaang, Q., Stouthamer-Loeber, M., & Van Kammen, W. B. (1995). The influence of deviant peers on the development of boys' disruptive and delinquent behavior: A temporal analysis. *Development and Psychopathology, 7,* 715–726.

Klein, M. W. (1971). *Street gangs and street workers.* Englewood Cliffs, NJ: Prentice-Hall.

Kupersmidt, J. B., Coie, J. D., & Howell, J. C. (2004). Resilience in children exposed to negative peer influences. In K. L. Maton, C. J. Schellenbach, B. J. Leadbeater, & A. L. Solarz (Eds.), *Investing in children, youth, families, and communities: Strengths-based research and policy* (pp. 251–268). Washington DC: American Psychological Association.

Kupersmidt, J. B., DeRosier, M E., & Patterson, C. J. (1995). Similarity as the basis for companionship among children: The roles of sociometric status, aggressive and withdrawn behavior, academic achievement, and demographic characteristics. *Journal of Social and Personal Relationships,* 12, 439–452.

Leont'ev, A. N. (1981). The problem of activity in psychology. In J. V. Wertsch (Ed.), *The concept of activity in Soviet psychology* (pp. 37–71). Armank, NY: Sharpe.

Lipsey, M. W., & Derzon, J. H. (1998). Predictors of violent or serious delinquency in adolescence and early adulthood: A synthesis of longitudinal research. In R. Loeber & D. P. Farrington (Eds.), *Serious and violent juvenile offenders: Risk factors and successful interventions* (pp. 86–105). Thousand Oaks, CA: Sage.

LoSciuto, L., Rajala, A. K., Townsend, T. N., & Taylor, A. S. (1996). An outcome evaluation of Across Ages: An intergenerational mentoring approach to drug prevention. *Journal of Adolescent Research, 11*, 116–129.

Lyon, J. M., Henggeler, S. W., & Hall, J. A. (1992). The family relations, peer relations, and criminal activities of Caucasian and Hispanic-American gang members. *Journal of Abnormal Child Psychology, 20*, 439–449.

Maguin, E., & Loeber, R. (1996). Academic performance and delinquency. In M. Tonry (Ed.), *Crime and justice: A review of research* (Vol. 20) (pp. 145–264). Chicago: University of Chicago Press.

Maxfield, M. G., & Widom, C. S. (1996). The cycle of violence: Revisited 6 years later. *Archives of Pediatric and Adolescent Medicine, 150*, 390–395.

McPartland, J. M., & Nettles, S. M. (1991). *Using community adults as advocates or mentors for at-risk middle school students: A two-year evaluation of Project RAISE*. Report No. 17. Baltimore: Center for Research on Effective Schooling for Disadvantaged Students.

Novotney, L. C., Mertinko, E., Lange, J., & Kelley Baker, T. (2000). *Juvenile mentoring program: A progress review. Juvenile Justice Bulletin*. Washington, DC: Office of Juvenile Justice and Delinquency Prevention.

O'Donnell, C. R. (1980). Environmental design and the prevention of psychological problems. In M. P. Feldman & J. R. Orford (Eds.), *The social psychology of psychological problems* (pp. 279–309). New York: Wiley.

O'Donnell, C. R. (1992). The interplay of theory and practice in delinquency prevention: From behavior modification to activity settings. In J. McCord & R. Tremblay (Eds.) *Preventing antisocial behavior: Interventions from birth through adolescence* (pp. 209–232). New York: Guilford Press.

O'Donnell, C. R. (1995). Firearm deaths among children and youth. *American Psychologist, 50*, 771–776.

O'Donnell, C. R. (2000). *Youth with disabilities in the juvenile justice system: A literature review.* Clemson, SC: Consortium on Children, Families, and the Law, Clemson University, Institute on Family and Neighborhood Life.

O'Donnell, C. R. (Ed.) (2003). *Culture, peers, and delinquency.* New York: Haworth Press.

O'Donnell, C. R., Lydgate, T., & Fo, W. S., (1979). The Buddy System: Review and follow-up. *Child Behavior Therapy, 1*, 161–169.

O'Donnell, C. R., Manos, M. J., & Chesney-Lind, M. (1987). Diversion and neighborhood delinquency programs in open settings: A social network interpretation. In E. K. Morris & C. J. Braukman (Eds.), *Behavioral approaches to crime and delinquency: Application, research and theory* (pp. 251–269). New York: Plenum Press.

O'Donnell, C. R., & Tharp, R. G. (1982). Community intervention and the use of multi-disciplinary knowledge. In A. S. Bellack, M. Hersen, & A. E. Kazdin (Eds.), *International handbook of behavior modification and therapy* (pp. 291–318). New York: Plenum.

O'Donnell, C. R., & Tharp, R. G. (1990). Community intervention guided by theoretical developments. In A. S. Bellack, M. Hersen, & A. E. Kazdin (Eds.), *International handbook of behavior modification and therapy* (2nd ed.) (pp. 251–266). New York: Plenum Press.

O'Donnell, C. R., Tharp, R. G., & Wilson, K. (1993). Activity settings as the unit of analysis: A theoretical basis for community intervention and development. *American Journal of Community Psychology, 21*, 501–520.

Patterson, G. R., & Dishion, T. J. (1985). Contributions of families and peers to delinquency. *Criminology, 23*, 63–69.

Patterson, G. R., & Yoerger, K. (1997). *A developmental model for late-onset delinquency. In* W. Osgood (Ed.), *Motivation and Delinquency* (pp. 118–177). Lincoln, NE: University of Nebraska Press.

Phillips, E. L. (1968). Achievement place: Token reinforcement procedures in a home-style rehabilitation setting for "pre-delinquent" boys. *Journal of Applied Behavior Analysis, 1*, 213–223.

Poole, E. D., & Rigoli, R. M. (1979). Parental support, delinquent friends, and delinquency: A test of interaction effects. *Journal of Law and Criminology, 70*, 188–194.

Rhodes, J. E. (2002). *A critical view of youth mentoring: New directions for youth development #93*. San Francisco: Jossey-Bass.

Rhodes, J. E., Grossman, J. B., & Resch, N. L. (2000). Agents of change: Pathways through which mentoring relationships influence adolescents' academic adjustment. *Child Development, 71*, 1662–1671.

Roberts, H., Liabo, K., Lucas, P., DuBois, D., & Sheldon, T. (2004). Mentoring to reduce antisocial behavior in childhood. *Education and Debate, 328*, 512–514.

Rogoff, B. (1982). Integrating context and cognitive development. In M. E. & A. L. Brown (Eds.). *Advances in developmental psychology* (Vol. 2) (pp. 125–170). Hillsdale, NJ: Lawrence Erlbaum Associates.

Royse, D. (1998). Mentoring high-risk minority youth: Evaluation of the Brothers Project. *Adolescence, 33*, 145–159.

Sampson, R. J., Raudenbush, S. W., & Earls, F. (1997). Neighborhoods and violent crime: A multilevel study of collective efficacy. *Science, 277*, 918–924.

Scudder, R. G., Blount, W. R., Heide, K. M., & Silverman, I. J. (1993). Important links between child abuse, neglect, and delinquency. *International Journal of Offender Therapy and Comparative Criminology, 37,* 315–323.

Schwendinger, H., & Schwendinger, J. (1982). The paradigmatic crisis in delinquency theory. *Crime and Social Justice, 17,* 70–78.

Shannon, L. W. (1988). *Criminal career continuity: Its social context.* New York: Human Sciences Press.

Simons, R. L., Johnson, C., Beaman, J., Conger, R. D., & Whitbeck, L. B. (1996). Parents and peer group as mediators of the effect of community structure on adolescent problem behavior. *American Journal of Community Psychology, 24,* 145–171.

Slicker, E. K., & Palmer, D. J. (1993). Mentoring at-risk high school students: Evaluation of a school-based program. *School Counselor, 40,* 327–334.

Steinberg, L. (1986). Latchkey children and susceptibility to peer pressure: An ecological analysis. *Developmental Psychology, 22,* 433–439.

Taylor, A. S., LoSciuto, L., Fox, M., Hilbert, S. M., & Sonkowsky, M. (1999). The mentoring factor: Evaluation of the across ages' intergenerational approach to drug abuse prevention. *Child & Youth Services, 20,* 77–99.

Tharp, R. G. (2003). Juvenile delinquency: Culture and community, person and society, theory and research. In C. R. O'Donnell (Ed.), *Culture, peers, and delinquency* (pp. 1–11). New York: Haworth Press.

Tharp, R. G., Estrada, P., Dalton, S., & Yamauchi, L. (2000). *Teaching transformed: Achieving excellence, fairness, inclusion and harmony.* Boulder, CO: Westview Press.

Tharp, R. G., & Gallimore, R. (1988). *Rousing minds to life: Teaching and learning in social context.* New York: Cambridge University Press.

Tharp, R. G., & Wetzel, B. J. (1969). *Behavior modification in the natural environment.* New York: Academic Press.

Thompson, L. A., & Kelly-Vance, L. (2001). The impact of mentoring on academic achievement of at-risk youth. *Children & Youth Services Review, 23,* 227–242.

Thornberry, T. P. (1998). Membership in youth gangs and involvement in serious and violent offending. In R. Loeber & D. P. Farrington (Eds.), *Serious and violent juvenile offenders: Risk factors and successful interventions* (pp. 147–166). Thousand Oaks, CA: Sage.

Thornberry, T. P., Lizotte, A. J., Krohn, M. D., Farnworth, M., & Jang, S. J. (1991). Testing interactional theory: An examination of reciprocal causal relationships among family, school, and delinquency. *Journal of Criminal Law and Criminology, 82,* 3–35.

Thornberry, T. P., Lizotte, A. J., Krohn, M. D., Farnworth, M., & Jang, S. J. (1994). Delinquent peers, beliefs, and delinquent behavior: A longitudinal test of interactional theory. *Criminology, 32,* 601–637.

Thorne, G. L., Tharp, R. G., & Wetzel, R. J. (1967). Behavior modification techniques: New tools for probation officers. *Federal Probation, 31*, 21–27.

Tierney, J. P., Grossman, J. B., & Resch, N. L. (1995). *Making a difference: An impact study of Big Brothers Big Sisters.* Philadelphia: Public/Private Ventures.

Tolan, P. H., & Guerra, N. G. (1994). Prevention of delinquency: Current status and issues. *Applied & Preventive Psychology, 3*, 251–273.

Van Patton, D. E. (1997). *TeamWorks evaluation project report.* Portsmouth, NH: Dare Mighty Things.

Vygotsky, L. S. (1978). *Mind in society: The development of higher psychological processes.* (Eds. and Trans. by M. Cole, V. John-Steiner, S. Scribner, & E. Souberman). Cambridge, MA: Harvard University Press.

Vygotsky, L. S. (1981). *The genesis of higher mental functions.* In J. V. Wertsch (Ed.), *The concept of activity in Soviet psychology.* Armank, NY: Sharpe.

Warr, M. (1993). Parents, peers, and delinquency. *Social Forces, 72*, 247–264.

Warr, M. (1996). Organization and instigation in delinquent groups. *Criminology, 34*, 11–37.

Washington State Institute for Public Policy (2002). *Preliminary findings for the Juvenile Rehabilitation Administration's mentoring program.* Olympia, WA.

West D. J., & Farrington, D. P. (1973). *Who becomes delinquent?* London: Heineman Educational Books.

White, H. R., Pandina, R. J., & LaGrange, R. L. (1987). Longitudinal predictors of serious substance use and delinquency. *Criminology, 25*, 715–740.

Whiting, B. (1980). Culture and social behavior: A model for the development of social behavior. *Ethos, 8*, 95–116.

Widom, C. S. (1989). Does violence beget violence? A critical examination of the literature. *Psychological Bulletin, 106*, 3–28.

Wilson, H. (1980). Parental supervision: A neglected aspect of delinquency. *British Journal of Criminology, 20*, 203–235.

Zimmerman, M. A., Bingenheimer, J. B., & Notaro, P. C. (2002). Natural mentors and adolescent resiliency: A study with urban youth. *American Journal of Community Psychology, 30*, 221–243.

SECTION III

Education and Teacher Development

Lois A. Yamauchi

Editor

CHAPTER 6

Culture Matters: Research and Development of Culturally Relevant Instruction

Lois A. Yamauchi

In 1989, Roland Tharp published a seminal article in the *American Psychologist* entitled, "Psychocultural Constraints and Constants: Effects on Teaching and Learning in Schools," in which he described how students' cultural backgrounds influence learning and other experiences in school. Tharp suggested how schools could be redesigned to better serve students who come from groups that traditionally have not been successful in formal education. Sometimes labeled "home-school match," "culturally compatible education" or "culturally relevant instruction," this perspective advocates behavior change on the part of school personnel rather than solely depending on students to adjust to school expectations.

Understanding cultural influences on learning as well as developing culturally relevant instruction have been integral to Tharp's lifelong work. For example, as the director of the Kamehameha Early Education Program (KEEP) for 20 years, Tharp led efforts to apply findings from anthropological research on Native Hawaiian[1] families and socialization to designing literacy instruction for Hawaiian children. Later, he was principal investigator of an 11-year project to generate principles of culturally relevant practices for American Indian students, based largely on his work in the Pueblo of Zuni, New Mexico.

Most recently, as the director of the Center for Research on Education, Diversity and Excellence (CREDE), he and his colleagues developed a set of core principles that should guide the design of effective practice for students from culturally and linguistically diverse backgrounds. One of the principles is Contextualization, the notion that learning is promoted when students connect new information with what they already know from home, school, and community (Tharp, Estrada, Dalton, & Yamauchi, 2000). This includes both teaching in ways that are consistent with familiar socialization patterns and using curriculum that integrates academic concepts with what students already know.

The purpose of this chapter is to review research on culturally relevant instruction and to highlight current issues. In doing so, I include Tharp's research on this topic, but also review relevant research that has emerged among others working in this area. In the next section, I review definitions of the term "culture" as a starting point of this discussion.

What Is Culture?

Culture is often described in varied and vague terms (Jackson & Meadows, 1991). As a number of scholars have pointed out, part of this problem may stem from the nature of culture as something that is rarely discussed among its members except in cases of cultural clashes with outsiders or when socializing novice members (Brislin, 1993; Erickson, 1997; Jackson & Meadows, 1991). Although there is no single definition upon which all social scientists agree, there is consensus regarding certain aspects or features of culture (Banks, 1994).

First, social scientists tend to agree that culture is something that is learned and shared among a group of people (Rohner, 1984). Brislin (1993) suggests that cultural knowledge is passed down from one generation to the next. Social scientists also agree that culture is the product of human construction rather than what is available in nature (Banks, 1994; Brislin, 1993; Erickson, 1997). Many cite Herskovitz's (1948) definition of culture as "the man-made part of the environment" (p. 17). For example, the local climate is typically not considered part of culture. However, when a group of people lives in a tropical environment, they develop strategies for keeping cool and expectations for dress (usually lighter clothing) that would be considered part of their culture. This reflects consensus that social scientists have about another aspect of culture—its inclusion of intangible human products, such as ideas, symbols, assumptions, beliefs, perspectives on life, and ways of interacting and problem solving. In their review of over 160 definitions of culture available in the 1950s, Kroeber and Kluckhom (1952) concluded that "the essential core of culture consists of traditional (i.e., historically derived and selected) ideas and especially attached values" (p. 161).

There is much controversy about whether or not culture includes artifacts. Since the cognitive revolution in the social sciences, theorists have tended to emphasize how artifacts are used or what they mean to a group, rather than the material objects themselves (D'Andrade, 1996). Cole (1999) noted that he and others are attempting to break away from the dichotomy between artifacts and the more cognitive aspects of culture. In doing so, he conceptualizes "the cultural medium in which human beings live as an environment transformed by the artifacts of prior generations, extending back to the beginning of the species" (p. 77). This is consistent with Geertz's view that human thought includes both processes inside the head and also those that occur in public places through symbols such as words, gestures, and artifacts (Cole, 1999). Thus, the distinction between material and cognitive elements blurs because artifacts reflect cognitive processes.

Evidence for Culture's Influence on Schooling

Theoretical Foundation

I now turn to a discussion of the theoretical and empirical support for the assumption that culture matters in classrooms and schools. Based on the ideas of Vygotsky (1978), sociocultural (also called cultural-historical) theory is helpful in understanding culture's influence on schooling. Sociocultural theory suggests that all higher[2] psychological functioning—e.g., one's ideas, beliefs, thoughts, and ways of problem solving—have their roots in social interaction. By engaging in joint activity with more experienced others through symbols, such as language, children and other novice members of a community eventually appropriate those symbols. More proficient members assist novices in performing the tasks and roles of their culture. Over time, less assistance is needed, until eventually learners can perform the behaviors independently. In this way, children and other novice community members appropriate the values, beliefs, ideas, and perspectives of the adults and other more experienced people with whom they interact.

Applied to schooling, the sociocultural perspective can explain why some groups of students perform poorly on standard measures of academic achievement or have other negative experiences in school. The notion is that all students learn—but what and how they learn may differ across groups, depending on who students interact with and the kinds of expectations, beliefs, and knowledge that are emphasized in those interactions. According to the sociocultural perspective, students may be less successful in school because of a lack of fit between what students are accustomed to in their homes and communities and what is expected at school. When educators incorporate more of what students expect and know from their home and community experiences, student motivation and learning may increase.

In sociocultural theory, the term "intersubjectivity" is used to refer to shared meaning that develops among people who have a history of interaction (Tharp et al., 2000; Vygotsky, 1978). This includes shared perspectives, values, beliefs, and expectations. When teachers and students come from different cultural backgrounds there tends to be less intersubjectivity between them and cultural clashes or misunderstandings are more likely to occur. Such is the case when students have less experience with the majority culture, as classrooms expectations tend to be based on the norms of the majority culture (Dyson & Genishi, 1991; Heath, 1983; Tharp et al., 2000).

Cultural Misunderstandings

Results of many studies indicate that students from non-majority backgrounds tend to misunderstand classroom expectations and are often misunderstood by their teachers (e.g., Erickson, 1980; Foster, 1992; Heath, 1983; Phillips, 1972). For example, Heath (1983) studied the difficulties encountered by working class African American and European American children when they came to school. At home, African American children were encouraged to be creative with their toys. Toys and other materials were used flexibly for whatever purposes and in whatever contexts they were needed. When African American children came to preschool, they often did not understand teachers' expectations that materials had particular places to be kept. They also misunderstood teachers' expectations for what Heath called "space-function ties."

> [The African American children from Trackton were] puzzled by the space-function ties the teachers expected them to recognize and obey. When told to "play," they interpreted play as improvisation and creation, and these called for flexibility in the mingling of materials and the mixing of items from different parts of the room. A truck which had detachable parts and was kept in the puzzle corner was to be taken to the sand box where water and sand could be mixed, the tires changed, and spare truck parts hauled. If a particular piece of a puzzle looked like a wrench or a jack for a truck, or a spoon for feeding a doll, Trackton children went to the puzzle shelf to incorporate it in their play. Teachers despaired when they found what they classified as *puzzles* in the sandbox or the doll corner [italics in original]. (pp. 273–274)

In another example of a lack of intersubjectivity, Heath found that working class European American students often did not understand why their teachers asked them to make up endings to stories or to invent fictitious tales. At home, this would be considered lying, something that might result in punishment. Children from these communities were better at answering questions about factual events because this kind of talk was more consistent with what they experienced at home. Thus, the nature of activities working class African American and European American children experienced prior to coming to school shaped the expectations they had about classroom activities. When these expectations were different from what teachers had in mind, students were less successful in school and were more often labeled as less capable by educators.

Changing School Activities to Promote Cultural Relevance

To address concerns about differences between teachers' and students' understandings about school, some programs have adjusted school activities to better fit what students are accustomed to at home. For example, in trying to understand how to improve the educational achievement of Native Hawaiian students, Tharp and his colleagues at KEEP analyzed the adjustments in expectations and values that Hawaiian children needed to make in order to be successful in school. There were two simultaneous program goals: to restructure classrooms so that they would be more compatible with what students expected based on their home and community experiences and to better assist students in adopting new ways of interaction and thinking that were required for school learning.

KEEP researchers found that socialization patterns among Hawaiian youth, particularly patterns of interaction among youth and adults, were different from participation structures typically found in classrooms (e.g., Gallimore, Boggs, & Jordan, 1974; Jordan, 1985). Their research indicated that household chores were often conducted by children as a group, with the oldest sister leading and delegating responsibilities to her siblings. There also appeared to be less direct child-adult interactions in the Hawaiian households than was typically expected in school. Yet, when these children came to school, students were expected to interact directly with an adult (the teacher) and to work independently rather than with groups of peers. Applying these findings, KEEP classrooms were rearranged so that the activities capitalized on students' more collective orientation, by emphasizing peer assisted cooperative learning. In these settings, students were highly engaged in their school work and scored higher on achievement tests than peers in public schools (Au & Jordan, 1981).

KEEP researchers also found that the language children used in their homes and communities differed from what was expected in school. At home, children often spoke Hawai'i Creole English, known informally as "Pidgin English." Further, students often experienced a conversational pattern "talk story" that is characterized by overlapping speech and co-narration. Overlapping speech occurs when talk is initiated before the current speaker has finished his or her turn in the conversation. Co-narration refers to more than one person telling an account. These two features of children's language patterns were at odds with the expectations of classroom discussions in which a child is often required to speak only when called on by the teacher, and only one person speaks at a time (Au & Jordan, 1981). When KEEP teachers allowed children to engage in overlapping speech and to participate with them as co-narrators of discussions, student participation and reading achievement increased.

The classroom does not need to exactly replicate what is found in children's homes. For example, although the anthropological research suggested that students might not have interacted directly or frequently with many adults, KEEP developers still wanted students to be comfortable interacting with their teachers in school. Jordan (1985) describes how they implemented a strategy at KEEP for extending what was already familiar or comfortable to students. In the case of attending to adults, their ethnographic research suggested that there were contexts in which the Hawaiian children focused on particular adults in particular situations.

> The teacher shares some role markers and behaves in some ways like adults to whom the children are accustomed to attending, but she also wants their attention in some circumstances that differ from those in which they are accustomed to giving it, as when they are asked to attend to detailed verbal instructions given to a large group of children—a totally foreign experience. However, the extension is not pushed too far, and they are not asked to attend to the classroom adult for long periods of time, exclusive of attending to their peers. (Jordan, 1985, pp. 114–115)

Four Important Cultural Dimensions

The KEEP research is significant because it illustrates the different ways culture influences the experiences of students in classrooms. Although cultures differ in a number of ways, there are four cultural dimensions that are helpful in understanding how cultures vary and make a difference in classrooms settings (Tharp et al., 2000). These four dimensions are (a) individualism versus collectivism, (b) role expectations, (c) power distance, and (d) language and genres.

Individualism versus collectivism. The first dimension of individualism vs. collectivism refers to the extent to which a culture tends to emphasize the rights and interests of the individual over that of the group. For example, KEEP researchers found that Hawaiian children tended to be more collectivist. Students did not want to be singled out, for either praise or punishment, and youngsters spent a lot of time inside and outside of the classroom attending to peers. To accommodate students' home experiences, classroom activities were changed to emphasize a more collective orientation where students were encouraged to help their peers. This increased motivation and achievement (Au & Jordan, 1981).

Other studies have found that many Native American, Asian American, African American, and Latino students, as well as those from more traditional and rural communities, tend to have collectivist values and respond well to small group activities (Tharp et al., 2000). In her classic study of Papago Indian youth and their experiences in off-reservation schools, Phillips (1972) found that Papago Indians were the most engaged when activities were structured as peer-oriented, student-directed work groups.

Role expectations. Cultures differ regarding expectations of various roles, most notably in sex roles and the role of the teacher. Regarding sex roles, in some cultures, there is more overlap between the roles of men and women; whereas, for other groups these roles are more distinct (Hofstede, 1980). Although KEEP researchers found that Hawaiian students were the most productive working in groups comprised of both boys and girls, this was not the case for the American Indian children with whom KEEP researchers worked in the Navajo Nation (Jordan, Tharp, & Vogt, 1985). Navajo Indian students refused to work in mixed groups. When students were placed in small groups comprised of both girls and boys, the children divided the work themselves and completed their assignments by collaborating with same-sex partners. This was consistent with traditional division of labor within the Navajo community.

Cultures differ regarding role expectations of teachers. An example is evident in the roles of teachers in Papahana Kaiapuni, a kindergarten through grade 12 program conducted using the Hawaiian language as the medium of instruction (Yamauchi, Ceppi, & Lau-Smith, 2000). Kaiapuni began in 1987 to promote the indigenous language after it had been banned from schools and other governmental agencies for nearly a century (Yamauchi, Ceppi, & Lau-Smith, 1999). Many of those involved in Kaiapuni consider it to be a form of culturally relevant instruction (Yamauchi et al., 2000). In addition to instructing students in the Hawaiian language, Kaiapuni educators strive to integrate Hawaiian culture with classroom activities and view their roles as part of a large extended family (Yamauchi et al., 1999; Yamauchi & Wilhelm, 2001). In enacting this role, they spend a lot of out-of-school time with their students and their students' families and continue to feel responsible for students even after the youngsters have moved to the next grade level. The teachers in the Hawaiian language immersion program report that being an "auntie" or "uncle" to their students is part of their role as their teacher. These aspects of Kaiapuni teachers' roles contrast with that of the more western approach that draws more distinct boundaries between home and school.

Power. Cultures differ regarding who has power and whether people are tolerant of power differences. This latter difference, coined "power distance" by Hofstede (1980) has implications for classrooms and schools. Hofstede's studies of the national culture of 50 countries indicated that some groups are more accepting of differences in power, whereas other cultures try to minimize power differences. For example, the U.S. is considered relatively less tolerant of power differences. Even though there are great inequities within the U.S. society, the general culture of the U.S. is one in which people try to empower those who do not have much status. In classrooms, this may take the form of teachers trying to empower students by giving them choices regarding what they want to study or with whom they want to work. Other cultures, for example many Asian societies, are more accepting of power differences. In general, people in these cultures do not think it is necessary or appropriate to give more power to those who have less. For example, Spencer-Oately (1997) compared British and Chinese graduates students and their tutors regarding their perceptions of appropriate student and teacher behaviors. All participants expected that students would yield less power; however, Chinese students and tutors felt stronger about maintaining power differences. They were more likely to agree that teachers should correct students and express dissatisfaction with students' performances, but that students should not do the same of their teachers.

Although I have not found any published studies measuring power distance among Hawaiians, Pukui, Haertig, and Lee's classic text on Hawaiian culture (1972) describes that traditionally Hawaiian youth were expected to respect the authority of their elders by watching silently as they were taught:

"Nānā ka maka. Ho'olohe. Pa'a ka waha. Ho'opili."
"Observe. Listen. Keep the mouth shut. Imitate."

> Such was the tenet of old Hawai'i. The elders well knew that. "*I ka nānā no a 'ike*, by observing, one learns. *I ka ho'olohe no a ho'omaopopo*, by listening, one commits to memory. *I ka hana no a 'ike*, by practice one masters the skill."
>
> To this final directive was added: Never interrupt. Wait until the lesson is over and the elder gives you permission. Then—and not until then—*nīnau*. Ask questions [italics in original]. (p. 48)

Similarly, when I interviewed Hawaiian immersion teachers about their experiences in the program, they often mentioned Hawaiian immersion teachers tend to wield more authority than in a typical public school classroom. Many of these teachers still expect students to be silent observers when they are first learning a skill. These issues of power may be related to why KEEP researchers found that

Hawaiian students often were not accustomed to engaging in extended discussions with adults.

Language. The fourth cultural dimension that makes a difference in classrooms and schools is language (Tharp et al., 2000). The languages students speak and write at home may or may not be the same as the languages used and promoted in school. In some schools, students may be bilingual speakers of both a first language (e.g., Spanish) and the language of instruction (e.g., English). In other cases, students may have little prior experience with the language used in school. For example, students who are recent immigrants may have little or no background in the majority language spoken by their teachers in school. Although they were exposed to Standard English in the community, most KEEP students came to school speaking Hawai'i Creole English, a language that is different from the Standard English spoken and promoted by teachers. Research suggests that promoting students' first language assists the learning of a second language (Cummins, 1991; Snow, 1990; Collier, 1987). In addition, second language learning in school can be either an additive or subtractive process (Lambert, 1981). In the additive case, students learn a new second language and retain their first. Unfortunately, many U.S. schools do not support students' first language adequately so that the process of learning English becomes subtractive. As students learn English, they do so at the expense of their first language.

Even when students speak the language used in school, they may not be familiar with the social use of language in the classroom. Foster (1992) found that African American and European American students differed in their oral presentations at sharing time. European American children's presentations resembled a short lecture about the features of an object or event and tended to fit European American teachers' expectations for the activity. This contrasted with the more dramatic style of African American children, whose sharing presentations were often longer, more elaborate, and conveyed a series of events using dialogue, gestures, and sound effects. Teachers interrupted African American students more and judged their presentations to be less appropriate. When teachers adjust their expectations of classroom talk, to be more consistent with students' home and community language use, student participation, motivation, and learning increases (e.g., Au & Jordan, 1981; Foster, 1992). As was the case in KEEP, educators may also increase success by more explicitly teaching students about the new ways of communicating at school, rather than expecting them to arrive at the classroom door already able to use language in these ways.

Three Issues in Culturally Relevant Instruction

I now discuss three issues that relate to research on culturally relevant instruction: (a) insider-outsider researcher tensions, (b) stereotyping and simplification, and (c) addressing the needs of heterogeneous classrooms. In doing so, I reflect on my experiences as a researcher studying the development of culturally relevant instruction for Native Hawaiians and Zuni American Indians (e.g., Yamauchi, 1993, 2003; Yamauchi et al., 1999, 2000, 2004; Yamauchi & Tharp, 1995).

Insider-outsider tensions. One of the issues facing those who study culturally relevant instruction, as well as other issues related to culture, is the influence of one's own status as a relative insider or outsider to the community of interest. Many have criticized the role of white researchers studying non-white communities. Troyna and Carrington (1989) suggest that there are three areas of concern in this context. The first involves the politics of interviewing and administering tests to non-white participants, when their racial background does not "match" the researcher's:

> [The argument] follows that production of research data…is likely to be inhibited, distorted and inferior unless "racial matching" is achieved, precisely because of the unequal power relationship between interviewer and respondent and/or by radical differences in their life experiences and cultural frames of reference (Troyna, 1998, pp. 97–98).

The second concern involves the potential for outsiders to misunderstand participants and to be less committed or able to interpret responses of those from other communities (Troyna & Carrington, 1989). For example, I have often worried that my status as a non-indigenous researcher might inhibit my ability to understand my participants' intentions and behaviors. I have tried to rectify this by using indigenous informants and by discussing my research interpretations with participants and other community members. There is always the threat, however, that I have missed something or that my participants and informants will not point out my errors.

Troyna and Carrington (1989) suggest that a third concern is that outsiders, in their case, white researchers, place a focus or "gaze" on non-white participants that may contribute to the persistence of racist attitudes. Those who apply this perspective argue that social science theory has only included non-white peoples as deviations from the norm (Troyna, 1998). By making other communities the focus of their work, researchers may objectify their participants for the advancement of their own status and careers. At all of the sites where I worked, I met community members who were suspicious of my role as a researcher from outside their community. Some were concerned that once the data were collected, I would abandon them and use the information in ways that would not benefit their community. These are legitimate concerns, given the history of non-indigenous researchers studying indigenous peoples and the often negative consequences. To address these concerns, I try to be explict with community members about what I hope to gain and how I hope to accomplish those goals. I also solicit community input regarding what they want to know about their own schools and communities, and look for ways that I can make contributions. For example, I have volunteered as a part-time teacher, taken minutes at meetings, written grant proposals, and organized and funded teachers to attend conferences. I have also collaborated with community members to conduct and present research (e.g., Yamauchi, Kurose, Forman, Kaloi, & Carroll, 2004; Yamauchi & Wilhelm, 2001).

Even when researchers share the same ethnic or racial background with their participants, it may not be clear that they are entirely insiders. Mehra (2001) described her research on the experiences of Asian Indian students and their families in American schools. Although she shared many things in common with her participants, including their Asian Indian background, language, status as a relative newcomer to the U.S., and participation in cultural activities; she also viewed herself as an outsider because she did not have children, was often viewed as more western and different from her student participants, and was not familiar with American schools.

A number of scholars believe that the insider-outsider dichotomy is too simplistic, given the complexities of identity and community development (e.g., Mehra, 2001; Rogoff, 2003; Wright, 1998). As Rogoff points out, many people participate in more than one community, and their involvement and status changes over time:

> People of Mexican descent living in what is now the United States are not entirely outsiders to European American communities; the practices and policies of the two communities interrelate. Similarly, an anthropologist who spends 10 or 50 years working in a community participates in some manner and gains some local understanding. Youngsters who grow up in a family with several cultural heritages…have some insider and some outsider understandings of each of their communities. Overlaps across communities also come from the media, daily contacts, and shared endeavors. (p. 25)

Indeed, my own experiences as a researcher have changed my status and role in the communities where I have worked. For example, after several years participating as a researcher and teacher educator at a high school situated in a rural community with the largest population of Native Hawaiians in the world, I no longer view myself as a total outsider to this community nor do I identify completely as an insider. Connolly (1996) and Kaomea (2001) emphasize that individuals have multiple and layered identities. As a Japanese-American female researcher who was raised in Hawai'i, I am not only Japanese-American, nor am I just female, a researcher, or a person from the islands. In similar ways, the identities of my participants are multi-faceted and layered, and our interactions reflect these complexities.

Stereotyping and simplification. Culturally relevant instruction involves incorporating pedagogy that is consistent with the knowledge, expectations, and socialization patterns of students who often do not come from a dominant societal group. A second issue to consider in this area is the tendency to over-generalize cultural characteristics. As Tharp and colleagues (Tharp et al., 2000) caution:

> Any description of a "culture" can only refer to the central tendencies of its members. In any culture, there are enormous individual variations. There will always be individuals from any culture who no doubt look much more like the members of another group than their own. (p. 107)

González (1999) suggests that culturally relevant approaches may lead to stereotyping because this often entails a focus on sociolinguistic and other "microinteractional processes" (p. 432) rather than on how schools perpetuate societal inequities. She argues that focusing on a cultural mismatch approach tends to represent groups in a static way. To address these concerns, she and her colleagues emphasize neo-Vygotskian ideas of distributed cognition which represent knowledge as mediated across individuals, artifacts, activities, and settings rather than isolated within one person's head (González, Andrade, Civil, & Moll, 2001). Their "funds of knowledge approach" involves three activities by teachers: (a) ethnographic analyses of students' households; (b) examination of classroom practices, and (c) participation in after school study groups with a goal of connecting household funds of knowledge to the curriculum (González et al., 2001; Moll & González, 1994; Moll & González, 2003). For example, in one project, teachers interviewed and made participant observations of their students' households to determine the existence of varied forms and use of mathematical knowledge in everyday life (González et al., 2001). Teachers then met with community members to discuss these practices and to brainstorm how to integrate this information into the curriculum. González and colleagues argue that a funds of knowledge approach represents culture as "lived contexts" (p. 118) rather than in static and simplistic ways, by emphasizing community members' practices and their own interpretations of these activities.

Gutiérrez and Rogoff (2003) are also concerned about stereotyping in research on culture and education. They argue that focusing on participation over time in specific cultural activities, rather than on cultural traits, can guard against overgeneralizations and stereotypes about groups. The extent to which individuals participate in different cultural activities influences their appropriation of inherent expectations, values, and skills. As discussed earlier, this perspective takes into account that over time individuals often vary the amount and type of their involvement in a particular activity. According to the authors, such a historical description of individuals' participation in cultural activities is a better indicator for how a person appropriated various ways of thinking, believing, and expecting, compared to attributions of such to membership in a particular ethnic, cultural, or community group.

In my own work, I have found that I must maintain a constant balance of being mindful of cultural tendencies whilst also being cognizant of individual variation within groups and across time. For example, while working in the Pueblo of Zuni, New Mexico, I found that communication in the Zuni language with other community members appeared to be a culturally-valued practice (Yamauchi, 1993). In addition, most Zunis were bilingual in the Zuni and English languages. However, whether someone used either language with other Zunis was dependant upon the context (e.g., whether non-speakers were present, the reasons for the communication), and this was evident for the teachers in my study. Although nearly all of the students in their classes were Zuni speakers, only two of the four Zuni teachers used the indigenous language frequently during instruction. These two teachers used Zuni to engage students in casual conversation, to explain abstract concepts, and to incorporate examples from the Zuni culture.

During instruction, the other two Zuni teachers appeared to only use their indigenous language as a last resort, when students didn't understand multiple attempts to communicate in English (Yamauchi, 1993). When I interviewed one of these teachers about her language use, she said that the Zuni language and culture belonged in the home and that it was the responsibility of parents to teach these to their children. For her, school was a place to learn English and about the majority (non-Zuni) culture, and she tended to use the language with students who were not strong English language speakers or were confused about the content. (I should note that in a follow-up interview one year later, this teacher told me that she was using more Zuni in the classroom with all students, after seeing students' positive reaction to this practice on one of the videorecordings I made of her class.) Thus, although speaking in Zuni with other community members was a culturally endorsed practice, it was more accurate to discuss the contextual features that led individual members to enact this practice instead of making a blanket assumption for all Zunis and all situations.

Weisner, Gallimore, and Jordan (1988) view culture as providing individuals with adaptive solutions that may be drawn upon, if the specific context favors such an option. For example, they found that, although care of younger siblings by older children was a culturally valued practice among Hawaiians in general, a family may or may not apply this to their own circumstances, depending upon the context (e.g., some older siblings were not suitable). Thus, a focus on activity settings can be a means of guarding against stereotyping because such an approach emphasizes the specific context in which culturally valued practices may or may not be used by particular individuals (Gallimore, personal communication, June 8, 2004).

Heterogeneous classrooms and settings. The final issue I address is the development of classroom activity settings to meet the needs of heterogeneous classrooms. As our nation's population continues to diversify, educators will increasingly find themselves working in classrooms that reflect this cultural plurality. As described in the previous section, there will also be variation of individuals within cultural groups, as well as differences across settings for the same people. Yet, a major premise of the culturally relevant approach is to tailor instruction to the background of students. Given such diversity, how can this be accomplished?

A simple answer to this question is diversity itself, this time in regards to classroom activity settings (Tharp et al., 2000). Activity settings are the contexts of human interaction and joint production (O'Donnell & Tharp, 1990; Tharp & Gallimore, 1988). One way to describe these settings is in terms of the "who" "what," "when," "where," and "why" of the contexts. The "who" refers to the people present. The "what" describes their actions, including any routines and scripts. The "when" and "where" describe the time and place. And the "why" represents the activity's objectives, participants' motivations, and interpretations. Tharp and others who advocate for culturally relevant instruction have criticized more traditional classrooms because of the lack of diversity in their activity settings. In these classrooms, the "who" is often limited to the teacher and a large group of same-age students (Tharp et al., 2000; Tharp & Gallimore, 1988). The students often sit in rows facing the teacher, as such an arrangement facilitates the dominant activities of the teacher lecturing and students completing assignments alone. Little time is provided for more genuine interactions between the teacher and students or among students themselves. The teacher may pose questions to the class, but these are typically "known answer" questions, those for which there is already an answer in mind (Mehan, 1979). Although some students participate readily in traditional classrooms, many others see little meaning in such activities and respond with low levels of motivation and achievement (Tharp et al., 2000; Tharp & Gallimore, 1988).

By diversifying classrooms activities, educators are more likely to engage a heterogeneous group of students. All students should have the opportunity to participate in activities that are culturally compatible with their own backgrounds, in addition to those that will extend their repertoires and competencies (Tharp et al., 2000). Instead of always conducting their classrooms using the same organizational structures (e.g., lecture, individual assignments completed at one's desk), educators can vary settings so that all students have opportunities to work with many different peers and the teacher, while engaged in a variety of activities. In addition to the traditional structures just described, classroom activities may be organized so that students have opportunities for discussions with the teachers and with peers, reading and writing alone and with others, conducting research, making presentations, drawing maps, participating in role plays, creating activities for peers, and so on. The time and place of instructional settings may also vary so that school activities extend outside of the walls of schools into the community, during and after school hours. The point is that there are many more ways to organize activity settings than is typically found in schools. When educators utilize just a few kinds of settings in their classrooms, it is unlikely that they will meet the needs of a diverse group of students.

These issues apply to my research on the Hawaiian Studies Program (HSP) at Waiʻanae High School. The HSP is a voluntary academic program for students in Grades 10 to 12 that incorporates the learning of Hawaiian values and knowledge with more traditional western curriculum in science, social studies, and English (Yamauchi, 2003). I first became interested in the program because of the heterogeneity of students and instructional settings. Although the majority of students in the HSP are of Hawaiian ancestry, there is much variation within this group in regard to cultural identification and participation in cultural activities. In addition, students come from a wide range of backgrounds in terms of socioeconomic status, academic achievement, and motivation. For example, some HSP participants are honor's students, others are in special education, and some are at-risk for dropping out of school. Because they attend a large high school where academic tracking is used, many of the HSP students would not have known each other, had they not been in the program together.

One of the major ways that HSP teachers have diversified their instructional activity settings is by instituting weekly community fieldwork (Yamauchi, 2003). Every Thursday, all HSP students and their teachers work with community members to conduct research and service projects (Yamauchi, Billig, Meyer, & Hofschire, 2004). For example, three groups of students work with professional archaeologists to document and excavate cultural sites within the Wai'anae Valley. The results of this work have become part of the State record and used by students and other community members to testify against commercial development of the area. Other students and teachers study the environmental effects of diverting water from Wai'anae Valley streams, participate in projects at the local health center, learn about canoe making and Hawaiian maritime culture, and work with botanists to study and restore native plants to the community forests and shorelines.

The activity settings created by HSP fieldwork involve a variety of people—peers, teachers, and community members. The community members often assist HSP youth in their academic, career, and personal endeavors and become role models for students. What is produced in these field settings is often valued and used by the community (e.g., archaeological maps and reports, scientific data, health related services). Activities are meaningful to students and promote the development of a range of skills and knowledge. They take place at various sites, promoting the notion that there are many places throughout the community where school knowledge and skills can be applied. An external program evaluation found that HSP students were motivated by these contexts (RMC Research Corporation, 2003). In addition, compared to peers who were not in the program, HSP students more strongly reported (a) feeling valued by their community, teachers, and peers; (b) believing that they make a difference in community outcomes; (c) having career skills, and (d) being interested in and knowledgeable about Hawaiian history and culture (RMC Research Corporation, 2003; Yamauchi et al., 2004).

Thus, to order to promote positive outcomes among heterogeneous students, classroom activity settings should be diverse. However, this does not mean that a variety of *any* type of activities will result in learning. The Five Standards for Effective Pedagogy are research-based principles of instruction for teaching students from culturally and linguistically diverse backgrounds that can guide the development of activity settings that promote student learning (Tharp et al., 2000). The Five Standards are: (a) Joint Productive Activity: teachers and students working together to produce tangible and intangible products, (b) Language and Literacy: developing language and literacy across the curriculum, (c) Contextualization: connecting instruction of new information with what students already know from their prior home or school experiences, (d) Challenging Activities: promoting students' thinking in complex ways that goes beyond rote memorization of facts, and (e) Instructional Conversation: teaching through dialogue. (See Doherty, Hilberg, Pinal, & Tharp, 2003; Tharp et al., 2000; Tharp et al., 2004 for more detailed discussions of the standards and evidence of their effectiveness.)

There are many instructional examples from the HSP that exemplify enactment of the Five Standards (Yamauchi, Wyatt, & Carroll, in press). For instance, while engaged in the archaeological fieldwork, students collaborate with community archaeologists to produce maps of cultural sites (Joint Productive Activity). There are opportunities for them to discuss and write about their findings and for the archaeologists and teachers to provide feedback and other support of students' language development (Language and Literacy). The activities involve complex problem solving (Challenging Activities) in work that is culturally relevant and integrated with students' other prior experiences (Contextualization). Finally, the smaller size and joint productive nature of the activities lend themselves well to conversations about abstract concepts and ideas (Instructional Conversation). Therefore, diversification of settings is important, but in consideration of other aspects of activity, as well.

Conclusion

This chapter reviewed research and issues related to culturally relevant instruction. It was inspired by Roland Tharp's contributions to our understanding of the influence of culture on education. When Tharp began his work in this area over 30 years ago, little was known about these issues, and many did not acknowledge the role of the cultural context on teaching and learning. Since then, however, research has accumulated that demonstrates that culture does matter in classrooms and schools. When the instructional context is changed to be more compatible with students' background, their participation, satisfaction, and learning tends to increase.

Tharp and others in this field have helped us to see that there are at least four dimensions along which cultures vary and make a difference in school (Tharp et al., 2000). The first dimension, individualism versus collectivism, refers to the extent to which a group places importance on individual or group concerns and achievement. This is important given that more traditional classrooms tend to emphasize individual performance and learning. The dimension of role expectations is also significant, particularly regarding sex roles and the role of the teacher. The third dimension, power, brings to our attention that culturally influenced notions about who should wield authority (e.g., the teacher alone; the teacher and students) can influence academic outcomes. Finally, language differences, both in terms of the languages spoken in and outside the classroom and the social uses of language, may be sources of cultural conflict or congruence.

Although these four dimensions have been identified, they have not been equally studied. In classroom contexts, we know the most about individualism versus collectivism and language differences. In contrast, less research has focused on role expectations and power. Most of the research in these latter two areas is descriptive and highlights what currently exists in classrooms and for particular groups. Research is needed to investigate the effects of changing classroom role expectations and power structures on student and teacher outcomes.

As the body of research on culture and education has accumulated, so has our knowledge of the complexity of these issues. For example, the entrance of non-majority researchers into the field has helped us to see that cultural biases influence our research choices and interpretations. Although the distinction between "insiders" and "outsiders" is more complicated than may have originally been construed, it serves us well to reflect on how our identities, and those of our participants, influence the research process. A focus on such issues also reminds us that it is important that research benefits communities and that community members are included in decisions about (a) what is researched, (b) how research is conducted, and (c) how results are used. So-called "insider research" and collaborations between those who are more and less familiar with focal communities are valuable and should be highlighted.

Another issue that has gained attention is regarding stereotyping and oversimplification. Although the term "culture" is used to refer to that which is shared among a particular group of people, we know that there will always be individual variation within any one group (Tharp et al., 2000). In addition, most people participate in many different groups, and their participation in various cultural activities changes over time (Gutiérrez & Rogoff, 2003; Rogoff, 2003). One means of guarding against stereotyping is to use the activity setting as the unit of analysis. Activity settings are specific contexts of human interaction and productivity (O'Donnell & Tharp, 1990; Tharp & Gallimore, 1988). Analysis of why one setting produces change in behavior, while another does not, may help us to unpack the specific ways in which the cultural context influences behavior.

A focus on activity settings can also help us to address the growing diversity of our classrooms. Some may feel that the increasing student diversity is at odds with a culturally relevant approach. However, as Tharp pointed out, our classroom activity settings have tended to be homogenous, benefiting only a small segment of society. By diversifying instructional settings, more students will have the opportunity to feel comfortable in school. All students should have the opportunity to experience learning in ways that are congruent with their cultural background, in addition to participating in settings that promote appropriation of new skills and expectations. Research that focuses on the diversification of activity settings is needed.

Finally, I note that behavior change in any setting is difficult. In schools, we are interested in promoting student learning and other positive behavior change. Achieving such outcomes, particularly for students who have had limited success in school, may require radical reorganization of classroom activity settings. Any modification of classroom organization will involve change in teachers' behaviors. Thus, we also need to understand strategies for changing educators' behavior toward enactment of culturally relevant instruction. Tharp and Gallimore (1988) and two other chapters in this book (Datnow, Stringfield, & Castellano, this volume; Saunders & Goldenberg, this volume) address the complexities of initiating and sustaining change among teachers. The issues raised by those authors should be considered in concert with the ones raised here.

Notes

I wish to thank Valerie Dutdut, Julie Kaomea, Angela Straub, Tasha Wyatt, and Tomoko Yoshida for their assistance. I am also grateful to Barbara DeBaryshe, Ernestine Enomoto, Ron Gallimore, Cliff O'Donnell, Cecily Ornelles, and Tracy Trevorrow for feedback on earlier drafts of this chapter. While preparing this manuscript, I was supported under the Education Research and Development Program, PR/Award R306A6001, the Center for Research on Education, Diversity & Excellence (CREDE), as administered by the Office of Education Research and Improvement (OERI), National Institute on the Education of At-Risk Students (NIEARS), U.S. Department of Education (USDoE). The contents, findings, and opinions expressed here are those of the author and do not necessarily represent the positions or policies of OERI, NIEARS, or the USDoE.

1. In this chapter I use the terms Hawaiian and Native Hawaiian interchangeably to refer to those of Hawaiian or part Hawaiian ancestry.

2. Vygotsky (1978) distinguished between lower and higher psychological functioning. Lower psychological functioning, which includes learning by association and sensorimotor learning, occurs among humans and other animals. Vygotsky believed higher psychological functions distinguished humans from other animals.

References

Au, K. H., & Jordan, C. (1981). Teaching reading to Hawaiian children: Finding a culturally appropriate solution. In H. Trueba, G.P. Guthrie, & K.H. Au (Eds.), *Culture in the bilingual classroom: Studies in classroom ethnography*. Rowley, MA: Newbury House.

Banks, J. A. (1994). *Multiethnic education: Theory and practice* (3rd ed.). Boston, MA: Allyn and Bacon.

Brislin, R. (1993) *Understanding culture's influence on behavior*. Fort Worth, TX: Harcourt

Cole, M. (1999). Culture in development. In M. H. Bornstein & M. E. Lamb (Eds.), *Developmental psychology: An advanced textbook* (4th ed., pp. 73–123). Mahwah, NJ: Erlbaum.

Collier, V. P. (1987). Age and rate of acquisition of a second language for academic purposes. *TESOL Quarterly, 23*(3), 617–641.

Connolly, P. (1996). Doing what comes naturally? Standpoint epistemology, critical social research and the politics of identity. In E. Lyon & J. Busfield (Eds.), *Methodological imaginations*. Basingstoke, UK: MacMillan.

Cummins, J. (1991). Language development and academic learning. In L. Malavé & G. Duquette (Eds.), *Language, culture, and cognition* (pp. 161–175). Clevedon, UK: Multilingual Matters.

D'Andrade, R. (1996). Culture. *Social Science Encyclopedia* (2nd ed., pp. 88–119). New York: Routledge.

Doherty, R. W., Hilberg, R. S., Pinal, A., & Tharp, R. G. (2003). Five standards and student achievement. *NABE Journal of Research and Practice, 1*, 1–24.

Dyson, A. H., & Genishi, C. (1991). *Visions of children as language users: Research on language and language education in early childhood*. Berkeley: CA: Center for the Study of Writing.

Erickson, F. (1997). Culture in society and in educational practices. In J. A. Banks & C. A. Banks (Eds.), *Multicultural education: Issues and perspectives* (3rd ed., pp. 32–60). Boston: Allyn and Bacon.

Foster, M. (1992). Sociolinguistics and the African-American community: Implications for literacy. *Theory in Practice, 31*(4), 303–311.

Gallimore, R., Boggs, J. W., & Jordan, C. (1974). *Culture, behavior and education: A study of Hawaiian-Americans*. Beverly Hills, CA: Sage.

González, N. (1999). What will we do when culture does not exist anymore? *Anthropology & Education Quarterly, 30*(4), 431–435.

González, N., Andrade, R., Civil, M., & Moll, L. (2001). Bridging funds of distributed knowledge: Creating zones of practices in mathematics. *Journal of Education for Students Placed at Risk, 61*(1 & 2), 115–132.

Gutierrez, K. D., & Rogoff, B. (2003). Cultural ways of learning: Individual traits or repertoires or practice. *Educational Researcher, 32*, 19–25.

Heath, S. B. (1983). *Ways with words: Language, life, and work in communities and classrooms.* New York: Cambridge University Press.

Herskovitz, M. J. (1948). *Man and his works: The science of cultural anthropology.* New York: Knopf.

Hofstede, G. (1980). *Culture's consequence: International differences in work-related values.* Beverly Hills, CA: Sage.

Jackson, A. P., & Meadows, Jr., F. B. (1991). Getting to the bottom to understand the top. *Journal of Counseling and Development, 70*, 72–76.

Jordan, C. (1985). Translating culture: From ethnographic information to educational program. *Anthropology & Education Quarterly, 16*, 105–123.

Jordan, C., Tharp, R., & Vogt, L. A. (1985). *Compatibility of classroom and culture: General principles with Navajo and Hawaiian instances.* Honolulu, HI: Kamehameha Schools/Bishop Estate Center for the Development of Early Education.

Kaomea, J. (2001). Dilemmas of an indigenous academic: A Native Hawaiian story. *Contemporary Issues in Early Childhood, 2*, 67–82.

Kroeber, A. L., & Kluckhom, C. (1952). *Culture: A critical review of concepts and definitions.* New York: Vintage Books.

Lambert, W. E. (1981). Bilingualism and language acquisition. In H. Winitz (Ed.), *Native language and foreign language acquisition* (pp. 9–22). New York: New York Academy of Science.

Mehan, H. (1979). *Learning lessons.* Cambridge, MA: Harvard University Press.

Mehra, B. (2001). Research or personal quest? Dilemmas in studying my own kind. In B. Merchant & A. Willis (Eds.), *Multiple and intersecting identities in qualitative research.* (pp. 69–82). Mahwah, NJ: Erlbaum.

Moll, L., & González, N. (1994). Lessons from research with language-minority children. *Journal of Reading Behavior, 26*, 439–456.

Moll, L., & González, N. (2003). Engaging life: A funds-of-knowledge approach to multicultural education. In J. Banks & C. Banks (Eds.), *Handbook of research on multicultural education.* (2nd ed., pp. 699–715). San Francisco: CA: Jossey-Bass.

O'Donnell, C. R., & Tharp, R. G. (1990). Community intervention guided by theoretical developments. In A. S. Bellack, M. Hersen & A. E. Kazdin (Eds.), *International handbook of behavior modification and therapy.* (2nd ed., pp. 251–266). New York: Plenum.

Phillips, S. U. (1972). Participant structures and communicative competence: Warm Springs children in community and classroom. In C. Cazden, V. John, & D. Hymes (Eds.), *Functions of language in the classroom* (pp. 370–394). New York: Teachers College Press.

Pukui, M. K., Haertig, E. W., & Lee, C. A. (1972). *Nānā i ke kumu: Look to the source.* Honolulu, HI: Hui Hānai.

RMC Research Corporation. (2003). *Waiʻanae High School Hawaiian Studies Program.* Denver, CO: Author.

Rogoff, B. (2003). *The cultural nature of development.* New York: Oxford.

Rohner, R. P. (1984). Toward a conception so culture for cross-cultural psychology. *Journal of Cross-Cultural Psychology, 15,* 111–138.

Snow, C. E. (1990). The development of definitional skills. *Journal of Child Language, 17,* 697–710.

Spencer-Oatley, H. (1997). Unequal relationships in high and low power distance societies: A comparative study of tutor-student role relations in Britain and China. *Journal of Cross-Cultural Psychology, 15,* 111–138.

Tharp, R. G., & Gallimore, R. (1988). *Rousing minds to life: Teaching, learning, and schooling in social context.* Cambridge: Cambridge University Press.

Troyna, B. (1998). "The whites of my eyes, nose, ears...": A reflective account of "whiteness" in race-related research. In P. Connolly & B. Troyna (Eds.), *Researching racism in education: Politics, theory, and practice.* Buckingham, UK: Open University Press.

Troyna, B. & Carrington, B. (1989). Whose side are we on? Ethical dilemmas in research on 'race' and education. In R. Burgess (Ed.), *The ethics of educational research.* Lewes, UK: Falmer Press.

Vygotsky, L. S. (1978). *Mind in society: The development of higher psychological processes.* (Eds. and Trans. by M. Cole, V. John-Steiner, S. Scribner, & E. Souberman). Cambridge, MA: Harvard University Press.

Weisner, T. S., Gallimore, R., & Jordan, C. (1988). Unpackaging cultural effects on classroom learning: Native Hawaiian peer assistance and child-generated activity. *Anthropology and Education Quarterly, 19,* 327–353.

Wright, C. (1998). 'Caught in the crossfire': Reflections of a black female ethnographer. In P. Connolly & B. Troyna (Eds.), *Researching racism in education: Politics, theory, and practice* (pp. 67–78). Buckingham, UK: Open University Press.

Yamauchi, L. A. (2002). Standards of effective pedagogy for students of culturally diverse backgrounds: Examples from Native Hawaiian classrooms. In E. Tamura, V. Chattergy, and R. Endo (Eds.) *Asian and Pacific Island American education: Social, cultural, and historical context.* South el Monte, CA: Pacific Asia Press.

Yamauchi, L. A. (2003). Making school relevant for at-risk students: The Waiʻanae High School Hawaiian Studies Program. *Journal of Education for Students Placed at Risk, 8,* 379–390.

Yamauchi, L. A., Billig, S. H., Meyer, S., & Hofschire, L. (2004). *Student outcomes associated with service-learning in a culturally relevant high school program.* Manuscript submitted for publication.

Yamauchi, L. A., & Carroll, J. H. (2003, September). *Fostering Hawaiian youth wellness through community involvement in a high school program.* Paper presented at the Kamehameha Schools Research Conference on the Education and Well-Being of Hawaiians, Kahuku, HI.

Yamauchi, L. A., Ceppi, A. K., & Lau-Smith, J. (1999). Sociohistorical influences on the development of Papahana Kaiapuni, the Hawaiian language immersion program. *Journal of Education for Students Placed At Risk, 4,* 25–44.

Yamauchi, L. A., Ceppi, A. K., & Lau-Smith, J. (2000). Teaching in a Hawaiian context: Educator perspectives on the Hawaiian Language Immersion Program. *Bilingual Research Journal, 24,* 385–403.

Yamauchi, L. A., Kurose, M., Forman, D., Kaloi, L., & Carroll, J. (2004, March). The Hawaiian Studies *Program at Waiʻanae High School: Community partnerships to promote civic engagement.* Roundtable discussion presented at the National Service-Learning Conference, Orlando, FL.

Yamauchi, L. A., & Tharp, R. G. (1995). Culturally compatible conversations in Native American classrooms. *Linguistics and Education, 7,* 349–367.

Yamauchi, L. A., & Wilhelm, P. (2001). E ola ka Hawaiʻi i kona ʻōlelo: Hawaiians live in their language. In D. Christian & F. Genesee (Eds.), *Case studies in bilingual education* (pp. 83–94). Alexandria, VA: TESOL.

Yamauchi, L. A., Wyatt, T., & Carroll, J. H. (in press). Enacting the five standards of effective pedagogy in a culturally relevant high school program. In A. Maynard & M. Martini (Eds.), *The Psychology of Learning in Context: Cultural Artifacts, Families, Peers, and Schools.*

CHAPTER 7

The Contribution of Settings to School Improvement and School Change: A Case Study

William M. Saunders
Claude N. Goldenberg

Efforts to improve schools have been around since the days when schools were first established. Reformers since the Enlightenment have sought to improve teaching, learning, and the operation of the institutions designated to prepare the young to assume their adult roles (Butts, 1955). It has now been more than 20 years since *A Nation at Risk* precipitated the most recent wave of school reform (National Commission on Excellence in Education, 1983). Its release triggered untold thousands of efforts, at all levels of government and among private and public entities of all sorts, to improve the functioning and effectiveness of U.S. schools. The record of success is, to say the least, mixed (Sarason, 1990).

Discussions about improving our schools have involved numerous questions about the content of schooling; for example, "How do we most effectively teach reading?" "What mathematics should be taught at the elementary grades?" They have also included questions about the processes of school improvement; such as, "What processes actually lead to improved school performance?" "How do schools successfully engage in those processes?" Both the content of schooling and the processes of school improvement are obviously important, since worthwhile content without effective processes is fruitless, and effective processes devoid of worthwhile content is pointless. In this chapter, however, we focus primarily on process, the *how* of school change. For the past decade our research team has been studying school change, assisting schools to make changes, and documenting processes and outcomes as schools attempt to improve teaching, learning, and achievement in culturally and linguistically diverse schools and communities. Improving professional development has been at the heart of our work. In particular, we have tried to establish school settings for ongoing professional development embedded within a larger school wide improvement effort. While there is a growing literature documenting the benefits and challenges of ongoing, school-based professional development (Scherer, 1998), there remains a need for descriptions and analyses of how to make such school settings work.

Our research and development have been greatly informed by the work of Roland Tharp and his many contributions to the behavioral and organizational change literature. In particular, *Rousing Minds to Life* (Tharp & Gallimore, 1988) directed our attention towards the fundamental challenge of creating schools that are vibrant and productive learning contexts for both teachers and students. Along with the work of Sarason (1972), *Rousing Minds* also provided the theoretical and empirical basis for our concentration on school settings as vehicles for school and teacher change. Behavior is maintained, or changed, in relation to the network of settings and relationships in which we participate. Institutional organizations, like schools for example, are comprised of multiple "activity settings." Making constructive changes in such institutions involves improving existing activity settings, creating new ones, establishing supportive linkages between them, and sustaining them over time. In schools, the central activity setting is the classroom wherein teachers and students engage in the process of teaching and learning. Improving schools is at least in part a matter of establishing, connecting, and sustaining activity settings for teachers that maximize their performance in the classroom (Goldenberg, 2004).

One of the problems we find in schools is that many settings exist, but their potential power to influence behavior for the better is rarely, if ever, understood. All schools have faculty meetings and many have department and/or grade level meetings, for example. Our experience has been that these meetings are dominated by bureaucratic, procedural, social, and personal matters far removed from the core concerns of teaching and learning and how to improve both. Thus, it has been a substantial challenge to identify, operationalize, implement, test, and replicate processes that reliably rouse such school settings to life.

This chapter is a case study of a school that we have worked with over the past several years—Pine Elementary School (pseudonym). Like other schools we are currently studying, Pine has shown significant achievement gains. Like other schools we are currently studying, those gains seem to be a result of several factors, first and foremost of which is the creation, maintenance, and refinement of weekly settings in which teachers meet to construct goals, analyze student work, plan and discuss instruction, and evaluate outcomes. In fact, as we will describe shortly, Pine is a particularly strong demonstration of the power of such professional development settings. Drawing on teacher focus group data collected over the last five years—from the very beginning of our work with Pine until the present—we document from teachers' perspectives how these settings were established, connected to one another, and sustained over time. Case studies of this sort are relevant to school change research because the literature currently has so few prospective studies of the change process (Fullan, 2000). We also think the Pine case study helps illustrate the research and model building that continues to benefit and grow from the work of Roland Tharp.

The chapter includes background information on our previous and current school change project and a brief description of the achievement and process data we analyzed that drew our attention to Pine as an informative case study of settings. We describe the methods we used to analyze the focus group transcripts, and then present our analysis of the development of settings at Pine organized under three topics: Establishing Settings, Connecting Across Settings, and Sustaining Settings. The chapter closes with a discussion of the relevance of this case study.

Background

Getting Results Model and Research

Thus far, we have conducted two phases of research. During Phase 1, we developed a school change model that produced substantial changes in teaching and learning at one elementary school in Southern California, which served primarily Latino children and families (Goldenberg, 2004; Goldenberg & Sullivan, 1994). We refer to this model as the *Getting Results Model* (GR Model). Over a six-year period, the school shifted from being the lowest achieving school in the district to surpassing district averages on both standardized tests and performance-based assessments. The GR Model utilizes five elements to promote changes in educators' instructional behaviors and attitudes, and student outcomes. These elements include: *goals* that are set and shared, *indicators* that measure success; *assistance* by capable others, *leadership* that supports and pressures, and *settings* that allow staff to get important things done. *Settings* is a superordinate concept in the model. Within the context of these settings, the other change elements work in concert to improve teaching, learning, and achievement in *any* targeted curricular area.

During Phase 2, we successfully implemented the *Getting Results Model* at nine schools (a scale-up study) and produced achievement gains similar to those obtained at the original pilot school (McDougall, Saunders, & Goldenberg, 2003; Saunders & Goldenberg, 2004). Phase 2 research also involved refinements to the model and the development of specific settings designed to ensure effective application of model elements—goals, indicators, assistance, and leadership. Settings include Academic Achievement Leadership Teams (AALT), Grade Level Teams (GLT), and GR Principals' meetings (see Saunders, O'Brien, Marcelletti, Hasenstab, Saldivar, & Goldenberg, 2001, for descriptions of these settings). In addition, GR staff provided on-site assistance to support schools' efforts to establish and maintain these settings, including monthly one-on-one meetings with the principal and participation in AALT meetings. GR staff also provided annual leadership training institutes for school leadership teams, and developed and helped schools implement beginning, middle and end-of-the-year assessments.

Phase 2 involved three levels of research and evaluation. First, at all nine GR schools and six comparison schools (all of which are located in the same school district), we collected annual achievement data based on state mandated standardized tests from 1997 through 2002 and administered annual surveys to certificated staff from 1998 to 2002. Although comparable at baseline, 2002 achievement and survey results showed significant differences favoring GR schools (Saunders & Goldenberg, 2004). Second, between 1998 and 2001, principal interviews, teacher focus groups, and on-site observations were conducted at four GR and three comparison case study schools. During the 2001–2002 school year, an external evaluator collected and analyzed all data from 1998 through 2002 and evaluated each school on the model elements. On average, ratings for GR schools were significantly higher than those of comparison schools on all elements (McDougall, Saunders, & Goldenberg, 2002). Third, we have been analyzing available data for each of the four GR case study schools in order to better understand and illustrate the similarities and differences in the change process that emerged at each school. Pine is one of the four GR case study schools. As we describe next, the evidence seems to suggest that while all model elements were successfully implemented at Pine, that which distinguishes Pine from other GR and comparison schools is their strong implementation of goals and settings.

Pine Elementary School:
Demographics, Achievement, and GR Implementation

Like all current *Getting Results* schools, Pine Elementary school is located in a densely populated metropolitan area of southern California and is a member of one of the largest school districts in the country. The community surrounding Pine is comprised of single-family homes, large apartment complexes, condominiums, and numerous large and small commercial outlets. To the south lies a primarily affluent, English-speaking neighborhood, and to the north lies a more modest, lower income, primarily Spanish-speaking neighborhood. Pine enrolls approximately 550 students, 55% of whom are Latino, 27% are Caucasian, 14% are African-American, and 2% are Asian. Seventy-three percent of Pine students qualify for free or reduced-priced lunches. Forty-four percent are English language learners (ELLs), 80% of whom come from Spanish-speaking families. With the exception of teachers added as part of state-wide class-size reduction, Pine staff has remained fairly stable over the past several years: average years teaching at Pine and total years teaching experiences are approximately 7 and 10, respectively. Midway through the 2001–2002 school year, at the request of the local superintendent, the principal (one of the most active principals in the GR Network) left Pine to become principal at a new school. Her replacement, a veteran principal who was familiar with GR research, welcomed the opportunity to participate in the GR Network.

Achievement levels at Pine have risen steadily across the last several years. As shown in Figure 1, Pine achievement levels in 1997 (averaged across reading, math, language, and spelling and across grades 2–5) were virtually identical to that of the District: 36.88 and 36.48 Normal Curve Equivalents (NCEs) or

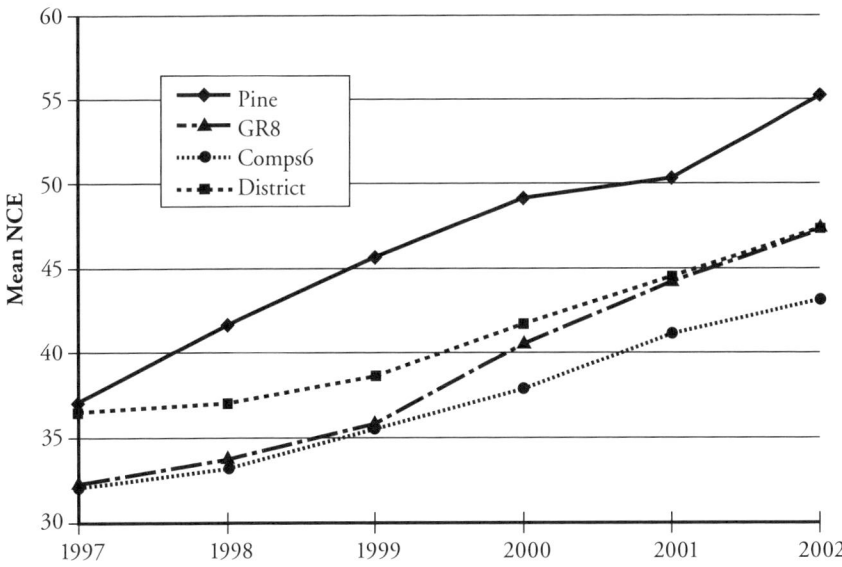

Figure 1. Pine academic achievement on Stanford 9, 1997–2002. Pine Normal Curve Equivalent means compared to other GR, comparison, and district schools.

27th and 26th National Percentile Ranks (NPRs). By 2002, however, Pine students were performing at levels significantly above the District averages: 55.15 and 47.29 NCEs (60th and 45th NPRs). The gain at Pine across the five-year period (18.27 NCEs) was slightly larger than the average gain among all other GR schools (15.12 NCEs), and substantially larger than the average gain among comparable schools (11.01 NCEs) and the District overall (10.82 NCEs).

The above average achievement gains at Pine (i.e., above GR averages) run parallel to the above average ratings Pine received in the external evaluation. On average, GR schools were rated significantly higher than comparison schools on each of the five elements, and Pine was rated significantly higher than the other GR schools on Goals, Leadership, and Settings (see Figure 2). Differences between Pine and other GR schools, reported in standard deviation units are .66, .59, and .74 for Goals, Leadership, and Settings, respectively.

In order to explore this pattern of results further, we also analyzed teacher surveys. The survey contained a subset of questions related to each model element. Teachers rated items based on a five-point scale. Similar to the external evaluator's ratings (see Figure 3), the 2002 survey results indicated that, on average, teachers at GR schools rated their schools significantly higher on most model elements than teachers at comparison schools. Pine teachers rated their school higher than teachers at other GR schools, specifically for Goals and Settings.

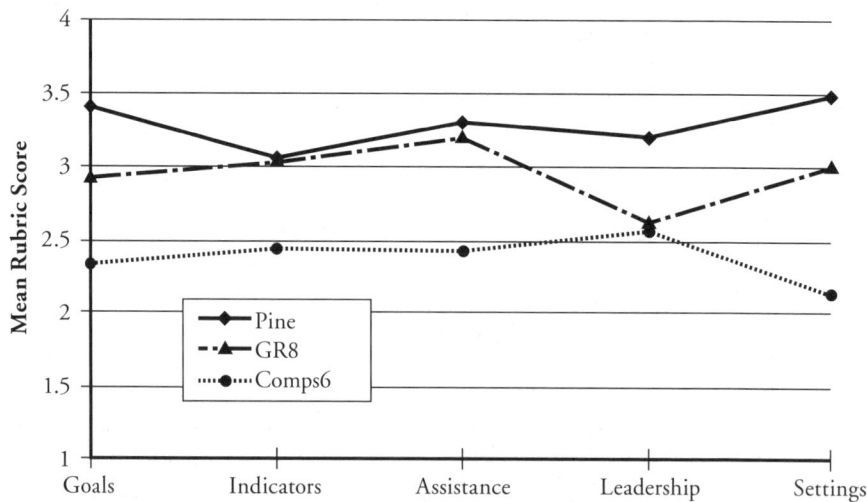

Figure 2. External evaluator's ratings of Getting Results Model elements.

In sum, our analysis of both teachers' ratings and the external evaluator's ratings converged on the same finding: The two model elements that distinguish Pine from other GR and comparison schools are Goals and Settings. In order to investigate this finding further, in particular, the prominent role of Settings, we analyzed transcripts from teacher focus groups conducted at Pine during the Spring semesters of 1998, 1999, 2000, and 2001. We also analyzed transcripts from a teacher focus group conducted at Pine as part of a different project during the Fall of 2003. Finally, we reviewed results of grade level meeting evaluations completed at Pine and all other GR schools during the Spring of 2003. The 2003 data allow us to examine Pine teachers' most current perceptions of Pine settings. Focus groups were conducted by the second author (1998, 1999, 2003), another researcher (2000), and the external evaluator (2001) and involved approximately six teachers in each group. Each year, in accord with guidelines provided by our research staff, principals recruited teachers to form focus groups that were as representative as possible. This included some teachers who were in school leadership positions and others who were not, those from lower, middle and upper grades (K–1, 2–3, and 4–5), and with varying years of experience.

The first author analyzed the transcripts. First, he read all transcripts and compiled all excerpts in which teachers talked about one or more of Pine's major school settings: grade level meetings, leadership team meetings, faculty meetings.

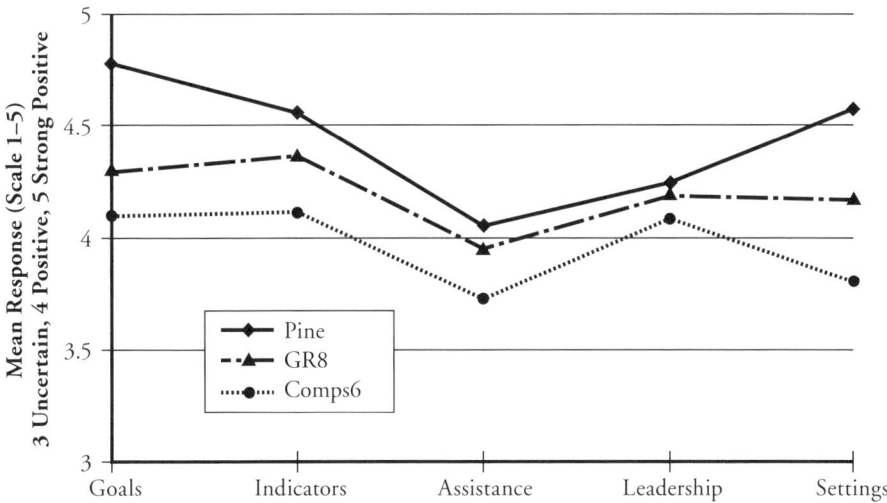

Figure 3. Teachers' ratings of Getting Results Model elements.

Second, excerpts were grouped chronologically, and the first author prepared a written analysis based on excerpts that seemed to best characterize and illustrate teachers' changing perceptions of these settings on a year-by-year basis. Third, excerpts were re-grouped thematically, and the first author prepared a revised analysis based on excerpts that seemed to best characterize and illustrate, from Pine teachers' perspectives, the processes of establishing, connecting, and sustaining settings.

Development of Settings at Pine

Establishing Settings

Like most schools in the district, Pine had weekly faculty meetings that were held after school for approximately one hour every Tuesday. This was the only professional development setting in existence at Pine during the 1997–1998 school year. The principal planned all faculty meeting agendas, and topics included a vast array of items. Everything related to school business, district policies, and professional development was addressed during this one time and place when the staff gathered together. If electricians were coming to install new wiring, the principal reviewed the schedule of work during a faculty meeting. If the district had established new policies regarding report cards, the coordinator explained the new policies during a faculty meeting. If a group of teachers had been sent to a conference on writing instruction, the group shared what they had learned at a faculty meeting. (Below is an excerpt from the focus group meeting. In this and other excerpts throughout the chapter, we use a "T" to denote a teacher speaking. However, because of the way these data were transcribed, we are unable to identify when a particular teacher spoke more than once.)

> T: I think we have had [a packed agenda] at every single faculty meeting, and speaking only for myself, sometimes, no every time to me, it feels very overwhelming because I'm the kind of person who needs to focus on one thing and work it through and know that I understand what's going on. And when I am bombarded, [or] it feels like I am bombarded—this is very personal—then I lose my focus....

> T: I think one of the other problems also is that our faculty meetings are at the end of the day. And by that point it is really hard to focus, you know, on technical information and process it. By that time you are tired, and sometimes it doesn't matter the way it should. (Teacher Focus Group, Spring 1998)

The litany of state and district initiatives intended to improve student achievement simply compounded the congestion of faculty meetings. The State had reduced class-size, established new content standards, revamped curricular frameworks for language arts and math, mandated literacy instruction trainings for all teachers, and significantly changed its language of instruction policies (Proposition 227). The district had undergone yet another administrative reorganization, hired a new superintendent, and mandated new promotion and retention policies, as well as student intervention programs, assessments, and language arts and math curriculum. The teachers' sense of being bombarded was understandable. Unfortunately, they saw themselves and their principal as virtually powerless against the onslaught of state and district forces.

> T: It's still not in her control. As much as she...is a very experienced teacher, but as far as an administrator saying this is how its gonna be.... She's not the authority.
>
> T: She has other people higher to answer to. She doesn't get to make those decisions. (Teacher Focus Group, Spring 1998)

Despite the sense of futility, however, teachers seemed more than willing to move forward, and without reservation. They expressed confidence in their colleagues. This was not a staff rife with factions and dissension. At the same time, there simply was no infrastructure of settings that allowed them to turn their intentions into concrete accomplishments.

> T: We really, the staff here really wants to do it. It's not that there's anybody who doesn't want to do it.
>
> T: There's nobody bitter on our staff. Everybody is motivated.
>
> T: It's kind of like, tell us what you want and then *let us do it*.
>
> T: We're ready.
>
> T: We'll do it. (Teacher Focus Group, Spring 1998)

The first steps, then, involved establishing two core Getting Results (GR) settings: The Academic Achievement Leadership Team (AALT) and Grade Level Team Meetings (GLs). Regarding the former, the principal recruited a representative from each grade level to serve on the AALT. Regarding the latter, the principal instituted a physical education program that would allow grade level meetings to take place while students were participating in the physical education program. During the focus group conducted the following spring, Pine staff were asked about what they were doing to improve student achievement.

> Interviewer: What sort of things are going on at Pine now to try and improve student achievement?
>
> T: We have grade level meetings. Teachers at the grade levels meet once a week to talk about…ways to improve students' learning, setting goals, carrying through with those goals and talking about the curriculum.
>
> T: We've all been working on a pacing [plan] for each grade level so that we are trying to, all of us, work on the same thing at approximately the same time
>
> T: We have a leadership team. One teacher at each grade level is on the team and we talk about setting school wide goals and other issues. (Teacher Focus Group, Spring 1999)

That the teachers immediately mentioned grade level meetings and the AALT is noteworthy, indicating that both settings had been sufficiently established in the day-to-day work of the school.

The launch of grade level meetings was successful in at least two important ways. First, as evident in the teachers' explanation, grade level meetings, as a setting, had a clear purpose: to improve students' learning. Second, that purpose had been translated into action, into specific things to do: "setting goals" and "working on a pacing [plan]." It would be so easy to underestimate the fundamental importance of these accomplishments. Most school settings founder for lack of purposeful activity. Either the purpose of the setting fails to get translated into concrete actions or the concrete actions lack the guidance of a clear purpose. Neither was the case at Pine.

Prior to the standards movement and the development and publication of state content standards, GR schools authored their own grade level standards or expectations. That process corresponded directly to one of the GR Model elements: Goals that are set and shared. When state standards were developed and mandated, we encouraged schools to review those standards carefully in their grade level teams. We suggested that the teachers reorder the standards, and translate them, as necessary, into terms all teachers could understand. At Pine, this document became known as the "pacing plan," and each grade level team authored one. Pine staff took this undertaking seriously, viewed it as a valuable collective product, and actually used it in their grade level meetings to guide their discussions of teaching. Several teachers in the focus group that spring described their grade level team's work on their pacing plan. For example:

> One of the things we did in fifth grade is we had actually worked out a graph which shows what week we're doing what story, what skills go with that story, what writing

activity goes with that story, what phonics skills, what spelling, what vocabulary, what comprehension, what inference questions pertain to that piece. So we have the whole year charted basically and we are going pretty well by that chart. I have always done it personally, but it has always been just my own. Now it's shared and we're all doing it.
(Teacher Focus Group, Spring 1999)

Perhaps the most important comment in this fifth grade teacher's account is the very last utterance: "Now it's shared and we're all doing it." The team had effectively engaged in the process of reviewing the standards; they systematically identified and then aligned all the language arts skills and activities; they produced a collective product; and, most importantly, they used it to guide their teaching and meeting discussions. Another teacher in the focus group reiterated the change they had experienced, "We're all more focused on what we need to be doing for the children" (Teacher Focus Group, Spring 1999).

The success of grade level meetings at Pine during that first year of implementation could not have happened without effective work completed outside grade level meetings. This is evident both in (a) what was and (b) what was *not* mentioned in the focus group that spring. Regarding the latter, teachers made no critical comments about the operational details that were so central to making grade level meeting time happen. The principal and her administrative staff were responsible for taking care of most of these details, including scheduling grade level meetings, establishing the P. E. program, purchasing the equipment, hiring and training the P. E. staff, and making sure the program functioned effectively. All of these details had to be addressed so that grade level meetings could take place regularly and dependably. When administration fails to address these details, teachers know it, and they are not hesitant to talk about it. Such was not the case at Pine.

Teachers did comment on the work of the AALT and that of the principal in helping to establish the grade level meetings.

> Interviewer: Any factors that have helped move [this] ahead?
>
> T: Our AALT, I think, has really done a really good job.
>
> T: A fine job.
>
> T: Absolutely.
>
> T: Um, pulling all of this together.
>
> Interviewer: Has the AALT played...a leadership role in this?
>
> T: ...Guidance.
>
> Ts: (laughter) (Teacher Focus Group, Spring 1999)

The Academic Achievement Leadership Team will be discussed further in the next section. Here it is important to note two things. First, staff recognized the AALT's role in the success of the grade level meetings "pulling all of this together." At same time, however, teachers seemed hesitant to applying the term "leadership" to the work of the AALT, characterizing it instead as "guidance." Teachers in the focus group registered this subtle, semantic shift (guidance rather than leadership). That is evident in their laughter, which is often a marker of sensitive topics (Schegloff, 1987). Indeed, this ambivalence towards teacher leadership dissolved over subsequent years, as we will see shortly.

Teachers in the focus group were not ambivalent about elaborating on the leadership role of the principal. Productive settings, settings wherein teachers get things done, require accountability. The GR Model defines leadership as a balance between support and pressure. As discussed earlier, the principal's support involved providing time for regular grade level meetings. Her pressure, on the other hand, involved holding grade level teams accountable for doing what they said they were going to do.

> Interviewer: What's been the principal's role in all this?
>
> T: She's the force behind it.
>
> T: The hammer behind the wedge
>
> T: Yeah.
>
> T: And I don't mean that unkindly either.
>
> T: She applies pressure to the extent of this is what you have to do, how are you going to do it, now that you've decided how to do it, go do what you just said you're gonna do.
>
> T: Makes us accountable. (Teacher Focus Group, Spring 1999)

In sum, Pine's first-year implementation of grade level meetings illustrate several aspects of establishing settings effectively. Grade level meetings were assigned a clear purpose (improving achievement), they involved a worthwhile, shared task (developing goals and a pacing plan), they were guided by the leadership team, and they were both supported and held accountable by the school principal. They were also supported by and connected to other Pine settings, the topic of the next section.

Connecting Across Settings

With the establishment of grade level meetings and the AALT, and the continuing faculty meetings, Pine had three settings in operation. Among these three, grade level meetings were the most important, specifically because they focused most directly on teachers' instruction. Grade level meetings function, however, within the larger school-wide context. To be effective, the larger school-wide context must support grade level meetings. There must be strong connections between grade level and other school-wide settings and most importantly between the grade level setting and the classroom setting.

From the beginning, connections were made at Pine between grade level meetings and both faculty and leadership team meetings. In the focus group following the first year of implementation, teachers mentioned the importance of instituting grade level meetings school-wide. Every grade level was involved. Every grade level had a representative on the AALT. Teachers viewed this as an opportunity to establish greater continuity. As they explained, that continuity was enabled by the seemingly simple but critical provision of sharing during faculty meetings and within AALT meetings.

> T: We also share whatever we have talked about in our grade level meetings at faculty meetings, as well.
>
> T: Right, right. So that we can build some continuity and see what each grade level is doing.
>
> T: That [also] happens at the AALT. The representatives will share what is happening at [each] grade level. And that meets once a month—the AALT. (Teacher Focus Group, Spring 1999)

In fact, the principal revamped her faculty meetings specifically to allow for grade level sharing. She moved all instruction-related items to the top of the agenda, including time for teams to report on the content and focus of their grade level meetings, and she moved all operational items that had often consumed her faculty meeting to the bottom of the agenda (or in many cases, to the weekly bulletin or memos). AALT meetings operated in much the same way, providing a portion of time for each grade level representative to share what their team was doing. Both the sharing in faculty meetings and AALT meetings reinforced the idea that this was a school wide effort. Teachers' descriptions spoke specifically to the issue of coherence:

> T: A lot of these things are overlapping.
>
> T: It used to be that everyone was on their own in their classroom and [now] with the grade level meetings and school-wide faculty meetings and in-services we're working towards…
>
> T: Yes.

> T: We started in grade levels mostly and now we're trying to synchronize with all grade levels, so that we're sharing, each grade level is sharing what it is they're doing to see if we can unify the whole thing. (Teacher Focus Group, Spring 1999)

In the first focus group conducted prior to implementation of grade level meetings, teachers expressed frustration over the lack of opportunities to digest, follow-up, and dialogue about district in-service trainings. However, grade level meetings helped minimize that frustration, providing time for teachers to share, discuss and assist one another in the actual implementation of methods and techniques introduced during in-service trainings and workshops. For example, one teacher said, "To a certain extent, part of the grade level meetings, too, is to discuss the pros and cons and how to implement some of these things that we bring back from the [inservice] workshops" (Teacher Focus Group, 1999).

The connection between grade level meetings and AALT meetings is important. Consistent with the triadic model (Tharp & Gallimore, 1988), each setting requires its own supporting setting. Teaching in the classroom is supported by grade level meetings, grade level meetings are supported by leadership team meetings, and leadership team meetings are supported by monthly GR principals meetings, including collective meetings of all principals and one-on-one meetings between each principal and GR staff. By design, the leadership team should help distribute leadership. The principal typically plays the central role on the leadership team—providing direction, seeking input, building consensus, establishing deadlines, listening and providing feedback to members, and facilitating cross-grade level sharing and discussion. Leadership team members then play the same role within their grade level meetings. Leadership team meetings should function as a setting that supports the grade level setting. As the teachers described it, the connection between AALT and grade level meetings became stronger and increasingly productive over time.

> T: Our AALT meets monthly. This year [our principal] gave us an agenda, all the things to have done in our weekly grade level meetings. So now, those grade level meetings are on task, you know. Last year they were also, we started getting a lot done, but now, we have to look at the schedule and say, okay by this week we're supposed to have these things done, so today we need to do this.
>
> T: It's more focused. (Teacher Focus Group, Spring 2000)

GR researchers and principals developed a protocol that outlined a series of steps grade level teams might take to analyze student work and identify specific

The Contribution of Settings to School Improvement

needs to which instruction might be targeted. That protocol was discussed at monthly principal meetings, the Pine principal shared it with her AALT, and then some of the AALT representatives began using it in their grade level meetings.

> [Our principal] started asking us to bring something that our grade levels were working on, so now at our grade level meetings.... Like a perfect example, at my grade level, we've all kind of committed to bringing work samples every week. Every week, as soon as we get in there, we're looking at work, you know, right away. So it's very student based, you know. How are you getting that done? And why isn't this working? Which is good for us. (Teacher Focus Group, Spring 2000)

The most important setting-to-setting connection is between grade level meetings and the classroom. In grade level meetings, teachers identify student needs, set goals, plan and discuss instruction, and analyze student work. To the extent that grade level teams engage in these activities productively, they affect what teachers do in the classroom. According to Pine teachers, grade level meetings had a positive effect on their teaching. In the excerpt below, teachers attribute their improved focus in the classroom to the improved focus of grade level meetings.

> T: Our classrooms are much more focused now than they have been.
>
> T: For sure. (all laugh)
>
> T: Oh yeah.
>
> Interviewer: What is this a result of?
>
> T: A combination of things.
>
> T: I think the AALT members were kind of forced—(someone laughs) Which helped though. I mean it was a big help to keep us focused and to keep a continued focus throughout every week—to keep our mind on a certain aspect of what we need to work on.
>
> T: And setting goals every week. Besides all the big school goals that we created in grade levels and as a school at the beginning of the year, every week we're making weekly goals at each grade levels. Agreeing on them, writing them down, adhering to them the following week, following up on them—all based on student needs. (Teacher Focus Group, Spring 2001)

The excerpt above illustrates the connection between grade level meetings and the classroom, but it also references the connection between the leadership team setting and the grade level meetings. A bit earlier in the discussion from which the above excerpt was taken, one of the teachers commented that grade level meetings had improved, specifically because the AALT was taking time during its meetings to plan and prepare written agendas for each meeting: "Grade level meetings are very well planned and organized. And they have agendas. And the agendas are reviewed and checked at the AALT. And suggestions are made. And revisions are made" (Teacher Focus Group, Spring 2001). The focus group also revealed that the principal required leadership team members to provide her with a copy of the agenda for each meeting. She also regularly attended grade level meetings—to participate, and also to check that teams were staying on task and accomplishing what was stated on the agenda. The principal improved the focus of leadership team meetings (spending more time on developing and refining agendas for grade level meetings), which helped sharpen the focus of grade level meetings, which in turn contributed to increased focus in the classroom.

Over time, the connection between grade level meetings and the classroom strengthened as Pine teachers' increasingly focused on results. For example, in the excerpt below, a teacher describes how the second grade team shared lessons, analyzed samples of student work, and provided demonstrations during their meetings. However, these activities seem to be driven by a common purpose: identifying and then implementing in the classroom those teaching strategies that worked best.

> We shared different lessons. Like in second grade, one week maybe someone would bring journals. The following week maybe different work samples of language arts, and maybe someone would demonstrate a lesson—whatever's working in the classroom. Because different things were working in different classes—and then, when you find out what's working in one class, then you can try it in the other classroom, and so eventually everybody's doing the same thing because it works. (Teacher Focus Group, Spring 2001)

At the heart of this process—sharing lessons, trying them in the classroom, identifying what works, and then collectively implementing—is the connection between grade level meetings and the classroom. That which is discussed in meetings has a direct bearing on what teachers do in the classroom, and what teachers experience in the classroom has a direct bearing on the discussions and activities of subsequent meetings. When this connection is maintained, grade level meetings take on increasing continuity, driven by the collective effort to identify and implement teaching that best addresses specific student needs.

> T: First we evaluate the student work and as we evaluate the student work we look at strengths and weaknesses. Then we decide on what kind of instruction we're gonna try in the classroom. And we try the instruction in

the classroom, and then we go back and re-assess to see if the instruction is working. If it's not working we just, we try to take a different approach until we meet those goals and those standards and objectives.

Interviewer: Would that be true in [kindergarten and Grades] 1, 2, 3, 4?

T: Absolutely. (Teacher Focus Group, Fall 2003)

Sustaining Settings

Pine settings have sustained over the last five school years (1998–1999 through 2002–2003). There were approximately 200 meetings each year. Each grade level team met three times each month for 45 to 50 minutes, for a total of 30 meetings per year. The AALT met once a month for 90 minutes, for a total of 10 meetings each year. In addition, 1 to 2 faculty meetings were held each month for 30 to 60 minutes, for a total of 20 meetings each year. How does a school go about sustaining all of these settings? At least three variables emerge as important from our analysis of Pine: leadership, resilience, and productivity.

First and perhaps foremost, Pine has maintained strong leadership over the past five years. Our observations at the school suggest that the principal at Pine (both the original and the current principal) consistently made these settings a top priority. In addition, Pine has maintained a very stable and highly committed AALT (3 of its 6 members have, with the support of their grade level teams, remained in their position over the entire five year period). Among the many indicators of strong leadership is one that is easily overlooked: being able to successfully address all the seemingly mundane operational details upon which these settings depend. For example, at the beginning of each of the last five years, the Pine principal and the AALT prepared a schedule of all meetings for the year. With very few exceptions, each meeting scheduled was conducted. All meetings had a designated leader (leadership team member, principal, other administrator or teacher). With very few exceptions, there was also a written agenda that was prepared ahead of time, used during the meeting, and stored in the principal's binder. Consistent leadership was also indicated by the continuation of the physical education program that provided the weekly time for grade level meetings.

Pine also seems to be a particularly strong example of distributed leadership. Teachers in the Fall 2003 focus group mentioned both their sense of empowerment and also their school's culture of leadership.

T: We're very empowered here when you think about it because at grade levels we make a lot of decisions about how we're gonna go forth.

T: And we are supported.

T: I think there is a culture of leadership. Whether you're the AALT rep for your grade level or whether you're the head of another committee, you know that you have a job. And whatever level your job is, if it is Assistant Principal, AALT leader or a supporting member in your grade level team, you know that your job is important, and it builds on this culture of leadership at the school. (Teacher Focus Group, Fall 2003)

The above teacher's explanation of this "culture of leadership" seems to include two important elements. On the one hand, Pine staff recognized that leadership positions are jobs with specific responsibilities to be fulfilled. At same time, the staff recognized the importance of everyone's role including those in non-leadership or supportive positions. Our observations at Pine corroborate the teacher's descriptions. Among teachers, even among those who sometimes do not get along, we have never observed anything but consistent mutual respect between school leaders and others in the school community. Teachers who are not in leadership roles vest their colleagues with license to lead, in addition to fulfilling their responsibilities as members of grade level and school-wide teams.

One last point regarding leadership concerns the principal's support and pressure. Teachers in focus groups credited both the original and current principals for sustained support of the staff's efforts. These conversations included discussions about the original principal's application of pressure. Although some teachers were somewhat put off by the principal's pressure and wondered if they were being singled out, most teachers seemed to view the pressure as beneficial. For example, one teacher described how the principal consistently provided positive feedback, but always followed it up with a challenge.

"Sure, you're doing it good. It's beautiful. You're doing a great job. Now, here's the challenge. Challenge question: Bonus!" You know, there's always that little star at the bottom, "Try this. Bonus!" (laughter). "What standard are you working on?" "Great bulletin board. What standard does that project address?" You know, that's like the big thing I'm always thinking about now. But, it, that's a great thing. I love it. I mean, I don't love it. (laughter). You know, it's just, it's a good thing. Of course it's good for us. You know, but it's a little intense. (Teacher Focus Group, Spring 2001)

Other teachers in the focus group followed up on this characterization, corroborating their colleague's assertion that the principal's challenging questions were a good thing.

T: Well, it just forces you to focus. It forces you to think

T: I was just going to say that.

> T: About, why am I teaching this? Why am I teaching it this way? Is it necessary, and do I need to add this, or should I add this?
>
> T: Yeah, it— It's getting the results.
>
> T: Mmhm.
>
> T: Sometimes it's uncomfortable to be pushed that hard. But, it's getting the results and ultimately that's what our job is all about. (Teacher Focus Group, Spring 2001)

We cannot definitively establish how the original principal's pressure, specifically her capacity to deliver challenging feedback to her teachers, helped sustain settings during her tenure at Pine. However, it seems likely that it served to communicate her expectations to her teachers.

> I think that's the case with a leader. They always let you know that you have this much to grow, you know? I mean, no one's going to say, "You're perfect. That's it. Stop right there." …It's only normal, I think. We need to grow. (Teacher Focus Group, Spring 2001)

Conceivably, the principal's feedback continued to provide a sense of direction to Pine staff and its settings, which were established from the beginning to improve student achievement and support teachers' professional development and growth.

Settings also sustained at Pine because the leadership and staff did not appear to have allowed themselves to get overly distracted by numerous external mandates that could have easily derailed the effort. Each year, they faced new state and district requirements with resilience, modifying and adapting what they were doing in order to fold in new reading and math programs, new reading and math assessments, new reading and math coaches, district authored and annually revised reading and math pacing plans, and so on. Each year, focus group discussions revealed teachers' concerns about the litany of mandates, as well as the pressure to produce ever increasing test scores.

> T: I think we're all sort of overwhelmed that there's so much to teach, and there's not enough time in each day.
>
> T: And they keep pushing literacy, and then they push math and then, you know, well wait a minute, there's science, there's social studies, there's health, and there's never enough time to teach everything. (Teacher Focus Group, Spring 1999)

In the Spring 2000 focus group, teachers talked about the disappointment they felt when the pacing plan they developed the previous year had to be replaced by the district's pacing plan. One teacher noted,

> We had put a lot of time in making our monthly plan and then the District came out with their plan, and it was kind of like, "Oh well, throw yours away and use this because if you don't, you're going to be up a creek. "(Teacher Focus Group, Spring 2000)

The teachers also talked about the pressure they felt from the district.

> T: There's a lot of pressure from the District right now. It's just, you know, pressure, pressure, pressure.
>
> T: It's a kind of pressure that I feel as a seasoned teacher, that's not necessary. I think it can be done in a much different way, in a much healthier way. And I see the pressure on teachers when it comes to standardized tests. I don't think that's the true indicator of what's really going on. I think it's very unhealthy. (Teacher Focus Group, Spring 2000)

In short, Pine teachers battled the same potential distractions and pressures that all other schools in the district faced, but we have no evidence to suggest that those distractions and pressures ever overtook Pine settings or ever seriously threatened the staff's efforts to improve achievement. If anything, focus group evidence suggests that Pine settings may have actually helped teachers deal with the mandates and pressures. For example, one teacher shared, "Just getting together with your grade level and talking about some of these things that make you feel overloaded ....You don't feel so alone" (Teacher Focus Group, Spring 1999).

How and why did settings sustain at Pine? Year after year, teachers felt these settings, particularly grade level meetings, were valuable and productive. Every focus group from 1998 through 2001 started with the same open-ended question: "What sort of things are going on at Pine now to try and improve student achievement?" Every year following implementation of grade level meetings (1998–1999), the very first responses to that question mentioned grade level meetings. Pine teachers have used these settings to accomplish things that they felt improved student achievement. Perhaps the lesson here is that settings have a reasonable chance of sustaining from one year to the next, if teachers perceive them to be productive and worthwhile. The evaluation of grade level meetings conducted at the end of the 2002–2003 school year suggested that this is the case at Pine. While results were generally positive at all GR schools, Pine teachers (n=24) consistently rated their grade level meetings higher than teachers from other GR schools—on average, approximately .65 standard deviations higher than means based on all respondents (n=491). For example, when asked, "Do grade level meetings contribute to the larger effort at your school to improve achievement?" Most Pine teachers said, "Definitely Yes" (Pine mean: 5.75, All GR schools mean: 5.18, sd, .82, scale 1–6; 6=definitely yes, 5=mostly yes).

Moreover, most Pine teachers responded very positively to the question, "Did grade level meetings have a positive effect on your classroom teaching this year?" (Pine: 5.75, All GR schools: 5.10, sd, .89). Finally, most Pine teachers responded very positively to the question, "Did your grade level meetings enhance your professional relationships with other teachers at your grade level this year?" (Pine: 5.88, All GR schools: 5.21, sd, .88)

We also know that Pine teachers continue to view their grade level meetings as productive, based on the Fall 2003 focus group.

> T: [We] formulate an objective. Assess for that objective. Look at the result. Did we meet the objective? No…let's go ahead and, you know, do it again. We all know this process.
>
> T: Very focused.
>
> T: We all know what we're doing at this meeting. We all know what we're doing at next week's meeting. We have an idea of what we will be doing, you know, two months from now.
>
> Interviewer: Is that school-wide? Is not just something at one grade level only?
>
> T: School-wide. (Teacher Focus Group, Fall 2003)

In fact, when asked specifically about continuing to strive for high levels of academic achievement, teachers remarked that the staff's expectations have increased, that they have seen positive results each year, and that grade level teams work closely together to meet those expectations.

> Interviewer: How does the faculty feel about striving for high levels of academic achievement?
>
> T: I think we have higher expectations.
>
> T: Totally.
>
> T: We've been going up over the last, what is it, six years or so? Since we've been part the Getting Results group, we've been going up on our assessments every year. So we already have the mind set. We expect (pause) to do really well.
>
> T: I think it's something that we pride ourselves in, you know, knowing that we're gonna meet with our grade level and together we're fighting for this common goal, you know, and it all comes together as a school.
>
> T: I know my grade level, when I was in second grade, we were really tight and in first grade we are really tight. Very cohesive.
>
> Interviewer: So if you had to characterized the academic climate for the school?

> T: Very academic. Very high expectations. (Teacher Focus Group, Fall 2003)

For Pine teachers, at least at this point in time, high expectations, results, and grade level meetings are tightly linked together. Such perceptions are probably both a product of and a promising condition for sustaining settings over time.

Conclusion

A generation ago, Sarason (1996) identified a gap in the school reform literature that still largely exists: the absence of comprehensive, systematic, and prospective descriptions of the school change process. Likewise, in his review of evidence that a collaborative school culture was related to student learning, Fullan (2000) commented that a "fundamental problem" was a lack of information about the development of such reform:

> The researchers who reported these results examined schools…once they were "up and running." We know nothing about how these particular schools got that way, let alone how to go about producing more of them. (Fullan, 2000, p. 582)

The ever-growing school change literature includes valuable portraits of changed or changing schools (e.g., Chasin & Levin, 1995; Heckman, 1996; Lieberman, 1995; Wagner, 1994). A recent and helpful trend in teacher professional development has focused more on actual instruction and learning in classrooms (e.g., Clark, 2001; Lieberman & Miller, 2001). However, what has been missing is a more detailed view of the change process, together with its results and outcomes, including measured student achievement.

We have been trying to fill this gap by simultaneously working with and studying schools using a model of school reform that focuses on establishing shared goals for student achievement, indicators to measure success, mutual assistance among professionals, and strong but supportive leadership to keep the process moving forward. Central to this effort is the concept of "settings." It is in settings such as grade level meetings and leadership team meetings, as we have tried to illustrate here, that these elements come together and influence the thinking and behavior of teachers. Settings provide an arena in which colleagues work together to understand and accomplish shared goals, examine data about whether students are accomplishing goals, and provide each other with assistance to accomplish the goals. Without settings, the other elements in our "change model" would be mere abstractions. But in the context of settings—stable, predictable, practical vehicles for joint, productive work—the elements create a dynamic that can lead to improved teaching and learning.

Understanding the phenomena we have attempted to document in this case study has of course been enriched by the work of many others, not least that of Tharp and colleagues. This work serves as a clear reminder that teachers' work—indeed, the work in which we all engage—cannot be seen in isolation, removed from the broad network of relationships that define who and what we are. Strategic use of this network can provide us with powerful tools for improving teaching, learning, and schools themselves.

Note

Funding provided by the Spencer Foundation and the Center for Research on Education, Diversity, and Excellence (CREDE), U.S. Department of Education.

References

Butts, R. (1955). *A cultural history of Western education: Its social and intellectual foundations.* New York: McGraw-Hill.

Chasin, G., & Levin, H. (1995). Thomas Edison Accelerated Elementary School. In J. Oakes & H. Quartz (Eds.), *Creating new educational communities, schools, and classrooms where all children can be smart* (pp. 130–146). Chicago: University of Chicago Press.

Clark, C. (Ed.). (2001). *Talking shop: Authentic conversation and teacher learning.* New York: Teachers College Press.

Fullan, M. (2000). The three stories of educational reform. *Phi Delta Kappan, 81,* 581–584.

Goldenberg, C. (2004). *Successful school change: Creating settings to improve teaching and learning.* New York: Teachers College Press.

Goldenberg, C., & Sullivan, J. (1994). *Making change happen in a language minority school: A search for coherence* (Educational Practice Report No. 13). Washington, DC: National Center for Research on Cultural Diversity and Second Language Learning.

Heckman, P. (1996). *The courage to change: Stories from successful school reform.* Thousand Oaks, CA: Corwin.

Lieberman, A. (Ed.). (1995). *The work of restructuring schools: Building from the ground up.* New York: Teachers College Press.

Lieberman, A., & Miller, L. (Eds.) (2001). *Teachers caught in the action: Professional development that matters.* New York: Teachers College Press.

McDougall, D., Saunders, W., & Goldenberg, C. (2003). *Inside the black box of school reform: The role of leadership and other change elements at getting results schools.* Paper presented at the annual conference of the American Educational Research Association, Chicago, IL, April.

National Commission on Excellence in Education. (1983). *A nation at risk: The imperative for educational reform.* Washington, DC: U.S. Dept. of Education.

Sarason, S. (1972). *The creation of settings and the future societies.* San Francisco: Jossey-Bass.

Sarason, S. (1990). *The predictable failure of educational reform: Can we change course before it's too late.* San Francisco: Jossey-Bass.

Sarason, S. (1996). *Revisiting "The culture of the school and the problem of change."* New York: Teachers College Press.

Saunders, W., & Goldenberg, C. (2004). *Getting Results school change model: Achievement and process outcomes, 1997–2002.* Unpublished manuscript. California State University, Long Beach.

Saunders, W., O'Brien, G., Marcelletti, D., Hasenstab, K., Saldivar, E., & Goldenberg, C. (2001). Getting the most out of school-based professional development. In P. Schmidt & P. Mosenthal (Eds.), *Reconceptualizing literacy in the new age of multiculturalism and pluralism* (pp. 289–320). Greenwich, CT: IAP.

Schegloff, E. (1987). Analyzing single episodes of interaction: An exercise in conversation analysis. *Social Psychology Quarterly*, 50, 101–114.

Scherer, M. M. (Ed.). (1998). Strengthening the teaching profession. [Special issue]. *Educational Leadership*, 55(5).

Tharp, R., & Gallimore, R. (1988). *Rousing Minds to Life.* Cambridge, England: Cambridge University Press.

Wagner, T. (1994). *How schools change.* Boston: Beacon.

CHAPTER 8

Extending Instructional Conversation

Gordon Wells
Mari Haneda

For more than two thousand years, educators have argued the need for a form of instruction in which learners are treated as active agents who, along with their teachers, engage in a form of discourse that aims for the enhancement of understanding rather than the one-way transmission of information (Goldenberg, 1991). However, it was not until Roland Tharp and Ronald Gallimore (1988) coined the term "instructional conversation" (IC) and provided an explicit model of what an IC entails that the significance of this rather general recommendation became the focus of systematic practice and research.

As a concept, instructional conversation "contains a paradox: 'Instruction' and 'conversation' appear contrary, the one implying authority and planning, the other equality and responsiveness" (Tharp & Gallimore, 1988). However, as they themselves acknowledge, this paradox is more apparent than real for, in many contexts outside the classroom, it is through instructional conversations that parents and subsequent mentors enable learners of all ages "to go beyond themselves" by engaging with them in joint activities and assisting them through action and talk with those aspects of the activity that they cannot yet manage alone (Vygotsky, 1934/1987). This being so, Tharp and Gallimore (1988) argue, "the task of schooling can be seen as one of creating and supporting instructional conversations, among students, teachers, administrators, program developers, and researchers" (p. 111).

In this chapter, we hope to further develop the theoretical rationale for the effectiveness of instructional conversation and provide some additional examples of what it can look like in the practice of educators who are exploring ways of bringing the principles of IC to bear in a variety of educational contexts. Most of the published examples of IC involve discussion of literary texts in primary classes; the examples we shall discuss range more widely across subject matter and age, from social studies in Grade 3 to a graduate class discussing cultural historical activity theory (CHAT) online. In these ways we hope to extend the appeal of instructional conversation to a wider range of educators.

Learning Through Interaction

Like Tharp and Gallimore, we follow Vygotsky in recognizing semiotic mediation in the context of jointly undertaken cultural activities as the principle means whereby learners appropriate the knowledgeable skills that those activities require and, in the process, develop their identities as members of the communities in which those activities are practiced. Shared meaning is made in many modalities, of course—in action, gesture, dance, music, and the visual arts—and in various multimodal combinations. However, linguistic discourse, both spoken and written, has a privileged status, in that it is not only one among the many semiotic systems through which culture is created and maintained; it also "serves as an encoding system for many (though not all) others" (Halliday, 1978, p. 2). Not only is it the principle medium for coordinating action, but it also provides the means for reflecting on action and for describing events and developing explanations of them; it thus allows humans to exercise some degree of control over the material and social world in which they live. It is for this reason that Halliday goes so far as to claim that discourse is "the process through which experience *becomes* knowledge" [italics in original] (Halliday, 1993, p. 96). And clearly instructional conversation has a central role to play in this process.

To enable the transformation of experience into knowledge to be organized most effectively, however, we need to understand why conversational discourse has this powerful epistemic potential. Here, the work of Bakhtin (1986) serves to complement Vygotsky's concept of semiotic mediation. Central to Bakhtin's work is his emphasis on the dialogic nature of language use. Every utterance, he points out, is oriented both to the anticipated response of its recipient as well as to the utterances that preceded. As he wryly observes, the one who utters "is not after all the first speaker, the one who disturbs the eternal silence of the universe. [On the contrary,] any utterance is a link in a very complexly organized chain of other utterances" (p. 69); it is filled with "dialogic overtones." In conversation, therefore,

> the unique speech experience of each individual is shaped and developed in continuous and constant interaction with others' individual utterances. This experience can be characterized to some degree as the process of *assimilation*—more or less creative—of others' words (and not the words of a language). Our speech, that is, all our utterances (including creative works) is filled with others' words, varying degrees of otherness or varying degrees of 'our-own-ness,' varying degrees of awareness and detachment. These words of others carry with them their own evaluative tone, which we assimilate, rework and accentuate. (italics in original)

Bakhtin was most interested in the dialogicality of literary utterances—complete novels or poems—but the above statement clearly applies equally to the child's first learning of his or her mother tongue, to the learning of a second language, and also to the learning of the registers of written language. Whatever the modality or genre of language use, we master it by appropriating the words and phrases—as well as the ways in which these resources are used in different situations and for different purposes—from the utterances of particular others, as we engage in dialogue with them.

However, it is not only the culture's way of using language that is learned through dialogue. Every utterance not only offers a "model" of language use, but it also provides evidence of the way in which, within a particular culture, experience is named, categorized and interpreted by the "meaning potential" of the language system. As Halliday (1978) emphasizes, in learning to talk, a child also learns *through* talk and thus assimilates the "world view" of the community in which he or she is growing up. Without his or her conscious awareness of the process, the child's participation in joint activities and in the linguistic interaction that accompanies, directs and comments on them transforms his or her raw experience into a personal construction of cultural knowledge. In other words, Bakhtin's concept of dialogicality applies equally to knowledge construction—as can be seen by substituting "knowledge" for "speech experience" in the immediately preceding quotation from his work.

But what this substitution also highlights is the fact that words, utterances, and the knowledge they encode are constructed and contributed by particular individuals on the basis of their unique trajectory of experience of participation in a particular range of activities within particular communities. Even when, through participation in the activities of schooling and, in some cases, of higher education, they have read the same texts and listened to similar teacher expositions of the same curriculum, they still each contribute their "own-ness" to their understanding of the topics studied and to the knowledge they are constructing.

It might seem, therefore, that each of us is confined to his or her own private world, condemned to misunderstand—or at least to differently understand—others' words and meanings and for the most part to be completely unaware of the subjective nature of our own idiosyncratic world model. Fortunately, however, this is not entirely the case. For most occasions of interaction also provide opportunities for the calibration of knowledge, as it is brought to bear on the issues and problems that inevitably arise in the prosecution of any joint activity. The result is that people who regularly engage together in joint activities eventually develop a degree of shared knowledge and overlapping meanings sufficient for their practical purposes. Indeed, this is one of the strongest forms of evidence for Vygotsky's insistence on the centrality of joint activity on all the timescales of development, from microgenetic to phylogenetic. Franklin (1996) captured this insight very succinctly when she proposed that knowledge is constructed and reconstructed in the discourse among people doing things together.

Not all discourse is aimed at knowledge construction, however. As Eggins and Slade's (1997) work on the analysis of casual conversation makes clear, a substantial proportion of conversation among family members, friends and colleagues is more concerned with establishing and maintaining social roles and relationships and with the consolidation of shared evaluative stances than it is with the calibration and construction of knowledge. If the latter is involved, it tends to occur implicitly and as an instrumental means toward the achievement of the social goals of the conversation. And for this reason, as teachers, we need first to focus on creating positive social and affective relationships among the members of our learning communities (Mahn & John-Steiner, 2002).

Nevertheless, there are occasions of conversation where collaborative knowledge building is explicitly one of the goals of the interaction and, in these conditions, participants' recognition of the occurrence of misunderstanding or disagreement can instigate a deliberate exploration of the nature and extent of the disagreement and an attempt to arrive at a common understanding. Bereiter (1994) terms this kind of interaction "progressive discourse," which he sees as the antidote to the relativism inherent in the idiosyncratic status of the knowledge constructed by individuals, as described above. In collaboratively undertaken progressive discourse, he argues, the aim is to achieve "a new understanding that everyone involved agrees is superior to their own previous understanding" (Bereiter, 1994, p. 7). This, it might be argued, is also the desired outcome of the teacher's intentional use of instructional conversation.

However, this still leaves unanswered the question as to how precisely participation in progressive discourse can lead to an enhancement of both individual and group understanding. In the next section, we shall attempt to sketch an answer to this question by further considering Bakhtin's concept of dialogicality and, more specifically, by exploring the implications of his argument that each utterance "is a link in a very complexly organized chain of other utterances" (1986, p. 69).

Constructing Knowledge With and for Others

One of the characteristics of any form of construction, material or symbolic,[1] is that it can be considered from two perspectives: the processes involved in its creation and the product that results. This is as true of utterances and works of art as it is of buildings and machines. With respect to utterances, these two perspectives can be described as "saying" and "what is said." Each contributes in its different way to the development of understanding.

> In uttering, the speakers' efforts are directed to the saying—to producing meaning for others. To do this, speakers have to interpret the preceding contribution(s) in terms of the information it introduces, as well as their own stance to that information; compare that interpretation with their own current understanding of the issue under discussion, based on their experience and any other relevant information of which they are aware; and then formulate a contribution that will, in some relevant way, add to the common understanding achieved in the discourse so far, by extending, questioning or qualifying what someone else has said. It is frequently in this effort to make their understanding meaningful for others that speakers have the feeling of reaching a fuller and clearer understanding for themselves. (Wells, 2000, pp. 73–74)

The process of speaking also produces "what is said," a perceptible signal that is generally available to all participants, and responding to it involves a comparable process, whether by others or by speakers themselves. For, as Bakhtin (1986) pointed out, to respond to an utterance is to interrogate the meaning of what is said, to evaluate its coherence and relevance, and to begin to formulate a further response.

In contributing to progressive discourse, then, a speaker is simultaneously adding to the structure of meaning created jointly with others and advancing his or her own understanding through the constructive and creative effort involved in saying and in responding reflectively to what was said. And, since a similar constructive effort is required to listen responsively and critically to the contributions of others, that too provides an opportunity to advance his or her understanding. It needs to be emphasized, though, that it is the joint attempt to construct *common* understandings that the participants recognize as superior to their previous understandings, as Bereiter (1994) put it above, that makes progressive discourse such an effective means for participants to enhance their individual understandings. For dialogue of this kind involves both the internalization of the meanings created in the inter-mental forum of discussion and the externalization of those intra-mental meanings that are constructed in response; it also constitutes a particularly clear instance of Vygotsky's (1981) insight that "the individual develops into what he/she is through what he/she produces for others."

To a very considerable degree, this account of the discourse of collaborative knowledge building applies also to instructional conversation. Certainly, the aim of such conversation is for the student participants to extend their understanding of the topic of conversation by relating the new information to their own and others' previous experiences, thereby making meaning with the new information. In addition, such conversations also extend the students' command of the language in which the discussion is encoded and of the relationship between topic and situation and the linguistic registers appropriate to them (Halliday & Hasan, 1985).

The main difference between the two genres of discourse is in the role played by the teacher in instructional conversation. Whereas the kind of progressive discourse that Bereiter (1994) describes does not assume that one of the participants is more expert than the others with respect to the topic under discussion, nor that one participant has the right or obligation to direct the course it takes, this is less the case with instructional conversation. As Tharp and Gallimore (1988) make clear, while the ostensible purpose of IC as practiced in elementary classrooms is to read the text and talk together about it, and while, on the surface, the flow of talk is conversational, there is in fact an underlying structure.

> The structure is provided by an explicit set of instructional objectives, devised by the teacher from the specific subject matter of the lesson, and the ever-present meta-objective, to increase comprehension and competence in discourse in the domain of instruction. (p. 136)

Does this crucial difference between the two types of discourse with respect to their participant structures outweigh their similarities with respect to their goals? We think not. While the instructional emphasis in instructional conversation is very much to the fore in the examples that Tharp and Gallimore (1988) quoted from ICs in the primary grades, it has the potential to transform into an emphasis on inquiry, in which the topics to be investigated and the means to be used are negotiated by teacher and students in collaboration. It is to an exploration of ways in which this transformation might be achieved that we now turn. We begin with a consideration of the "improvable object" as a focus for knowledge building.

The Value of an Improvable Object

Over the course of human history, the most frequent spur to collaborative knowledge building has undoubtedly been the emergence of a problem in the course of a group's engagement in a routine activity or the challenge of taking on a new goal for which no procedures or tools had already been invented. Such situations demand initiative and creativity; they also bring about a transformation or extension of existing knowledge and skills. A rather similar description also applies at the ontogenetic level in the learning of cultural practices by novice members of a community. In the latter case, however, more expert members can provide assistance in solving what the novice experiences as a problem and typically they do so in a manner that enables the newcomers to achieve mastery of the relevant knowledgeable skills so that they are eventually able to participate in the activity autonomously. Such assistance of performance was described by Vygotsky (1934/1987) as working in the learner's zone of proximal development.

In both cases, a key role is played by the object of the activity, where this is understood both as the end in view and as the product under construction. The attempt to find a way of moving toward the goal or of creating and making improvements to the product provides a joint focus for effort and attention and stretches all concerned to "go beyond themselves" in both skill and understanding. The same is equally true when dealing with intellectual problems as diverse as, for example, designing the layout of a new town or developing an explanatory theory of some phenomenon. An actual three-dimensional model of the terrain or a representation of the theory in the form of a text, a flow diagram or some multimodal combination, allows the collaborating participants to illustrate their arguments, test the consequences of their proposals and, in these ways, make improvements to the object on which they are working.

In the classroom, such improvable objects can take a variety of forms, as the teachers in the Developing Inquiring Communities in Education Project found, as they explored ways of approaching different curricular topics with an inquiry orientation. These ranged from a working model of a land yacht created by two girls in a fourth grade unit on technology (Wells, 2002) to the role-played enactment of the hearing of a First Nation's land claim before the Supreme Court of Canada, which was the culmination of a seventh grade's study of political history (Kowal, 2001). In these and other cases, which the teachers made the subjects of their own investigations (Wells, 2001), instructional conversations occurred at various points along the way: as the whole class or small groups brainstormed the form(s) their object-in-view might take; in the course of collecting or interpreting evidence; following group presentations of work in progress to the rest of the class; and, most importantly, in the whole class discussion that typically formed the conclusion of the unit as a whole.

Rather than draw from these already published studies, however, we prefer here to present two small ongoing projects from schools in Santa Cruz County in California, where Roland Tharp's ideas have significantly influenced the ways in which a substantial number of teachers are attempting to make connections between the home and community experiences of the student members of their diverse classrooms and the increasingly strictly mandated curriculum that they are required to teach. In both of the following studies, the teachers concerned were committed to creating opportunities for students to bring their experiences and ideas to the topics being investigated, while at the same time ensuring that the ensuing conversations contribute to their curricular objects-in-view.

The first project involves an ongoing collaboration between the first author and the teacher of a fourth-grade class in a culturally diverse urban community. While most of the students are from homes in which English is the first language, the class contains several who only started to learn English on entry to school. It was the teacher's concerns about the effectiveness of his program in meeting the needs of these students that, through the mediation of the student teacher assigned to his classroom, led to our collaboration.

Designing, Building, and Testing Model Cars

The first author's initial visit to Buzz Gray's classroom occurred in December, on the last day before the holiday break. I had been invited to an annual end-of-term event: the "lunch-box derby." For this event (which was related to the health and nutrition curriculum), the children had brought to school "vehicles" constructed from fruit and vegetables, with the aim of making them to go as far as possible when released down a ramp. As the children took turns in running their vehicles, we all noticed that some traveled a considerable distance while others fell apart as they reached the point where the ramp rested on the level floor of the classroom. The winning vehicle, which traveled 13 feet and 6 inches, was simply constructed from a banana and four oranges, with wooden skewers providing the axles. When all the runs had been measured and recorded, the teacher brought the class together to consider the results, which he represented on the whiteboard in the form of a simple frequency distribution of distances achieved. However, with the holiday just beginning, there was no time to further explore the significance of these results.

Early in January the first author contacted Buzz again with the suggestion that it might be worthwhile to capitalize on the interest generated by the lunch-box derby and to try to engage the children in a sustained investigation of the design of similar vehicles made from more durable materials. Buzz agreed and together we planned how to proceed. As with the lunch-box derby, the first aim we proposed to the children was to design and construct vehicles that would travel as far as possible from the end of the ramp. At the same time, however, we had a second aim in view, which was to encourage the children to identify and explain the design features that led to success.

Much was learned over the next three months, with the last hour of each week devoted to designing, constructing, and testing vehicles from scrap lumber, wooden and plastic disks of various kinds to serve as wheels, and wooden skewers or carriage bolts as axles. The children made considerable progress in working together in collaborative groups; they also learned quite a lot about using the various materials effectively. However, because there was such a variety of designs and such varying degrees of constructional success, it was not possible, in the time, to carry out controlled tests of potentially critical variables. From this, the adults learned that it would have been preferable to use more standardized materials and to take a stronger lead in directing attention to specific design features in order to highlight those that might be critical for success. This was what we decided to do in a second iteration with a new group of students at the beginning of the following school year.

This time, the lessons were scheduled for a 90-minute period earlier on Fridays and, as planned, we provided more standardized material, including commercially available construction kits. We also led them to understand the concept of controlling all but the experimental variable and taught them to average several runs to overcome inaccuracies of measurement. Over ten weeks, based on student suggestions, the effects of changing a number of variables were investigated: length of chassis, diameter of wheels, weight of vehicle, and the ramp's angle of incline. At the end of each lesson, some time was spent in reflecting on what had been learned from the morning's experiments. As can be imagined, this led to some very interesting class discussions, in which students came up with a variety of hypotheses using such explanatory terms as "momentum," "traction" and "friction." Following these discussions, the students were also asked to make entries in their journals about what changes they had made to their vehicles and what they had discovered as a result.

By the final lesson we had firmly established that the length of the chassis and the wheel diameter did not make a difference; on the other hand, we found that adding weight reduced the distance traveled across the carpet in the classroom whereas, when we took the cars out into the playground and tested them on its asphalt surface, adding weight made some cars go further than without the extra weight. On a different occasion we also found that increasing the angle of the ramp significantly lengthened the distance traveled. This prompted a lively discussion about the relationship between the force that gives the cars their momentum and the competing force that makes them slow down. Finally, we found that putting a drop of oil between each wheel and the axle enabled all the cars to travel further.

The following extract is taken from the final review, the aim of which was to reconsider all the variables that might make a difference as a prelude to inviting individual inventiveness in making a vehicle at home that would go as far as possible, with the trials to be held in the final session. In this and the following extracts, the following conventions are used: angle brackets "< >" surround passages for which the transcription is uncertain; an "x" indicates a word that was unintelligible; words in full uppercase indicate emphasis; italicized words indicate segments of speech that overlap; a hyphen "–" indicates an interruption, either by another speaker or by the current speaker making a new start; a period "." indicates approximately one second of pause; parentheses "( )" enclose glosses on meaning or nonverbal communication; and brackets "[ ]" enclose descriptions of action or contextual information.

Buzz led off the discussion by inviting students to suggest any features of their vehicles that should be treated as of particular importance; GW, the first author, joined in later. After several contributions, Jesse indicated that he wished to speak.

 Buzz: Jesse, what do you think?

 Jesse: Well, er– . this is my theory of why weight helps when you're on the asphalt–

 Buzz: What do you mean, theory?

 Jesse: My theory– like– . well it's not really x x x but it's like weight– .why weight causes x the asphalt . 'cos the asphalt has little bumps which x x – the little bumps make the cars go UP a little bit and that slows them down . but with weight . um it keeps the car um . going to– going THROUGH the x x

 Buzz: That's a good theory . . Hannah (nominating)

 Hanna: Er– I– . um– I've been thinking about it's um– because um– . because I said if you took er– . a bunch of <knobbly> tires and <went> on a bumpy road . if it would go faster or . um– . . like . so skateboards, they have smoother wheels . and if um you want to go FAST . then there's this ramp to do it on (makes gesture of going down a slope) and a real smooth– . people normally skate on . flat smooth ground (makes horizontal gesture) . [T: Uh– huh] if they want to go fast so I think– . and so I think it might have to be– if it's smoother– if they're going smoother it will go further than if xxx (voice drops away) .

 Buzz: OK . . . Well Jesse's brought up the word . "theory" . which is kind of like you're taking a guess on something which you do have some facts but it has never been PROVED . like he was saying "well we didn't PROVE that . but based on all the stuff that I was observing out there this is kind of my theory" . . Does anybody have a theory– this is like . out there . like the future thing– on how . you could make a car that would go . farther than that wall? (pointing to end

	of room opposite him) . . . without an engine, just using the ramp? . . . . How you could improve on them, I mean . . . Miguel (nominating)
Miguel:	Make the ramp . a little bit higher–
Buzz:	Ok, so make it more– we found– we found out that we can make cars . . go farther if the ramp's . on a bigger angle
Miguel:	–cos it's going to crash to the floor when– it's going to stop like this . *so we–*
GW:	Could I ask *a question?* Do you remember we've been talking about a sort of struggle between two . forces . one of them is friction, what was the other one that *we were–*
Many:	*Gravity*
GW:	Gravity, OK . so . why do you think they go further if we make the slope of the ramp steeper . what do we change when we change the slope?
Buzz:	Miguel again (nominating him from among those with hands up)
Miguel:	If you put it a little bit higher it's going to crash down on to the floor . but if you put like soft paper that goes like that (one hand moves up and down on the other indicating a cushioning effect) it might go along a bit like in a roller-coaster they go UP and they go DOWN but they don't crash *through x x–*
GW:	*Yes, but–* . why– why would making the slope of the ramp steeper .. make it go further? what's that changed in the struggle between the two forces?
Buzz:	Hasmin (nominating)
Hanna:	Because it makes it go faster
GW:	But why? . . . what's changed?
Hanna:	Because of the angle that the ramp is at–
Buzz:	It's going to go faster, we'll give you that but why is it going to go faster . what– what's making it go faster?
Several:	Gravity
GW:	Ok, so what's changed about gravity?
Buzz:	Oh, Jesse (nominating)
Jesse:	Well um . I think um– when gravity's <in> it has more force going down . so with more force it has more speed . that way it can go farther on the carpet
GW:	So if we were to have the ramp . . . like that (holding ramp vertically)
Many:	Oh (excitedly)
Jesse:	It would break

GW: It would go BOOM (demonstrating) . really fast because there's lots of gravity . but it wouldn't run along the floor because it would just go bump . so if we–

Sam: There's not enough friction (as the car travels down the ramp)

Ellie: It would fall

GW: That's right . well it wouldn't be just not enough friction . but it couldn't make the turn as it got to the floor (demonstrating turn from vertical to horizontal movement) if we had it absolutely upright

Buzz: Yes .. Miguel (nominating)

Miguel: This was falling <but> say you started off high <this was gravity> . so . it– could– it would be <really> softer <first> if you put a piece of paper right there (pointing to the bottom of the ramp) and taped it and it goes like that (showing a curved trajectory when reaching the paper) . like that (demonstrating on his open journal) . and then it could run away . it's going far . it would go far (gestures the trajectory of the roller-coaster)

There are several things to note about this discussion. First, and perhaps most important, is that it had a goal: to identify the design features that should be attended to when the children set about building their individual vehicles at home. Second, and related, was the fact that their suggestions arose from their experiences over the previous weeks in trying to determine which were the features that were important. But equally significant was the shift that had taken place in their thinking about those experiences. Rather than simply reporting how their group's vehicle had performed, they were beginning to offer explanations for what they had observed. Jesse's contribution was particularly significant in this respect. First, he offered an explanation as to why adding weight to the vehicles enabled them to go further on the asphalt when the opposite result had obtained in the carpeted classroom. And second, he characterized what he had to say as "my theory"—a technical term that had not previously been used by any one else. Buzz was quick to seize on this word, providing a gloss that might prompt others to present their ideas in similar terms.

A second interesting feature was the obvious enthusiasm for increasing the slope of the ramp as a way of making the vehicles go further. The session in which we investigated this variable caused great satisfaction, as every group's vehicle traveled considerably further when the slope was increased. In fact, in this condition, some of the more successful vehicles could not run their full course as they hit the wall at the far end of the room. In this final discussion, Miguel, the boy who first suggested this strategy, was also the one to suggest a way of overcoming the problem of the vehicles breaking apart when they were launched down a near vertical ramp. Drawing on his experience of riding the roller-coaster—a popular attraction at the Santa Cruz Boardwalk—he suggested attaching a sheet of stiff paper part way down the ramp to convert the sharp angle between the ramp and the floor into a gentler curve which the vehicles could safely traverse. Then, a few turns later, after Jesse had made the connection between gravity and the increased speed down the ramp, Miguel once again explained through words and gestures how the card attached to the ramp would allow the vehicles to maintain their increased speed and, as a result, to travel further across the floor. It is interesting to note, therefore, that Miguel was one of the small number of English language learners (ELLs) in the class, about whose progress Buzz had been concerned and that had led to the first author's initial visit to his classroom. Clearly, as far as Miguel was concerned, the invitation to speak from his own experience enabled him to make a really important contribution to the discussion, linking the children's shared interest in the practical investigation with the scientific concepts of gravity, momentum, and friction that the adults had intended they should begin to understand.

Learning Language and Learning Through Language

The preceding example was taken from a class in an urban classroom in the Central Coast area of California. While a substantial proportion of the children were growing up speaking both Spanish and English, most had already achieved a reasonable mastery of English. In the next example, taken from a third-grade class in a rural school not very far away from the first, all the children were from families of Spanish-speaking agricultural workers and were designated ELL. The program in which they were enrolled was described as "transitional bilingual," and Spanish was used as a medium of instruction for all content area instruction, English only being used in lessons designated as English language development (ELD).

At the time of the study carried out by the second author, Ms. Wilson, an experienced teacher, had been involved for eight years in a professional development project that promotes ELD through science inquiry. In accordance with her belief that language is best learned through firsthand engagement with subject matter, she devoted her ELD blocks to science inquiry. She created many opportunities for her students to engage in hands-on experiments to build a basis for developing academic registers, scientific reasoning skills, and thinking skills. In spite of their limited English proficiency (beginner to intermediate), her students were observed to participate in science inquiry competently by carrying out experiments, predicting, observing, keeping records of their observations, and interpreting results.

An inquiry approach, of course, may take different forms, ranging from a teacher-directed investigation to a more full-fledged one that is based on mutual negotiation between teacher and students with respect to the topic and the means for its investigation, depending on students' level of English language proficiency, their cognitive maturity, and the nature of the subject matter in focus. This example falls toward the former end.

The focus of the case study was to investigate the way in which Ms. Wilson attempted to adopt an inquiry approach to social studies in a unit on "community and change" with a secondary focus on science. This was a major undertaking for her. First, she needed to imagine what a hands-on inquiry might look like in social studies, which required a paradigm shift from her normal use of prescribed textbooks. Second, she needed to develop all the instructional materials by herself, which in the case of science inquiry were provided by the professional development project. Ms. Wilson spent half a year developing her thematic unit on "community and change" through collaboration with two colleagues at her school. We first provide a brief overview of the unit and then discuss instances of instructional conversation that can be considered also as cases of "exploratory talk" (Barnes, 1992), talk in which students explore their ideas with teacher guidance.

The focal unit was designed using a California Social Studies Standard under the heading of continuity and change: Students describe the area's physical and human geography and use maps, tables, graphs, photographs, and charts to organize information about people, places, and environments in a spatial context. Ms. Wilson wanted her students to develop map-reading skills and to understand the concepts of community and change particularly in relation to the local area. The challenge that she faced was to make these abstract concepts accessible to her young second-language students. She started with a brief teacher exposition about the typical parts of a community and quickly moved to ask her students concrete questions: where they lived, other communities they had visited, naming the geographical features, and the industry in the local community. In lieu of a hands-on experiment in science, she drew on her students' knowledge base and constructed shared discursive space about their local community. Having established this common ground and roused her students' interest, she introduced a map reading activity in the third lesson. The first excerpt of instructional conversation is taken from this introductory phase. In groups of four, the students were carrying out a vocabulary review game. Ms. Wilson visited each group in turn to explain how to read a topographic map of the local region.

1   T: I'm gonna come to your table, I think, it might be easier [while speaking she walks around with a big laminated map] So let's– you're gonna have to close your journals so that I can put this BIG map on your table

2   S1:   Whoopee

3   T: (lays a map down at a table) This is called a topographic map and what it shows–

4   S2:   xx

5   T: Right

6   S3:   Teacher we have to write in English *or Spanish*?

7   T: *English*

8   S3:   xx

9   T: Well that's fine however– however *x x*

10   S3:   *Teacher* <apopotes apopotes> (meaning unclear)

11   T: OK, see these little lines that look like a lot of squiggly lines

12   SS: Yes

13   T: OK, what these lines are showing.. is the hi– how high things are . so you notice *there's–*

14   S3:   *Teacher* xx

15   T: Excuse me . just let me finish explaining– there's some lines here but they aren't very close together as they get closer together that means it's . it's higher . so all of this (pointing to an area on the map) as you can see has a lot of really really close together lines which means these are the mountains . THESE are the mountains that we saw when we were– when we were walking . see here's [our] School right there (pointing to map) . here's the street where we crossed and we looked– and we looked to our left we looked straight out here . this is what we saw . . these are *mountains–*

16   S4:   *Cool*

17   T: – right there

18   S2:   That looks like a car with a little flag (pointing at the map)

19   T: Ok, where's the river . where's the Pajaro River? [students are scanning the map with their fingers looking for the river]

20   S4:   It's supposed to be <white> x

21 S1: PAJARO (pointing to the river on the map)

22 T: No (not clear who she was responding to)

23 S2: Here's xx

24 T: It's right here . here's the Pajaro River going all the way back . you can see it– it's coming ALL the way–

25 S4: From here

26 T: – from– from over here . so it goes all the way along here (tracing the river with her finger on the map) .. very long and *it goes out to–*

27 S3: *Teacher what are these?*

28 T: – if you go on it would go out to the ocean

29 S3: Teacher I one question, are these– Que es esto? [What is this?]

30 T: This is Riverside Road *so that's Riverside–*

31 S4: *Oh oh this is* Watsonville

32 T: – see there's the high school . yes, all of this is Watsonville . all of this all the way out to here now is Watsonville

33 S1: I like this (pointing to an area on the map)

34 S2: Here's high school

35 T: Here's the high school um there's the Plaza

36 S1: *Plaza*

37 S3: *The Plaza*

38 S4: HEY then I must live right here

39 S2: Where's my house?

40 S1: Mine's en by x Park Hospital

41 T: The hospital, except that's not really the hospital anymore

42 S3: I know, Teacher

43 T: The hospital is out by the airport now

44 S2: More over *here*

45 T: *This map* is– when this map was made that was the hospital but now the hospital is– . let's see Airport Boulevard [teacher and students are looking for the hospital] . yes, see here's Freedom Green Valley Road is right–

46 S3: Teacher, am I– if– if I am in Pinto Lake where would I live

47	T:	Pinto Lake is up here . so look look at all this . see this part with all these lines and over here there's more lines and all around *these–*
48	S2:	*Those* are all the Santa Cruz Mountains
49	T:	Not all of them . these are not the mountains . these are like hills
50	S3:	Hills
51	T:	And see this part is FLAT because it doesn't have a lot of wavy lines . and then this whole area is also very flat because it also doesn't have lot of wavy lines

As shown in the transcript above, an abstract map reading became a hands-on tactile activity when the students moved around the table and attempted to locate places on the map by physically feeling their way around the map. They intently examined the density of squiggly lines, gradually learned to locate local landmarks, and inferred the location of their houses on the map. Turn 19 marks a shift in the teacher's gradual hand-over to student exploration when she asks where the Pajaro River is. After a few failed attempts from the students, in turn 24 she shows where the river is on the map by tracing it from the mountain to the ocean. This tracing action prompted some of the students to start to engage in the same action and at the same time to make the connection between a long narrow winding line cutting across the map and the Pajaro River. For Marco (S4), it is not until turn 31 that he understands this correspondence. Ms. Wilson then goes on to identify places familiar to the students: the only high school in the area and the Plaza in the city center.

Turn 38 marks a transition to a more fully blown exploration of ideas when one of the students exclaims with enthusiasm: "HEY then I must live right here." For the next ten turns or so, one after another, the students try to find the location of their houses on the map. By this stage, it was they who were initiating the talk. One of the students says, "Teacher, am I– if if I am in Pinto Lake where would I live" (If I live close to Pinto Lake, where is my house on the map?). Despite grammatical inaccuracy, it is clear that the student is attempting to speculate. While this is quite a small step towards "exploratory talk," it is clear that the students in this group had started to grasp that the map represented the local area and that they were co-constructing their understanding with the assistance of Ms. Wilson.

After the map reading, more hands-on activities followed to reinforce the students' understanding of different representations of the local area. First, they colored their topographic maps of Watsonville according to landforms; then, based on their colored maps, they also constructed three-dimensional relief maps with play dough. In addition to this geographical component, Ms. Wilson attempted to introduce the notion of change, i.e., change in the local community, through picture comparison activities (photos of the community sixty years ago and now).

In addressing the notion of change from a different perspective, Ms. Wilson incorporated science. For this, she introduced two experiments that examined the effects of water and light on plant growth. The following excerpts, taken from the first experiment on the effect of light on plant growth under the with- or-without water condition, show that while the teacher selected the topic and experiments, she made sure to engage her students in "exploratory talk":

1   T: What do roots do for a plant?

2   Ss: Water

3   S2: They absorb the water.

4   S3: They drink water.

5   S4: And they– *they help the plant to grow*

6   S5: *They do something to xxx*

7   T: They help the plant get the water.

This short sequence is illustrative of Ms. Wilson's simultaneous focus on science content and language form. In turn 1, she poses an open-ended question, to which several students respond one after another, building on each other's responses until they come to an approximation of the right answer in turn 5. This type of co-construction of meaning was typical in this classroom; over successive turns, student responses achieved an increased sophistication in terms of syntactic complexity and accuracy of content. The response by the first student consists of only one content word, water. The second and third respondents develop this into a complete sentence with a propositional content: Roots absorb water. Building on the previous responses, the fourth student provides additional propositional content: They (roots) help plants to grow. To conclude this sequence, in turn 7, the teacher reformulates the answer by combining the two propositions that the students offered. This type of reformulation was one of the most typical discourse moves used by this teacher. Admittedly, this is not as sophisticated as Bereiter's (1994) "progressive discourse" nor is this excerpt built upon rigorous intellectual debate in an attempt to resolve disagreement. However, what is clear is that the students were constructing their understanding together both in content and language form.

In the next excerpt, having established the function of roots for plant growth, the teacher prompted the students to pose a question and predict the results of the experiment.

11   T: It says QUESTION (pointing to the workbook that she handed out to the students), what we want to know . now, we are going to leave one– box with no water– we're going to have– put water in the other box . what do you think we want to KNOW– if we do that experiment? . think about it

12   S1:   See if they grow.

13   T: We want to know if– ?

14   S2:   *They grow*

15   S2:   *They grow* without water

16   T: Say it again Felipe

17   S2:   They grow without WATER . .

18   T: If – these plants will grow without water . . does that sound like a good question?

19   Ss: *No*

20   Ss: *Yes*

21   T: Yes? .. raise your thumb up if you think that's a good question (demonstrates) rai–

22   Ss: [Variously show thumbs up/down]

23   T: Okay, we want to see if these plants will grow without water

24   S1:   *No*

25   S2:   *They won't* grow

26   T: So write that on the LINE

As she typically does, the teacher starts the discussion with a negotiatory question: "What do you think we want to know if we do that experiment." Building on the previous student's responses, Felipe (S2) offers a correct answer in turn 15. It appears that, in order to ensure that all students understand the question, she not only asks Felipe to repeat what he said in turn 15 but also reformulates his answer in turn 18, thus creating redundancy in language use. In turns 18 and 23, she makes an interesting move, asking the students to evaluate Felipe's proposition through doing thumbs up or down. This strategy was effectively used to help her students have ownership of the knowledge building process in spite of the constraints of their command of English. Also interesting is the fact that, in turns 24 and 25, two students immediately move to their prediction without needing a teacher prompt. Such voluntary predictions are considered to be an important step toward "progressive discourse," albeit a small one.

In sum, there were instances of instructional conversation in the two content areas, although they occurred in different group configurations. In geography, considering the unit as a whole, there was much teacher exposition used to explain new concepts, vocabulary items, and skills, as well as procedural talk used to give directions as to how to complete the activity at hand (e.g., map coloring, relief-map making). As presented in the first excerpt, instructional conversation occurred in a small group with the teacher in a map reading activity, where she helped students to make a connection between the physical features and landmarks of the local area and their representation on the map. This excerpt illustrated the way in which the students took turns spontaneously to locate their houses on the map; they were applying their newly acquired skills without being prompted. In science, on the other hand, it was in a whole class discussion during the predicting phase of the experiments that instructional conversation occurred. The question is why there were these differences between the occurrence of ICs in the two content areas. It can be speculated that while predicting results of science experiments was a well-established routine in Ms. Wilson's classroom, reading a map is not only an abstract activity, but it was also the first time it had been attempted in this class. This, in turn, may have necessitated the need for scaffolding in a more intimate setting than the whole class can afford. In other words, with young second-language students, both the degree of abstraction of a particular task and the familiarity with analytical procedures may affect where instructional conversation occurs. However, perhaps more significant are the similarities across the excerpts. That is, instructional conversation is more likely to occur when students are engaged in an activity, and are free to offer their opinions and explore their ideas in co-constructing common knowledge.

In both the case studies just presented, the instructional conversations occurred in the context of practical investigations where the object to be improved was the outcome of hands-on activity. In the next section, we briefly consider two rather different cases, in which student collaboration on the construction of a symbolic object extends the notion of instructional conversation still further.

Improving Symbolic Objects

The concept of an "improvable object" was first proposed by Scardamalia, who saw it as a central component of all the various realizations of the "knowledge-building community" that she, Bereiter, and their colleagues have been developing for schools, universities, hospitals, and businesses over the last two decades (Bereiter & Scardamalia, 1996; Scardamalia, 2000). In its first manifestation as the Computer Supported Intentional Learning Environmment (CSILE) (Scardamalia, Bereiter, & Lamon, 1994), the knowledge-building community was realized in a variety of classes, from Grade 1 through high school, in each case by means of a substantial number of networked computers linked to a central database. Instead of all students learning from the same textbook, they were encouraged, either individually or in small groups, to take on one aspect of a curricular topic and, on the basis of research of various kinds, to contribute their theories and questions to the central database, where their stored messages could be responded to by answers, comments, and further questions, or by competing theories, contributed by other members of the classroom community. In this way, the whole class could participate in collaborative knowledge building as they attempted to improve on the initial contributions.

Later realizations of this design principle, which use the connectivity of the Internet, enable distributed communities of older students or of professional workers to be created. Here too, a similar pattern of progressive knowledge building can be seen as participants treat each other's contributed observations and theories as objects that can potentially be critiqued and improved. Based on the success of these projects, Scardamalia urges teachers to ensure that all students become engaged in authentic knowledge work: "Don't relegate some students to an idea-free curriculum on grounds that they are too young or differently-abled or that they have a different kind of learning style. Instead, capitalize on diversity" (2000, p. 3).

Not all classrooms are equipped with the networked computers that underpin the CSILE that Scardamalia writes about. However, the principles can be reproduced in a variety of formats, as the following example shows.

Studying the Black Death

Having read about CSILE, Karen Hume decided to introduce the practice of collaborative knowledge building into her Grade 6 and 7 class. However, not having enough computers to reproduce the same format, she decided to use a large bulletin board instead. When questions arose in the course of their investigations, students posted them on the "Knowledge Wall" and, as in CSILE, other students continued the dialogue by posting comments or questions below the opening question. In this particular unit, her students were studying the Causes and Consequences of the Black Death in Medieval Europe and, in the materials they were reading, some students were intrigued by references to and illustrations of protective clothing worn by doctors. As these written notes show, the students used conjecture, evidence from published material and reasoning to attempt to construct a satisfying answer to their question.[2]

> Question: Why did an odd bird figure in a cloak protect doctors? (referring to an image from a history book showing a doctor clad in leather and wearing a beak mask that makes him look like a bird)
>
> Ian: I don't have a total answer for this, but the paragraph underneath the picture says that the bird mask is to filter out the polluted air, and the wand is to heal patients. Don't ask me why he/she wears a leather cloak.
>
> Eren: If what this guy is wearing is a mask, it might have actually helped him stay healthy.
>
> Alec: This is good Ian, but why a bird/man/penguin?
>
> Justin: At the end of the caption of the bird figure, in quotes, it claims, "doctors hoped to avoid the contagion by looking more like a crow than a man." Can anybody try to clarify the quote?
>
> Alec: Why a crow?
>
> Suzanne: People probably wanted to be birds because they saw that the birds weren't dying. This is because birds don't get fleas and fleas caused the Black Death.
>
> Matt: It was not the bird figure protecting the doctors like a god, but it is a form of disease proof clothing. The beak is an early form of gas mask, the cloak of heavy leather. The wand is for soothing the patients. The doctor is covered from head to toe, therefore keeping out the disease.
>
> Ray: Theoretically, the birdlike cloak thing might prevent the fleas from getting to the doctors skin, thus giving the individual the plague. The cloak was basically a shield.
>
> Suzanne: This could and probably is true, but I doubt the people of the time knew that.
>
> Jon: I think it is a witch doctor because of what he is wearing.
>
> Justin: It is just a doctor dressed in leather wearing an early edition of a gas mask. More like a doctor wearing a shield from the fleas.
>
> Suzanne: But Justin, the doctor didn't KNOW that fleas cause the disease, therefore he couldn't have been wearing it for protection. That's why I agree with Jon that yes, the doctor probably is a witch doctor. The bird suit only had a spiritual meaning.

Extending Instructional Conversation

Justin: I didn't say that he/she knew. I mean that the doctor was using the leather as a shield.

Ray: The birdlike figure of a god worked. Scientifically speaking, it protected the wearer by preventing the fleas from reaching the skin. It had religious value too. The power of the costume prevented the virus from taking over. COMBINATION Some guy who lived in a town saw his friends dropping like flies. He then decided to cover himself up with lots of clothes. He put clothes on that made him look like a bird. Some doctors noticed he didn't get the plague and thought it was a spirit who protected you when you wore the clothes. But what they didn't know is that it stopped the fleas from getting to you. Question solved.

Justin: Did the odd bird figure protect doctors? What is your source? How did these people have the technology when they did not know the cause?

Brad: No Justin, the bird man didn't protect doctors. It was the fact that all of their skin was covered and no fleas or rats could pass the disease on to them.

Colin: Brad, I must agree, with their bird suits on, the fleas infecting the patient could not penetrate the skin, spreading the disease.

Ray: The reason that they thought the suit protected was spiritual. The reason it actually protected them was that it kept the fleas off them. Please reread my previous notes.

Alec: This is crazy. It keeps going from spiritual focus to just plain protection and shield edge. Let us first try and get which one is correct. Maybe they're both right. I don't know.

Justin: It's not crazy. It keeps on doing that because we are arguing over spiritual and protection. They are both right because the doctor thought it was spiritual, but it was a shield.

Alec: Well put, Justin. I now understand why it keeps going. Thanks.

Amanda: Maybe that was what doctors wore all the time anyway.

Brad: Amanda, I really truly doubt that doctors wore that all the time because I remember reading something that said those costumes were first used during the Black Death.

This was certainly a form of instructional conversation—but with some important differences. First, the improvable object on which their conversation was focused was an answer to the question that they themselves had posed. Second, the conversation was carried on in writing, which gave participants time to think about their responses before posting them on the Knowledge Wall. Finally, this form of IC had been so well appropriated by the students that they no longer needed the teacher to organize it for them by asking questions and probing for further information. They had reached the stage in their zones of proximal development where they were able to practice autonomously what they had initially learned from participating in similar conversations orally with their teacher.

Improving a Virtual Object

The final example of working on an improvable object comes from a doctoral seminar, in which Knowledge Forum, the Web-based version of CSILE, was used to continue the instructional conversations carried on in class. The students readily took to the use of this tool for thinking and communicating, but their contributions tended initially to be more like individual monologues than contributions to a knowledge building dialogue. So, in an attempt to increase the dialogic nature of the postings, the first author, who was teaching the course, decided to introduce a different sort of challenge. Following a reading and in-class discussion of the role of artifacts in mediating action and learning, he proposed that the class undertake a joint project: to plan an ideal school in the virtual space of the Knowledge Forum and to explain the reasons for the organizational features they proposed.

The first difference in the subsequent dialogue was in the average length of contributions, which increased considerably as contributors provided much fuller justifications for their proposals or for their reactions to those of others. The second interesting finding was in the mean length of the discussion threads. This increased by 50 percent compared with those in earlier topics of discussion. And third, there was an increase in the proportion of contributions that made links and references to preceding notes in the thread. Taken together, it certainly seemed that working on an improvable (virtual) object led to more focused and cohesive "conversation" than did the discussion of any of the preceding topics in the course (Wells, 2003). Furthermore, as one of the class members, Martha, noted,

> Often, we don't get to share our experiences with the material in class (for various reasons: e.g., fear of embarrassment, fear of disapproval, inappropriate time/place, etc.). I think it's valuable for students to share their direct relations to the material and the classroom discussions in a way that is non-threatening. I believe that this encourages community-building.

As Martha makes clear in this comment, extending the instructional conversation to the asynchronous medium of the on-line Knowledge Forum had some important advantages in overcoming the inevitable constraints of real-time interaction. Thus, as many university teachers are discovering, harnessing the potential of the Internet to allow all students to contribute their ideas in a more thoughtful manner can significantly enrich collaborative knowledge building.

Building on this discovery, the first author decided to use the same tactic in a master's course for practicing teachers that he was teaching, mainly in distance mode, during the same semester. This group also took enthusiastically to the constructional task. Interestingly, where the doctoral seminar designed a high school and focused much of their attention on the organization of the buildings and rooms within them to allow for a variety of participant formats—students working on their own, in collaborating groups, or in teacher-led seminars—the teacher group chose to design an elementary school that also functioned as a community and adult education center. In their case, it was the challenge of creating functional connections between the various user groups that they found most stimulating and rewarding.

In both cases what was clear, however, was that working to construct a specific object brought our weekly readings alive and encouraged the students to go beyond the typically abstract discussion of the "implications" of the theories being studied. Constructing a particular—though virtual—school required them to consider how, in bricks and mortar, in the choice of resources and the ways they were to be used and—most importantly—in the social and professional relationships between the various groups involved, the theories being studied could be most effectively realized in practice. This, as both Dewey (1938) and Vygotsky (1934/1987) argued a century or so ago, is the true test of, and spur to, real understanding.

Conclusion

As we hope to have shown in this chapter, conversation is the essential mediator of cultural learning at any age, from infancy to adulthood, and in all settings in which people are engaged in joint activity. In the classroom context, however, the particular merit of *instructional* conversation is that it capitalizes on conversation as the means for students' systematic intellectual development and identity formation, by drawing on each student's personal experience, in school and out, and by bridging between class members' joint actions and their shared understanding. As a variety of observational studies of classrooms have shown, students' hands-on activities without conversation, in which the significance of what was done and observed is collaboratively explored, all too often leave no impression other than the "fun" experienced; but, equally, teacher-directed instructional talk which does not connect with action, ongoing or envisaged, is likely to be as quickly forgotten. By incorporating students' contributions as well as the instructional goals specified by the curriculum, instructional conversation functions as a crucible in which all the relevant ideas and experiences are brought together and melded into an improved understanding and potential for future action.

In a recent description of instructional conversation, Dalton and Tharp (2002) state:

> Ordinarily, IC takes place in small groups, though a teacher may have instructional conversations with larger groups or individuals. For example, teachers may work on a unit or thematic topic with the whole class, followed by small group ICs that focus on researching and analyzing selected aspects of the large group topic. Teachers combine ordinary conversation's responsive and inclusive features with assessment and assistance to help engage students and stimulate their learning. While any good conversation requires some latitude and drift in the topic, the teacher's leadership is used to focus on the instructional goal. While the teacher holds the goal firmly in mind, the route to the goal is responsive to student participation and developing understanding. (p. 191)

They also propose as one of the criteria of successful IC that the teacher "guides the students to prepare a product that indicates the instructional conversation's goal was achieved" (p. 191).

In the preceding examples we have illustrated these characteristics of IC and shown how they can be suitably adapted to a variety of educational settings, from a primary grade class to a doctoral seminar, across the curriculum from the physics of motion to change over historical time, and in different modes—speech, writing, or through computer-mediated communication. In each case we have also shown the importance of "an improvable object" (the "product" referred to above) in providing a focus for students' activity. In particular, as the last two examples show, when students take ownership of the creation and improvement of such an object, they can continue the instructional conversation without the need for the teacher's moment-by-moment participation, determining for themselves the extent to which their goal has been achieved.

As Tharp and his colleagues have strongly argued, instructional conversation is the epitome of assistance in the zone of proximal development. And, as such assistance should always do, IC provides opportunity for students to appropriate the different disciplinal modes of making meaning so that, over time, students become able to engage in such dialogue autonomously, in conversation with their peers, in transacting with written texts, and in thinking in the mode of inner speech. On these grounds, we fully concur with Tharp and Gallimore (1988, p.

111) when they write: "To most truly teach, one must converse; to truly converse is to teach."

Notes

Mari Haneda's research was supported by a Post-doctoral Research Fellowship from the Social Sciences and Humanities Research Council of Canada.

1. This distinction is largely conceptual as any form of construction has both aspects: as well as its material form any artifact also has symbolic significance with respect to the knowledgeable skills involved in its creation and use; equally, a symbolic artifact such as a theory can only function in the social world when embodied in a physical object such as a book or diagrammatic representation.

2. The gender imbalance in this discussion was at least partly due to the gender imbalance among the students. Seventeen of the twenty-four students in the class were male.

References

Bakhtin, M. M. (1986). *Speech genres and other late essays* (Y. McGee, Trans.). Austin: University of Texas Press.

Barnes, D. (1992). *From communication to curriculum* (2nd ed.) Portsmouth, NH: Boynton/Cook Heinemann.

Bereiter, C. (1994). Implications of postmodernism for science, or, science as progressive discourse. *Educational Psychologist, 29*(1), 3–12.

Bereiter, C., & Scardamalia, M. (1996). Rethinking learning. In D. R. Olson & N. Torrance (Eds.), *The handbook of education and human development* (pp. 485–513). Cambridge, MA: Blackwell.

Dalton, S. S., & Tharp, R. G. (2002). Standards for pedagogy: Research, theory and practice. In G. Wells & G. Claxton (Eds.), *Learning for life in the 21st century: Sociocultural perspectives on the future of education* (pp. 181–194). Oxford: Blackwell.

Dewey, J. (1938). *Experience and education*. New York: Collier Macmillan.

Eggins, S., & Slade, D. (1997). *Analysing casual conversation*. London: Cassell.

Franklin, U. (1996). *Oral introduction to the conference, Towards an Ecology of Knowledge*. Toronto: University of Toronto.

Goldenberg, C. (1991). *Instructional conversations and their classroom application* (Educational Practice Report 2). Santa Cruz, CA: The National Center for Research on Cultural Diversity and Second Language Learning.

Halliday, M. A. K. (1978). *Language as social semiotic: The social interpretation of language and meaning*. London: Arnold.

Halliday, M. A. K. (1993). Towards a language-based theory of learning. *Linguistics and Education, 5,* 93–116.

Halliday, M. A. K., & Hasan, R. (1985). *Language, context and text: Aspects of language in a social-semiotic perspective.* Geelong, Vic.: Deakin University (Republished by Oxford University Press, 1989).

Kowal, M. (2001). Knowledge building: Learning about native issues outside in and inside out. In G. Wells (Ed.), *Action, talk, and text: Learning and teaching through inquiry* (pp. 118–133). New York: Teachers College Press.

Mahn, H., & John-Steiner, V. (2002). The gift of confidence: A Vygotskian view of emotions. In G. Wells & G. Claxton (Eds.), *Learning for life in the 21st century: Sociocultural perspectives on the future of education* (pp. 46–58). Oxford: Blackwell.

Scardamalia, M. (2000). Can schools enter a knowledge society? In M. Selinger & J. Wynn (Eds.), *Educational technology and the impact on teaching and learning* (pp. 6–10). Abingdon, VA: Risk Management Consultants.

Scardamalia, M., Bereiter, C., & Lamon, M. (1994). The CSILE project: Trying to bring the classroom into World 3. In K. McGilley (Ed.), *Classroom lessons: Integrating cognitive theory and classroom practice* (pp. 201–228). Cambridge, MA: MIT Press.

Tharp, R., & Gallimore, R. (1988). *Rousing minds to life.* New York: Cambridge University Press.

Vygotsky, L. S. (1934/1987). Thinking and speech. (N. Minick, Trans.). In R. W. Rieber & A. S. Carton (Eds.), *The collected works of L. S. Vygotsky, Volume 1: Problems of general psychology* (pp. 39–285). New York: Plenum.

Vygotsky, L. S. (1978). *Mind in society: The development of higher psychological processes.* (Eds. and Trans. by M. Cole, V. John-Steiner, S. Scribner, & E. Souberman). Cambridge, MA: Harvard University Press.

Vygotsky, L. S. (1981). The genesis of higher mental functions. In J. V. Wertsch (Ed.), *The concept of activity in Soviet psychology* (pp. 144–188). Armonk, NY: Sharpe.

Wells, G. (2000). Dialogic inquiry in the classroom: Building on the legacy of Vygotsky. In C. Lee & P. Smagorinsky (Eds.), *Vygotskian perspectives on literacy research* (pp. 51–85). New York: Cambridge University Press.

Wells, G. (Ed.). (2001). *Action, talk, and text: Learning and teaching through inquiry.* New York: Teachers College Press.

Wells, G. (2002). The role of dialogue in activity theory. *Mind, culture, and activity, 9*(1), 43–66.

Wells, G. (2003). Creating an 'improvable object' through computer mediated communication. In R. Ottewill (Ed.) *Educational innovation in economics and business pedagogy, technology and innovation* (Vol. 8) Amsterdam: Kluwer.

CHAPTER 9

School Reform and the Education of Culturally and Linguistically Diverse Students

Amanda Datnow
Samuel C. Stringfield
Marisa Castellano

In their landmark book, *Rousing Minds to Life,* Tharp and Gallimore (1988), challenged us to see schooling in a social context. Building upon the work of Vygotsky, they combine theory and rich ethnographic data to argue for the need for fundamental changes in how we think about teaching and learning and call for a redefinition of school as a place "where all teach and all learn" (p. 268). Such a change, which implies very different ways of thinking about the behavior of teachers and students in the classroom, was seen as critical in order to bring about improved education for all students, most notably underachieving minority students.

Now, sixteen years since the publication of Tharp and Gallimore's (1988) book, children of color currently constitute the majority in 25 of the largest school districts in the United States, and the need to improve their education has never been more pressing. Many of these students represent multi-ethnic backgrounds and do not speak English as their first language. The majority of these students are from Hispanic and Asian countries, which produce a growing or at least steady number of immigrants each year. According to the 2000 U.S. Census, persons of color comprise the majority of the population of the State of California and similar trends are expected in Texas, Florida, and New York.

The questions are: "Does the current generation of school reform models serve these students effectively?" "If so, how?" "Do they in fact do this by redefining 'what school means' in positive and productive ways?" This chapter presents findings from a four-year case study of 13 multilingual, multicultural elementary schools, each of which implemented a comprehensive school reform model.

The roots of this study lie in two of the most rapidly developing areas in school improvement research: (a) identifying practices that improve education for culturally and linguistically diverse students, and (b) examining the implementation and outcomes of comprehensive school reform (CSR) models. It is important to note that this study—and the intersection of these two areas—was directly inspired by Roland Tharp, who approached us in 1996 about conducting a study of reform in a multicultural, multilingual school district. We had done prior studies of comprehensive school reform in a variety of contexts, but never specifically focused on cultural and linguistic diversity. This was a chance to break new ground.

The scale up of comprehensive school reform models has been occurring at an unprecedented rate, as evidenced by the fact that there are now dozens of school reform models (e.g., Success for All, High Schools that Work, Comer School Development Program, Accelerated Schools) being implemented in thousands of schools in the U.S. Their increased scale up was bolstered by the federal Comprehensive School Reform Demonstration Program legislation providing $150 million in 1998 (since increasing to $260 million in 2003) for the adoption of such models and by changes in Title I regulations allowing for the use of funds to support schoolwide programs (U.S. Department of Education, 2000).

Some argue that the current generation of CSR models provides the best hope for school improvement on a grand scale that has existed in the past several decades (Slavin & Madden, 1998). Though the reforms differ in their approaches to change, common among many of them is an interest in whole-school change, strong commitments to improving student achievement, new conceptions about what students should be expected to learn, and an emphasis on prevention rather than remediation (Oakes, 1993). Numerous reform models have also been associated with gains in student achievement (see Borman, Hewes, Overman, & Brown, 2002; Herman et al., 1999, Slavin & Fashola, 1998; Stringfield et al., 1997).

Despite these indicators of success, effectively "scaling up" or transferring innovations across school contexts is quite difficult, as the conditions in one setting are never the same as the conditions in the next (Elmore, 1996; Fullan, 1999; Hargreaves & Fink, 2000). Moreover, most of the nationally disseminated school reform designs were not developed specifically for multilingual or multicultural school contexts. However, all of the reforms emphasize improving outcomes for all students and most declare the need to respect diverse cultures. With the exception of Éxito para Todos, the Spanish version of Success For All (Slavin & Madden, 1999), there has been relatively little research on the effectiveness of CSR models in achieving successful implementation, let alone improvements in student achievement, in multilingual contexts.

Just how workable are these reforms in culturally and linguistically diverse contexts? The principles which we have drawn upon to address this issue in our study are those which are apparent in research on language education by Cummins (1989, 1998) and research on multicultural education by Sleeter and Grant (1994) and Banks (1995). Our framework is also informed by Roland Tharp's work on the "Five Standards for Effective Pedagogy," which guided much of the work of the Center for Research on Education, Diversity, and Excellence, which Tharp directed and of which this project was a part (Tharp, Estrada, Dalton, & Yamauchi, 2000).

First, Cummins' (1989) work is helpful in summarizing some important features of effective programs for linguistically and culturally diverse students. Drawing on an extensive review of the literature, he finds that effective programs have the following process characteristics: (a) allow for the development of students' native linguistic talents; (b) foster a sense of personal and cultural identity; (c) promote multiculturalism rather than assimilation; (d) employ materials relevant for minority students; (e) engage students in cooperative learning; (f) maintain high expectations for minority and white students; and (g) promote confidence in ability to learn.

Cummins is attentive to the need for students of color to have their histories and experiences confirmed by schools, rather than disconfirmed. What also makes Cummins' research distinctive is that he focuses on student empowerment through cultural pluralism, or the embracing of multiple cultures (Fillmore & Meyer, 1992). Because we believe these to be worthy goals of schooling, we are attentive to these issues in our research. However, the tenets that Cummins outlines are not just effective practices for students of color, but for all students.

These tenets are also evident in the work of researchers in multicultural education (Banks, 1995; Sleeter & Grant, 1994). Broadly stated, the term multicultural education is used to refer to "education policies and practices that recognize, accept, and affirm human differences and similarities related to gender, race, disability, class, and increasingly, sexual preference" (Sleeter & Grant, 1994, p. 167). Advocates of multicultural education believe that it should promote social justice and equity in the distribution of power among groups (Sleeter & Grant, 1994). For this to be accomplished, major school reform is required to establish a curriculum that reflects diverse perspectives, equitable teaching techniques, and a school culture that supports diversity (Banks, 1995). Cummins' (1989) recommendations regarding high expectations, valuing student backgrounds, and fostering cooperation and a positive self-concept are also found in the work of multicultural education researchers (e.g., Banks, 1995).

Finally, Tharp's principles for the effective education of at-risk students overlap considerably with these principles, but focus more directly on pedagogical strategies rooted in sociocultural theory (Tharp et al., 2000). In Tharp's work, we are able to find guidance of what we might look for at the classroom level in schools serving large numbers of linguistic and cultural minority students. Tharp characterizes effective classroom instruction as (a) facilitating learning through joint productive activity between teachers and students; (b) developing competence in the language and literacy of instruction throughout all instructional activities; (c) contextualizing teaching and curriculum in the experiences and skills of home and community; (d) challenging students toward cognitive complexity; and (e) engaging students through dialogue. We looked for examples of these as we observed in classrooms and interviewed teachers about their practice, and we were continually mindful of Tharp's argument that culturally compatible education improves the education of at-risk students. Taken together, these works guide us in assessing the workability and effectiveness of CSR models in multilingual, multicultural schools.

Method

This chapter draws upon data from the Scaling Up: School Restructuring in Multicultural, Multilingual Contexts Study, a research project which involved longitudinal case studies of 13 elementary schools in one culturally and linguistically diverse urban U.S. district ("Sunland County") over a four-year period from 1996 to 2000. (For a detailed description of the method of the entire study, see Stringfield, Datnow, Ross, & Snively, 1998). Table 1 includes descriptive data on each school in the sample.

Each of the schools was implementing a CSR model. The reform designs included three of the original New American Schools (NAS) models (Success for All/Roots and Wings, Modern Red Schoolhouse, and the Audrey Cohen College System of Education). Created by business leaders, NAS is a non-profit organization that has attempted to create large-scale reform by bringing a "menu" of school restructuring models to numerous partner districts (Kearns & Anderson, 1996; for a description of the NAS designs see Stringfield, Ross, & Smith, 1996). The schools we studied in Sunland also implemented three independent reform designs (not part of NAS) including the Core Knowledge Sequence, the Coalition of Essential Schools, and the Comer School Development Program (SDP). The appendix includes a brief description of each reform design. Our sample of 13 elementary schools involved two schools implementing each of the six re-

Table 1: Characteristics of School Sample

		Race/Ethnicity				Free-Lunch Status	LEP Status
	Size	Percent Afr. Am.	Percent Asian	Percent Latino	Percent White	Percent Eligible	Percent LEP
All Sunland County Elementary Schools	166,011	34	1	51	14	70.2	22.4
Success for All							
Mangrove	798	93	0	6	1	89	3
Nautilus	1,126	75	1	1	8	88	20
Orchid	1,411	72	3	18	8	86	19
Modern Red Schoolhouse							
Tupelo	1,025	11	1	71	17	79	37
Bay	609	2	1	71	26	29	18
Core Knowledge							
Cypress	1,188	1	1	91	7	72	33
Jetty	1,853	26	4	49	21	35	10
Audrey Cohen							
Key	885	1	1	79	18	46	22
Sawgrass	1,057	53	10	22	15	72	16
School Development Program							
Forest	950	11	2	77	9	88	44
Hibiscus	1,225	1	1	92	5	75	52
Coalition of Essential Schools							
Cedars	896	19	3	16	63	18	5
Limestone	946	7	4	52	37	30	14

forms, with the exception of Success for All, of which there were three schools in our sample.

These externally developed reform models array on a continuum from those which are geared more toward indigenous invention to those which are developed fully by the design teams. For instance, some models (e.g., Coalition of Essential Schools) are grounded in the belief that school reform should be locally developed, but offer guidance through the process and often a common set of principles or a model for schools to organize around. Other externally developed school restructuring designs (e.g., Success for All) take a more comprehensive approach, providing teachers with manuals, materials for students, training, and often also providing schools with implementation plans, suggested organizational structures, and governance models. A number of other external reforms (e.g., Core Knowledge) fall somewhere in between, providing some elements of a reform design, such as curriculum, but not all.

Our data collection for this study resulted in a total of over 300 interviews with school and district staff, union representatives, design team staff, parents, and students, as well as classroom and school observations. For this chapter, we carefully analyzed interview transcripts and drew upon the detailed case reports the research team had written on each school. To a more limited degree, we also drew upon field notes from classroom and school observations.

According to the case study methods of Yin (1989) and Miles and Huberman (1984) and the grounded theory approach of Strauss and Corbin (1990), data analysis proceeded following the theoretical propositions and research questions that led to the study. This process was facilitated by the fact that we had used the research by Tharp, Cummins, and others to develop interview questions and classroom observation queries, which noted the reforms' overall sensitivity to culturally and linguistically diverse students. For example, we asked questions such as "Do teachers employ a pedagogy that motivated students to use language to generate their own understandings?" and "Does the reform's curriculum foster a sense of personal and cultural identity?" and "What adaptations do teachers make to a reform to help it better suit their own learning needs or those of their students?" Asking questions which were aligned with our framework allowed for easy collapsing of data with code/question categories. The responses to these questions were subsequently synthesized into sections of school case reports which focused on these issues. After coding the data, we reduced the data within some codes to thematic categories to aid in within and cross-site analyses.

In the sections that follow, we first provide a description of the district and state context. We then proceed with a discussion of our findings on (a) how the reforms helped or hindered educators' efforts to address the linguistic needs of their student populations; (b) how the reforms helped or hindered schools' efforts to foster positive cultural identities for their students; and (c) how educators' social constructions of linguistically and culturally diverse students interacted with their perceptions of the reforms. In each of these sections, we point to examples from the schools we studied. We conclude with a summary of our findings and implications for policy, practice, and further research.

The District and State Context

Located in a sunbelt state, Sunland County Public Schools (SCPS) is one of the largest public school districts in the United States, serving more than 300,000 students. SCPS provides education to students from a richly diverse set of cultures and language groups. A significant number of the students are immigrants, and approximately 17 percent of the students speak English as a second language. The neighborhoods in the district include some of the wealthiest in the country and some of extreme poverty. Students reside primarily in urban communities, but some schools in the district serve students living in the suburbs.

In areas such as multicultural education, bilingual education, and site-based management, Sunland County schools has been at the forefront of educational innovation. When our study began in the 1995–1996 school year, Sunland County Public Schools' then-superintendent was very much in favor of promoting the use of externally developed reforms. His assistant superintendent was also a strong advocate for school reform and externally developed models. This leadership team brought the Comer School Development Program, Core Knowledge, and the Coalition of Essential Schools into the district in the early 1990s. In 1995, the district became one of the first NAS jurisdictions. Teams of educators from all district schools were invited to attend a "reform fair" and choose, or not choose, a reform design. In schools where 80 percent of the teachers voted to implement a NAS design, the district agreed to pay for teachers to be trained in the various designs, purchase materials for schools adopting NAS designs, and hire a full-time program facilitator for each school.

The district supported implementation of these reforms through their Office of Instructional Leadership. This office was staffed by regional directors to serve as "district liaisons" or as the connecting point between the schools and the various design teams. However, in late 1996, the district leadership changed dramatically, and agendas began to shift. The new school board and new superintendent's reform agendas were in the areas of school-to-work transitions, basic literacy, and ending social promotion. Externally developed reforms were no longer as well supported.

During the four-year period of our study, changes were also occurring rapidly at the state level, particularly in the areas of standards and accountability. First, in 1997–1998, the State expected all schools to teach to state curriculum standards in all subjects for grades kindergarten through grade 12. The state's high stakes accountability system also significantly increased in intensity in 1998, coinciding with the election of a new governor. These changing district and state leadership and policy contexts had a significant impact on the longevity of reform efforts in Sunland County, an issue which we take up in another paper (see Datnow, in press). In brief, at the end of our four-year study, five of the thirteen schools were still continuing to implement their reform designs with moderate to high levels of intensity. Reforms expired in six of the thirteen schools we studied; two other schools were still implementing reforms but at very low levels. While the turbulent district and state contexts were clearly a significant issue in the sustainability of reforms, as was how schools got into reforms in the first place (Datnow, 2000), the adaptability of the reforms to the multilingual, multicultural contexts was also an important factor, as we discuss below.

Linguistic Diversity and the Implementation of Comprehensive School Reforms

Most CSR models were not created with students who speak English as a second language in mind. Most of the reforms we studied did not include guidelines regarding the education of English language learners, though some design teams did offer assistance to educators in trying to best match the reform to their local demands. We found that educators in multilingual or bilingual schools had to make adaptations to almost all of the reforms in their schools, more successfully in some cases than in others. Not only did the extant needs of language minority students come into play, but also district and state policies with respect to limited English proficient (LEP) students.

Perhaps the most significant and successful adaptation to accommodate language diversity and foster students' native linguistic skills occurred at Cypress Elementary, a school implementing the Core Knowledge Sequence. The Core Knowledge Sequence is a list of topics and is not accompanied by materials or a teacher's manual. Rather, lesson plans are locally developed by teachers, thus allowing for substantial flexibility in methods of presentation. At this school, bilingual instruction of Core Knowledge topics in both Spanish and English enabled students to benefit from this curriculum reform, regardless of English language proficiency. Over 30 percent of the student population spoke English as a second language (ESL) and were mostly native Spanish speakers.

While the teachers at this school believed that this bilingual adaptation of Core Knowledge was successful, they had some difficulty finding age-appropriate materials on Core Knowledge topics in Spanish. Because of the demands required by teaching Core in both languages, the teachers elected not to teach all of the topics. Rather, they taught a selection of them. Meanwhile, the Core Knowledge Foundation suggests teaching all topics in the Sequence. It is notable that this school received a waiver to conduct two-way bilingual instruction, well known to be an effective approach for second language acquisition (Genessee, 1999), long before implementing Core Knowledge.

Another Core Knowledge school, Jetty Elementary, attempted to meet the needs of their LEP students through ESL instruction. Most of these students, who comprised 10 percent of the school population, were native Spanish speakers. One ESL teacher said that the ideas in Core were "way over the heads" of LEP students. Other teachers, however, believed that Core content could be easily adapted for LEP students using visuals, manipulatives, peer tutoring, and project-based learning. While the reform facilitator at this school did not see Core as explicitly enhancing the children's ability to speak their native language, she did think that the multicultural curriculum content gave students "a pride in their culture that would make them want to continue with their native language."

In general, this school's approach was to teach students to integrate fully into English as quickly as possible, and little instruction in the students' native language appeared to be provided. The reform did not explicitly or implicitly call this practice into question, nor was it necessarily in compliance with district and state regulations. The staff did not receive district or design team support in adapting Core to suit ESL requirements. Nevertheless, the school's practices were not, of course, consistent with Cummins' (1989) recommendation that students' native language abilities should be fostered. Most students reportedly exited self-contained ESL classes after kindergarten in this school and thereafter received pull-out ESL instruction. We also found that, consistent with prior research (Bascia & Jacka, 2000), the regular, non-ESL classroom teachers appeared to feel little responsibility to acquaint themselves with the cultural and linguistic background of their ESL students and instead saw them as the primary charge of the ESL teacher. ESL education and the needs of English language learners seemed to be a low priority in this school. An observation of an ESL classroom where much of the instruction of LEP students took place revealed a small room, crowded with over 30 students, and which lacked the resources of the regular classrooms.

While the two-way bilingual Core Knowledge program at Cypress was often held up in the district as an example of successful integration of a reform and bilingual education, another significant and apparently successful implementation of reform in a linguistically diverse context occurred at Hibiscus Elementary, a Comer SDP school. Over 50 percent of the school's students were classified as limited English proficient; the majority were native Spanish speakers. The Comer decision making process and principles were credited as leading to the development of a dual language program, an inclusion model for the instruction of LEP students, and a well functioning ESL committee. In the school-within-a-school dual language program, described by an administrator as "one of the biggest successes at Hibiscus," students were instructed half of the day in English and half of the day in Spanish. Elsewhere in the school, LEP students were encouraged to be fully integrated into the school, rather than separated in classes of their own. The principal explained, "We meet the needs of LEP children in the same way we meet the needs of everyone else in the school." The LEP committee focused on organizing the resources and support for LEP students to be successful in mainstream classes and to maintain their primary language skills.

Some other schools struggled to make reform adaptations to serve LEP students effectively, in some cases because of long-standing school practices and local policies. Teachers at Sawgrass Elementary, an Audrey Cohen school, felt that the design would be far more adaptable in a monolingual school, instead of the multilingual Haitian, Spanish, and English environment they were teaching in. They believed that the purpose-centered learning activities upon which the reform is based would be easier to present if all students understood English. A teacher at another school that implemented this reform, Keys Elementary, explained that since her first-grade students could not read in English, she read books to them, explaining the concepts in Spanish at times, and then writing the main points on the board for students to copy. However, there was little evidence that the students gained from this adaptation, and it seemed inconsistent with Cummins' (1989) call for maintaining high expectations for students and Tharp's (Tharp et al., 2000) suggestions for joint productive activity and opportunities for students to develop language competence.

The Audrey Cohen College design team was willing to make some adaptations to accommodate speakers of other languages, and local educators applauded their flexibility. In one case, a school-level facilitator for the reform called an Audrey Cohen College design representative to ask whether students could do the writing exercises in their home language. The design team representative said yes, emphatically stating that they wanted the children to be as comfortable as possible with the Audrey Cohen System. They allowed students to write in their "purpose record books" in their native language. However, the College did not provide any materials in Spanish or other languages other than English. This was because they reportedly believed that, "all students should be functional in English, the language of the business world," explained one principal.

The schools in Sunland that had the most difficulty adapting the reform to meet the needs of LEP students were schools that served a Haitian Creole population and were implementing Success for All (SFA). While SFA has a Spanish version of the program (hence, a significant LEP student accommodation), this was not helpful in the Sunland schools that served Haitian Creole students. Even so, the district's policies[1] prohibited reading instruction in students' native languages for as much time as SFA recommended (450 minutes weekly), and thus, the Spanish version, Éxito para Todos, could not be used in the schools with Spanish speakers. The SFA design team began working in collaboration with the district on an ESL adaptation specifically for Sunland County schools, but this significant effort took time and was only completed after some schools had attempted implementation of SFA for three years. The principal at Nautilus Elementary said, "It was like, going back and forth, and back and forth…and Hopkins said 'We're developing it. We're developing it. We're developing it.'" He was frustrated by the design team's inability to immediately respond to the needs of his school's population.

A second complication was that because the State required that LEP students be taught by ESL-certified teachers, the LEP students could not always be placed in reading groups according to level— a key component of the SFA program—as some teachers were not ESL-endorsed. Instead, the LEP students in the primary grades remained in self-contained classes that were heterogeneous by reading level. Another SFA school, Orchid Elementary, used this approach for several years and then eventually abandoned SFA in the ESL classrooms while continuing implementation in the rest of the school.

The principal at Nautilus permitted significant adaptations to SFA by ESL-certified teachers to adapt the SFA materials and strategies for use with their LEP students. The teachers rewrote some materials and replaced some of the SFA vocabulary with words that may have been more familiar to students. For example, the principal explained:

> Our teachers are writing their own Treasure Hunts. But they also modify it because ESL is an oral language development program and Roots and Wings is a reading pro-

gram. Certain parts of it you can do, and other parts you have to say, "Okay, I have to put this down and go with the ESL strategies." When a child moves in and out of the classroom to the resource room we want there to be some continuity.

He explained that an adaptation his school made to suit SFA to the needs of LEP students was to change the pacing: "When you're supposed to do a lesson in three days, it could take up to five." Teachers also occasionally dropped the SFA lesson plans in favor of using ESL strategies for oral language development. While developing oral language skills was a potentially positive adaptation, we found that the SFA curriculum was often significantly diluted for LEP students, again a school-level adaptation not in keeping with calls for high expectations made by Banks (1995) and Cummins (1989, 1998).

These complications notwithstanding, in numerous cases, some teachers saw the SFA pedagogical strategies and curriculum as very helpful for LEP students. One teacher at Mangrove Elementary thought that the program was helpful for LEP students because it gave students many opportunities to communicate with each other and with the teacher. Another teacher added: "In this program it is okay to have a classmate help you, and I like that. ESL kids need that." A teacher at another SFA school, Orchid Elementary, believed that SFA's focus on phonics was a major boost in improving the reading skills of English language learners.

Teachers in other schools also saw the various reforms as increasing opportunities to learn for LEP students' learning. One teacher at an Audrey Cohen school explained that the reform introduced a sort of universal language to many of their students who didn't speak English and thus enhanced her ability to meet LEP students' needs:

> Audrey Cohen was one of the few things that they could all do, because when we were speaking about safety, they could all participate. Some could write, some could draw, they would work in cooperative groups, so they felt successful. At least that's what happened in my room....It was something that they enjoyed, and they grew from it because it brought in a lot of vocabulary for these children.

On the other hand, another teacher said it was hard to expose these students to those unfamiliar words or "jargon" in the reform's materials or curriculum. Yet, she saw this as mainly a failing of the students, "who weren't getting it at home," rather than of the reform.

Teachers at several schools complained that because the district and state ESL policies meant that students were pulled out of class for ESL instruction, they were absent from regular classroom activities related to the reform. For example, at Tupelo Elementary, a school that was implementing the Modern Red Schoolhouse reform design for a brief time, teachers also told us that because LEP students were pulled out for instruction, they missed the content that was reflective of the reform. Teachers at this school also talked about feeling constrained by policies regarding ESL instruction, arguing that these laws inhibited the implementation of their restructuring design: "The whole idea of the Modern Red Schoolhouse is that you can play around with your classes. And Sunland County said [according to State law], 'no, you can't do this.' It was kind of squelched." Again, the need for LEP students to be instructed by ESL certified teachers, while an important equity safeguard, posed a constraint for reform implementation.

Irrespective of the constraints of a reform, not all schools appeared to fully comply with the district's home language instruction rule, as this depended on the availability of instructors in a student's home language and the number of students in a given school who needed to be served. For example, at one Coalition school, there were only a few students who spoke Urdu in a class of native Spanish speakers. We observed them learning Spanish during their home language instruction time instead of Urdu. The district faced a shortage of certified Urdu instructors who generally visited the school only every two weeks.

Cultural Diversity and the Implementation of CSR Models

The schools we studied were characterized by rich ethno-cultural diversity, serving students from Caribbean, Mexican, Central and South American, Cuban, Middle Eastern, Asian, Anglo, African-American, Haitian, and Spanish heritages, among others. Some schools served ethnically mixed populations, whereas as others served a predominance of one ethnic group. In either case, there was often significant diversity in the cultural or ethnic as well as immigrant backgrounds within each group.

In a number of cases, educators believed that their school's chosen reform design helped them to better affirm students' cultural backgrounds and promote multiculturalism in their schools. For example, an educator at Forest Elementary, a school implementing the Comer model, which is intended to address the developmental needs of children, explained that the reform has helped them become more sensitive to diverse family backgrounds:

> We are very sensitized to the families and we are learning more about their culture and understanding more and more why the parents and the children act the way they do. We have a significant Haitian population and their views on education are very different from our views or the Hispanic views.

The teachers also stated that Comer's unstructured nature allowed them to be more sensitive to various cultures in their curriculum: "The program allows us a lot of flexibility in the classroom," said one teacher, "so it allows us to bring more of a cultural awareness to the other children."

Similarly, at Hibiscus Elementary, another Comer school, teachers agreed that the Comer focus on the "whole child" made them more aware of their students' cultural and family backgrounds. As one teacher explained, the school celebrated cultural diversity through various classroom and school activities: "We had a parade in which the kids carried their country's flag. There were about fifty different countries. We also made cookbooks that the kids put together that incorporated some of their backgrounds." It is unclear how much of these activities were specifically a result of the Comer reform or whether they would have occurred anyway.

Educators at Hibiscus also saw the Comer reform as a way to break down racial barriers among students. The staff believed that the Comer philosophy promoted inclusion by encouraging children to focus on the similarities rather than the differences between races. "We always tell the kids we are a family," explained one teacher. Another teacher added: "What you don't see at Hibiscus is Hispanics hanging out just with other Hispanics and the Blacks with the Blacks and the Anglos with the Anglos. I mean we're friends with everyone." In general, there was a great deal of evidence that this school was attending to the needs of their culturally and linguistically diverse student population in positive ways. This may be attributable to the reform or to the philosophies of the staff themselves.

At the two schools that implemented Core Knowledge, educators overwhelmingly believed in the ability of the reform to effectively serve a multicultural population, though there were a small number of differing opinions. At Jetty, the student population was described by a staff member as "a multi-ethnic community, we are Hispanic, we are Anglo, we are Black…and just everything else under the sun." One educator believed that no multicultural adaptations were necessary for Core Knowledge because

> Core is a truly multicultural program the way it is written. Core gives everyone a sense of history about their own culture….For example, it goes back to the Middle African kingdoms and shows African American children that there is a rich culture that they came from that had a highly developed civilization….It gives them a pride in who they are….I mean, they are actually a thread in history. They're not somebody plopped down in February because it's Black History Month.

Another teacher described Core Knowledge as a "rounded curriculum where the kids learn about Central America and South America." However, one ESL teacher, expressing a minority opinion, said she would like to see more emphasis on cultural diversity in the Core curriculum: "In Sunland County we're supposed to be covering African American history and Hispanic heritage, but Core doesn't really address any of this. In Core, we just have one or two culturally diverse people mentioned and that's it." She said she approached the director of the Core Knowledge Foundation about this concern, and he explained that Core was only supposed to comprise a part of the curriculum, leaving time for the inclusion of a multicultural curriculum. On the other hand, the reform facilitator at the school argued that "E.D. Hirsch and the Core Knowledge Foundation have definitely tried to make it equitable to all cultures." Teachers at Cypress Elementary incorporated a Native American novel into their curriculum, and they praised Core Knowledge as a reform that allowed for such additions. Meanwhile, some teachers we interviewed viewed the curriculum as fairly static and did not see themselves as changing it in any way to adapt to new ethnic populations of students that might be coming to the school: "We'll continue teaching Core the way we did last year or the year before."

By and large, teachers in schools that implemented Success for All saw the SFA curriculum materials as up-to-date and representing students of diverse racial and ethnic backgrounds. As one teacher at Orchid Elementary explained, "That is the positive aspect of the program, that it is not based on Sally and Dick or always a white Anglo-Saxon child." Another teacher added: "Even the basal that they chose is really good…is excellent….Every story has a multicultural connection." On the other hand, one teacher felt constrained by the strict pace of the SFA lesson plan which she felt did not allow time to delve into a particular issue involving the diversity of her student population. Another teacher spoke of feeling like she was "sneaking in" activities such as bringing in chopsticks when the class was reading a story on China because she was told, "You're on Day 1, you do Day 1." The educators at this school saw themselves as celebrating cultural diversity and noted the activities of the "multicultural committee," which included Black History Month, Spanish Heritage Month, and Haitian Creole activities. These activities were not connected to SFA, and in general, reflected the school's cultural celebration orientation to the issue of multicultural education rather than an orientation that acknowledged cultural bias and social justice goals (Banks, 1995).

Social Construction of Ability, Race, and Language

In some cases, how teachers saw the multicultural, multilingual students in their schools influenced whether they saw the reform as workable in their contexts, as well as whether they more generally created an environment that was supportive of the education of culturally and linguistically diverse students. First, we found several examples of how the social construction of minority, immigrant students as low ability and lacking in basic skills served as a constraint in both educators' initial receptiveness to reform designs as well as in their subsequent implementation of them. The constraints that operated as a result of educators' constructions of student ability connected to language background, race, and culture were not unique to a particular school, or to a particular reform.

For example, a teacher at Keys Elementary, a school that worked with the Audrey Cohen College System of Education, found that the design was difficult to implement because, as one teacher stated, "the students are not high. They don't have high abilities. They come from second languages and they need a lot of basic drilling. They lack a lot of skills they need in order to do Audrey Cohen well." According to some teachers at this school, not only did students lack the innate abilities to do well with the reform's Purpose Centered System of Education, but they also came from a culture that did not ready them for taking responsibility for their own learning. Speaking from her own experience as a Hispanic, one teacher explained,

> They [the Hispanic students] need to take charge....They're not used to it. So we had a doubly hard time....I saw it in those kids that were American. They did do better. Right away they came up with something

for a lesson on inventions. Her view was applied to all Hispanic children, whether they were born in the U.S. or not, "because it comes with their culture."

Reinforcing this finding from another angle, the reform facilitator at this school argued that the program worked particularly well with gifted students, "who see beyond where they are now....They're the ones that read something in the paper and they worry about it.... And I don't find that to be typical with the other students." The comments by these educators reveal beliefs in intelligence or ability as a fixed entity and as innate, not as skills that were malleable through engagement in new types of learning activities. These beliefs in the importance of ability rather than effort led them to have little faith in the reform design.

Teachers at another Audrey Cohen school lamented that it was difficult to implement a reform that went beyond basic skills because the low income Caribbean, Hispanic, and Jamaican immigrant students in the school "have not been to the fire department, the zoo, to the library. They haven't been anywhere. They know nothing. They have no prior knowledge....They can't brainstorm because they have nothing to talk about. It's sad. But that's what we need. We need some kind of program that goes back to basics, phonics." It was quite clear that these harmful attitudes predated the reform and served as barriers to its successful implementation.

Even in schools that appeared to be generally inclusive and respectful of diverse cultures and languages, there was still evidence of some teachers' adherence to a belief in a racial or cultural hierarchy, where the majority culture was most highly valued. The following comment by a teacher in a Comer school is one example of this:

> When you are teaching something, for example, Thanksgiving, it's interesting to see how they celebrate Thanksgiving. And then at the same time you can introduce them to American traditions and customs. Students then understand that it's okay to share what you did in your country, but it's also important to know what the traditions and customs of this country are because they are now being a participant in this country.

One teacher spoke of parents who were "just coming off the boat" and the school's family center—a feature of their Comer implementation–as helping these parents. While the intent of the family center was certainly positive, it seems that more cultural sensitivity and respect could be used in describing the families served.

We were fortunate to find some counter examples in Sunland, as well. In some schools serving populations that were similarly comprised of low-income immigrant students of color, educators celebrated students' backgrounds and saw them as the building blocks of the reform. Educators at one Comer school explained that the Comer philosophy "helps us see the child as an individual. And we look for their strengths instead of weaknesses."

In the case of Cedars Elementary, involvement with the Coalition reform caused the principal to consider equity issues arising in the varied educational experiences of white students who comprised the majority and those of Hispanic and Black students. However, she had not yet succeeded in making these issues an imperative for the staff. The challenge to the principal was getting teachers to "walk the talk" of the Coalition even when classroom doors closed:

> There are some of us who see we need to do something differently. We have minority students in the building that need to be addressed and how to deal with their needs. If we change and continue to change…we need to look at our minority students, be they Hispanic or black.

Although the black students reportedly scored better at Cedars than black students attending schools elsewhere in Sunland County (who tended to be lower income), the achievement gap between black and white students troubled the principal, and she hoped to effect changes to address it.

We also found cases of teachers who defended the assets of culturally and linguistically diverse families in front of their colleagues. For example, at one Success for All school, a teacher in a focus group proclaimed that, "ESL parents tend to be very good....Usually parents who are new to the country want the best for their kids...." This was in response to another teacher's belief that ESL parents were less involved with the school.

In numerous schools, we also observed teachers holding high expectations of students' learning. The following serve as two examples: At Cypress Elementary, we observed teachers asking higher order math and science questions (e.g., "Just what is multiplication? How would you define what you're doing when you multiply?") and eliciting sophisticated student writing, in both Spanish and English (e.g., descriptive paragraphs following a literary model). This meets the "Complex Thinking" standard outlined in Tharp's Five Standards for Effective Pedagogy (Tharp et al., 2000). Similarly, at Hibiscus Elementary, classroom observations revealed positive attitudes by teachers and pedagogical strategies that tended to promote confidence in all students' ability to learn. Often activities were those in which all students could have been successful, regardless of their English language fluency or American acculturation. Students were encouraged to participate in discussions and to share and express their views.

Conclusion and Implications

The findings of this study reveal that implementing comprehensive school reform models in multilingual, multicultural school contexts can be both a rewarding and challenging enterprise—and this is likely precisely why Roland Tharp thought this would be an important research project. School reform can lead to a redefinition of "school" as a place where all teachers and students are engaged in continual learning (Tharp & Gallimore, 1988), or it can fail to change business as usual. Whether or not this occurred in the schools in our study was in part dependent on whether the reforms were adaptable to local contextual needs—and whether the schools exhibited a capacity for continual learning in the first place.

On a practical level, were the reforms adaptable to students' linguistic needs? Some schools found successful ways to use the reforms as vehicles to enhance the education of LEP students, or at least found ways to offer a quality bilingual education program in concert with a reform. In other cases, it appeared that a particular reform had little impact on a school's language acquisition program, which was usually not very effective to begin with. With the exception of Success for All, seldom did reform design teams provide more than limited guidance in adapting the reforms to multilingual or bilingual school settings. Most of the challenges arose in adapting reforms to suit the educational needs of English language learners and the policies regarding their instruction, particularly when reforms called for significant changes in teaching and learning or the organization of schooling.

The molding of reforms fit the linguistic diversity of school populations is a significant issue, as the demand for change and the number of limited English proficient students continues to grow, in both urban and rural areas. What makes these matters all the more tricky are the differences of opinion that surround bilingual education and how best to teach second language learners. Reform models, which bring their own theories about language, can conflict with local educators' beliefs about what is best for children. These issues become even more heated when they reach political levels outside the school, as often occurs regarding language diversity.

Were the reforms "culturally compatible," as Tharp might ask? Our data suggest that reforms were more easily accommodated to the cultural rather than the linguistic diversity of the student populations served by the schools. In some cases, the reforms allowed enough flexibility for educators to meet their own goals of multicultural education, if they had them. Materials or curriculum associated with most of the reform models, where provided, tended to be seen as reflecting diverse cultures—though we noticed that they were not always the cultures served by a particular school. In some cases, educators saw the reforms as helping them celebrate diversity, whereas in others, educators had difficulty seeing the connections between the reforms and multicultural education. Disappointingly, many of the educators we spoke with did not see multicultural education as more than a simple commitment to appreciating all cultures. Their chosen reforms did not push them (or they did not use them) to look at multicultural education as an overhaul of the schooling process—one that would involve changes in belief systems, school organization, curriculum, instruction, and expectations to ensure that students from diverse racial, ethnic, gender, and socioeconomic groups would experience educational equality (Banks, 1995).

Regarding the social construction of ability, race, and language, we found educators with two types of basic beliefs: One group of educators felt that the reforms did not fit their schools well because they did not "fix" the primary problems of the low-income, immigrant, language minority students they served. A second group believed student success could be nurtured. Educators in this latter category saw their chosen reform designs as in fact helping them better understand or value the cultures of children in their communities. These attitudes caused them to embrace, rather than resist, the reform. Both sets of attitudes point to the influence of social constructions of student achievement as applied differentially to students of diverse backgrounds (Oakes, Wells, Jones, & Datnow, 1997). As all of these illustrations reveal, educational reform requires behavioral and cultural change as well as organizational rearrangements. Unfortunately, prevailing attitudes about race, language, and ability, prevalent in schools and also in the larger society, were often not confronted when schools implemented reforms.

In conclusion, with respect to the education of culturally and linguistically diverse students, what often needs to change goes beyond curriculum or pedagogy. There is a need to challenge broader social constructs of ability, race, and language in order to provide improved educational opportunities for immigrant or minority students. As Tharp and Gallimore (1988) remind us, "the larger society is the context that hatches the activity setting of classrooms, but it is classrooms that produce the problem-solving styles and discourse meanings that prepare new citizens to operate in mature society" (p. 275). Comprehensive school reform models could take leadership in providing forums for inquiry around these issues (and indeed some do attempt this, such as the Coalition of Essential Schools). Equity and multiculturalism need to be explicit goals of reform efforts for them to be realized. Moreover, policymakers need to support these goals and provide resources and technical assistance in order to help achieve them in concert with externally developed reforms. This imperative will become more urgent as the demographic reality of cultural and linguistic diversity reaches more and more schools, as current trends indicate will happen. Multicultural education will then no longer be seen as a fringe extra or merely as a way to improve minority or immigrant student self-esteem, but as a practical method of fostering cooperation among members of society.

Appendix
Description of Comprehensive School Reform Models*

I. New American Schools

The Audrey Cohen College System of Education	*Developer:* Audrey Cohen College, New York. *Primary goal:* Development of scholarship and leadership abilities using knowledge and skills to benefit students' community and larger world. *Main features:* 1. Student learning focused on complex and meaningful purposes 2. Students use what they learn to reach specific goals 3. Curriculum focused on Constructive Actions (individual or group projects that serve the community) 4. Classes structured around five dimensions (e.g., Self and Others, Values, etc.) that incorporate core subjects For grades K–12. Materials and training provided.
The Modern Red Schoolhouse	*Developer:* The Modern Red Schoolhouse Institute, Nashville. *Primary goal:* To combine the rigor and values of little red schoolhouse with latest classroom innovations. *Main features:* 1. Challenging curriculum (Core Knowledge recommended in K–6) 2. High standards for all students 3. Emphasis on character 4. Integral role of technology 5. Individual education compact for each student For grades K–12. Some materials and training provided.

Table continued on next page.

Success for All/Roots and Wings	*Developer:* Robert Slavin, Nancy Madden, and a team of developers from Johns Hopkins University. Now based at the Success for All Foundation in Baltimore. *Primary goal:* To guarantee that every child will learn to read. *Main features:* 1. Research-based, prescribed curriculum in the areas of reading, writing, and language arts. 2. One-to-one tutoring; family support team; cooperative learning; on-site facilitator; and building advisory team. For grades K–6. Mostly all materials provided. Training required.
II. Independent	
Core Knowledge	*Developer:* E. D. Hirsch, Jr. (University of Virginia) and the Core Knowledge Foundation, Charlottesville, VA. *Primary goal:* To help students establish a strong foundation of core knowledge for higher levels of learning. *Main features:* 1. Sequential program of specific grade-by-grade topics for core subjects; the rest of curriculum (approximately half) is left for schools to design. 2. Instructional methods (to teach core topics) are designed by individual teachers/schools. For grades K–8. Curriculum guidelines provided. Training available but not required.
Coalition of Essential Schools	*Developer:* Ted Sizer, Brown University, Providence, RI. Now based in Oakland, CA. *Primary goal:* To help create schools where students learn to use their minds well.

Table continued on next page.

Main features:

1. Set of Ten Common Principles upon which schools base their practice
2. Personalized learning
3. Mastery of a few essential subjects and skills
4. Graduation by exhibition
5. Sense of community
6. Instruction and organization depend on how each school interprets the Common Principles (may involve interdisciplinary instruction, authentic projects, etc.)

For grades K–12. No materials. Range of training options mostly provided by regional centers.

Corner School Development Program	*Developer:* James Comer, Yale University, New Haven, CT. *Primary goal:* To mobilize entire community of adult caretakers to support students' holistic development to bring about academic success. *Main features:* 1. Three teams (school planning and management team, student and staff support team, parent team) 2. Three operations (comprehensive school plan, staff development plan, monitoring and assessment) 3. Three guiding principles (no-fault, consensus, collaboration) For grades K–12. Training and manual with materials.

This table draws information from *The Catalog of School Reform Models: First Edition.* Oak Brook, Illinois: Northwest Regional Educational Laboratory. http://www.nwrel.org/scpd/natspec/catalog.

Notes

The work reported herein was supported under the Educational Research and Development Centers Program, PR/Award Number R306A60001, as administered by the Office of Educational Research and Improvement, U.S. Department of Education. However, the contents do not necessarily represent the positions or policies of the National Institute on the Education of At-Risk Students, the Office of Educational Research and Improvement, or the U. S. Department of Education, and you should not assume endorsement by the Federal Government. We wish to thank the participants of the research study and our numerous colleagues at Johns Hopkins University and the University of Memphis who assisted with data collection and analysis. We also express our appreciate to Lindsay Travers and Mandira Raksit at the Ontario Institute for Studies in Education for their research assistance on this chapter. Please address correspondence to Amanda Datnow at datnow@usc.edu.

1. In Sundland County, the district provides basic subject area instruction in the home language (in 12 different languages) to ESL levels 1 and 2 for a period not to exceed 50 percent of the instructional time in the basic subject areas and language arts instruction in students' home languages for 150 minutes weekly. The rest of the basic subject area instruction is provided in English using ESL strategies.

References

Banks, J. A. (1995). Multicultural education: Historical development, dimensions, and practice. In J. A. Banks & C. A. McGee-Banks (Eds.), *Handbook of Research on Multicultural Education*. New York: Simon and Shuster Macmillan. pp. 3–24.

Bascia, N., & Jacka, N. (2000). *When every teacher is an ESL teacher (not)*. Paper presented at the annual meeting of the American Educational Research Association, New Orleans.

Borman, G., Hewes, G., Overman, L., & Brown, S. (2002). *Comprehensive School Reform and student achievement: A meta-analysis*. Baltimore, MD: Johns Hopkins University, Center for Research on the Education of Students Placed At Risk.

Cummins, J. (1989). *Empowering minority students*. Sacramento: California Association of Bilingual Education.

Cummins, J. (1998). Language issues and educational change. In E. Hargreaves, A. Lieberman, M. Fullan, & D. Hopkins (Eds.), *International Handbook of Educational Change*. London: Kluwer. pp. 440–459.

Datnow, A. (in press). The sustainability of externally developed reforms in changing district and state contexts. *Educational Administration Quarterly*.

Datnow, A. (2000). Power and politics in the adoption of school reform models. *Educational Evaluation and Policy Analysis, 22*(4), 357–374.

Elmore, R. E. (1996). Getting to scale with good educational practice. *Harvard Educational Review, 66*(1), 1–26.

Fillmore, L. W., & Meyer, L. M. (1992). The curriculum and linguistic minorities. In P. W. Jackson (Ed.), *Handbook of research on curriculum* (pp. 626–658). New York: Macmillan.

Fullan, M. (1999). *Change forces: The sequel.* London: Falmer Press.

Genessee, F. (Ed.) (1999). *Program alternatives for linguistically diverse students.* Educational practice report no. 1. Santa Cruz, CA: Center for Research on Education, Diversity, and Excellence.

Hargreaves, A., & Fink, D. (2000). Three dimensions of educational reform. *Educational Leadership, 57*(7), 30–34.

Herman, R., Aladjem, D., McMahon, P., Masem, E., Mulligan, I., O'Malley, A., Quinones, S., Reeve, A., & Woodruff, D. (1999). *An educators' guide to schoolwide reform.* Washington, DC: American Institutes for Research.

Kearns, D. T., & Anderson, J. L. (1996). Sharing the vision: Creating new American schools. In S. Stringfield, S. M. Ross, & L. Smith (Eds.) *Bold plans for school restructuring: The New American Schools designs* (pp. 9–23). Mahwah, NJ: Erlbaum.

Miles, M., & Huberman, M. (1984). *Qualitative data analysis.* Beverly Hills, CA: Sage Publications.

Oakes, J. (1993). *New standards and disadvantaged schools.* Background paper prepared for research forum on Effects of New Standards and Assessments on High Risk Students and Disadvantaged Schools. Cambridge, MA: Harvard University.

Oakes, J., Wells, A. S., Jones, M., & Datnow, A. (1997). Detracking: The social construction of ability, cultural politics, and resistance to reform. *Teachers College Record, 98*(3), 482–510.

Slavin, R. E., & Fashola, O. (1998). *Show me the evidence!* Thousand Oaks, CA: Corwin.

Slavin, R. E., & Madden, N. A. (1998). *Disseminating Success for All: Lessons for policy and practice, Revised technical report.* Baltimore, MD: Center for Research on the Education of Students Placed at Risk, Johns Hopkins University.

Slavin, R., & Madden, N. (1999). Effects of bilingual and second language adaptations of Success for All on the reading achievement of students acquiring English. *Journal of Education for Students Placed At Risk, 4*(4), 393–416.

Sleeter, C., & Grant, C. (1994). *Making choices for multicultural education.* New York: Macmillan.

Strauss, A., & Corbin, J. (1990). *Basics of qualitative research: Grounded theory procedures and techniques.* Newbury Park, CA: Sage.

Stringfield, S., Datnow, A., Ross, S., & Snively, F. (1998). Scaling up school restructuring in multicultural, multilingual contexts. *Education and urban society, 30*(3), 326–357.

Stringfield, S., Millsap, M., Yoder, N., Schaffer, E., Nesselrodt, P., Gamse, B., Brigham, N., Moss, M., Herman, R., & Bedinger, S. (1997). *Special strategies studies final report.* Washington, DC: U.S. Department of Education.

Stringfield, S., Ross, S., & Smith, L. (Eds.). (1996). *Bold plans for school restructuring: The New American Schools Development Corporation models.* Mahwah, NJ: Lawrence Erlbaum.

Tharp, R. G., Estrada, P., Dalton, S. S., & Yamauchi, L. A. (2000). *Teaching transformed: Achieving excellence, fairness, inclusion and harmony.* Boulder, CO: Westview Press.

Tharp, R., & Gallimore, R. (1998). *Rousing minds to life: Teaching, learning, and schooling in social context.* New York: Cambridge University Press.

U.S. Department of Education. (2000). Guidance on the Comprehensive School Reform Demonstration Program. Retrieved June 7, 2004 from http://www.ed.gov/programs/compreform/guidance/page_pg5.html?exp=0.

Yin, R. (1989). *Case study research.* Beverly Hills, CA: Sage Publications.

SECTION IV

Conclusion

Lois A. Yamauchi
Clifford R. O'Donnell

Editors

CHAPTER 10

Behavior Change in the Natural Environment: Everyday Activity Settings as a Workshop of Change

Ronald Gallimore

> The "treater" is rarely a psychiatrist or psychologist or social worker, but is rather the individual's parent or teacher or spouse or ward attendant or sibling or friend or employer....If the environment [setting of the intervention] is the hospital, these people are the nurses, doctors, or other patients; if...the school, they are the principal, teachers, or other pupils; if...the family, they are siblings, the spouse, or the parents.
>
> The traditional alternative is build a "new and artificial relationship" between the "treater" and the individual....This procedure is patently wasteful, if there is indeed an alternative form of intervention which mobilizes the potential power of [an individual's existing social relationships]....(Tharp & Wetzel, 1969, pp. 3–4)

Tharp and Wetzel's *Behavior Modification in the Natural Environment* crystallized new ideas and practices emerging in the helping professions. One of a handful that influenced a generation of psychologists (e.g., Bandura, 1969; Mischel, 1968), their book presented and illustrated a behavior change paradigm sharply contrasted to prevailing practice: The "natural environment" for Tharp and Wetzel included two components: (a) Interactions within existing social relationships, and (b) the *settings* in which those relationships were situated. Settings are recurring events in individuals' daily routines in which two or more people interacted around some joint activity; settings are found in families, schools, hospitals, jails, and other contexts to which an individual might have a connection or an occasion to occupy. Tharp and Wetzel argued that any setting in the natural environment, even a pool-hall (MacDonald, Gallimore, & MacDonald, 1970), sustains social relationships that might be mobilized for behavior change (see Evans, this volume, for additional discussion of this contribution and O'Donnell, this volume, for its influence on mentoring and delinquency prevention programs).

These were powerful ideas in the 1960s, and they remain generative five decades later. Originally, natural environment applications attended mainly to the particulars of interactions that occurred within settings. For example, reinforcement contingencies, modeling, instructing, and other means of behavior influence observed in existing social relationships and how they might be modified (Tharp & Gallimore, 1988). With increasing experience and research in natural settings, the importance of setting factors surrounding interactions became clear.

This chapter focuses on the aspects of *settings* in the natural environment which receive and host behavior change interventions. After a brief history of natural environment-situated interventions, there is a review of several conceptualizations of settings, why settings are resistant to change, and some propositions for changing natural environment settings to change behavior possibly worthy of more investigation.

A Little History

Intentional efforts to change behavior is as old as human history. The Romans employed contingencies to discourage unwanted behavior—execution by wild beasts, among others. This practice was gradually abandoned during Medieval times in favor of other approaches, such as bonfires to extinguish heresy. In the more enlightened times that followed, non-fatal dunking and bleeding were sometimes used to discourage non-normative behavior. Evangelism emerged in the late 18th and early 19th centuries that discouraged anti-social behavior with emotionally charged sermons on the wages of sin (Thompson, 1966). By the 19th century, hypnotism, magnetism, electricity, and catharsis, among other notions, came into vogue heralding the rise of several behavior change professions. Updated versions of some pioneering methods remain in the armamentaria of contemporary practitioners.

For the first half of the 20th century, psychotherapy in its several forms dominated behavior change theory, research, and practice. Patients visited the therapist's office, something almost never reciprocated. Facilities built in this era were often a rabbit-warren of tiny offices to afford as many individual sessions as possible. Lacking such a private office was equivalent to being excluded from the status of professional behavior changer.

The idea of working in the community did not spring full grown in a single moment. Earlier in the century, the idea of expanding practice to include community-interventions had emerged. However, there was little attention to the existing web of social relations used by to such good effect by Tharp and Wetzel (1969). Consider the Cambridge-Somerville Youth Study (Powers & Witmer,

1951) which assumed that trained professionals delivered intervention to the individuals following the then current and still widely used model (Roberts, this volume). Conceived in 1935 by the visionary Richard Clark Cabot, it was the first systematically conducted and evaluated "psychological intervention" in the natural environment. Matched-pairs of "troubled" and average boys in factory-dominated neighborhoods were randomly assigned to either a treatment or untreated group. For an average of 5 years, the treatment group received bi-weekly visits by social workers for counseling and assistance with family problems. Treatment group boys also received, in varying degrees, tutoring, access to social and community programs, and medical and psychiatric attention. The untreated group provided information to the researchers, but received no assistance.

In a follow-up conducted 30 years later, McCord (1978) compared the two treated and untreated groups on 57 outcome measures. On none of the outcomes did the treated group fare better than the untreated group. However, for 7 of the 57 the *untreated* group had statistically significant better outcomes than the treated group. For example, untreated men were less likely to have committed two or more crimes, less likely to suffer alcoholism, and exhibited fewer signs of serious mental illness.

McCord (1978) speculated that "interactions with adults whose values are different from those of the family milieu may produce later internal conflicts" (p. 288). In other words, it is possible that an unintended and negative effect of treatment was alienation from families and communities. In the 1930s no one in the Cambridge-Somerville Project assessed the participants' social environments well enough to directly test the validity of McCord's speculation.

Inattention to context began to change roughly five decades ago when disciplines that study, plan, and conduct intentional behavior change visibly broadened their perspective. A milestone event was the *1965 Swampscott Conference on the Education of Psychologists for Community Mental Health*, which is considered by many to be the "founding moment" for the field of community psychology (Merritt, Greene, Jopp, & Kelly, 1998). This shift was also pushed along by developments in psychological theory and research, for example, Mischel's (1968) argument that clinical psychology had been too preoccupied with internal states and traits and had ignored powerful environmental and contextual effects. Mischel's and other contributions (e.g., Bandura, 1969; Staats, 1968; Tharp & Wetzel, 1969) speeded the shift from a preoccupation with internal psychodynamics to a more balanced view of the impact of environments and social interactions. Talk therapy was out. Culturally aware, community behavioral interventions were in.

Behavior Modification in the Natural Environment (Tharp & Wetzel, 1969) included a chapter entitled "Resistances," an intentionally ironical choice since the authors were challenging the psychodynamic model. But resistances in this case referred not only to individual psychological defenses but also to cultural, institutional, familial, and interpersonal barriers to behavior change. To their great credit, Tharp and Wetzel reported in detail cases in which their intervention failed. The resistances described foreshadowed some of the most important ideas that have developed about the impact of settings on behavior, and on attempts to change behavior.

One of these important ideas is traced by O'Donnell (this volume). He documents how an early delinquency prevention program based on the work of Tharp and Wetzel, the Buddy System, contributed to an increase in delinquency among some youth in the program. Research on this iatrogenic effect in prevention programs led O'Donnell to propose a peer network model to show how family, school, and neighborhood relationships and settings influence the type of peer networks that youth form and how they affect delinquency.

Where the designers of the 1930s Cambridge-Somerville project might have neglected to take context into account, by the 1960s the research and practice communities began to recognize the benefits of doing so. As other chapters in this volume so clearly document, consideration of the everyday "settings" of interaction and activity is now commonplace. The era that opened with the publication of *Behavior Modification in the Natural Environment* might properly be called "The Age of Context."

Conceptualizing Settings

Ecological Factors

Using a meticulous system to record child activities throughout a single day, Barker and Wright (1951) demonstrated that individuals exhibited predictable behaviors within settings; individual behavior showed more variation across than within settings. In the fifteen years after Barker and Wright's study, evidence accumulated that variability across settings of an individual's behavior was more likely than consistency (Mischel, 1968). The implication was clear. It might not work very well to "treat" individuals in an office and hope that any behavior changes secured would automatically generalize across all the settings in their natural environments. Perhaps the settings themselves should be examined for their effects on behavior.

Settings of everyday life are constructed and work to elicit and maintain adaptive and normative behaviors. Distal and proximal ecological factors are powerful constraints on and enablers of what settings are constructed and sustained, and thereby on what behaviors are observed, just as Barker reported (LeVine, 1977; Super & Harkness, 1986; Weisner, 1984, 1998; Whiting & Edwards, 1988). Health or safety factors can influence routines, e.g., in neighborhoods where children must be protected from violence, racial discrimination and other urban ills. Transportation and communication required for work or other health, safety, and support requirements are additional features shaping routines, as are the number and complexity of domestic chores, including childcare (Whiting & Edwards, 1988; Wishart, Bidder, & Gray, 1981), and the costs and benefits of social support networks (Beresford, 1994a).

For example, ecological effects may be exaggerated for families accommodating children with developmental and behavioral problems: when delivery of treatments require parents to juggle work and transportation demands, or locate a durable setting in which to provide prescribed activities (Gallimore, Bernheimer, & Weisner, 1999; Gallimore, Keogh, & Bernheimer, 1999). In other words, no matter how powerful therapies might be, the odds of producing highly generalized behavior changes are not great if they run counter to the press of everyday settings. Interventions are much more likely to be sustained if they are woven into the fabric of everyday life (Bernheimer & Keogh, 1995).

Cultural Factors

Not only are settings and behavior within them influenced by the material ecology, cultural features play a powerful role as well. Culture is used here to refer to those schemata human beings use to understand and organize their everyday lives (beliefs and goals relating to the good and moral life, appropriate conduct of interpersonal and family relationships, etc.). The key idea is that settings, no matter how objectively defined and measured, may involve a subjective component because of the schema or lenses through which they are viewed by participants.

Seemingly identical settings can produce very different behavior depending on the cultural lenses through which they are perceived. For example, everyday domestic chores can become a context for teaching literacy and numeracy in households intent on preparing children for schooling and careers, e.g., asking young children to do counting games around setting the table, or helping with recipes (Rogoff, 2003). In families with parents who may not "see" the teaching/learning opportunities in everyday settings, children may be taught to do household chores quickly and efficiently but with a minimum of talk and minimal attention to their developmental potential (Gallimore, Goldenberg, & Weisner, 1993). Thus, "training" parents to interact differently with their children may be problematic because, not only is there no existing setting in which new interactive patterns could be situated, the behaviors to be learned may not fit available cultural schemata. Similarly, children from some communities may view conventional classroom settings through cultural lenses that create problems sufficient to affect short- and long-term achievement (Yamauchi, this volume). For example, small groups of Native Hawaiian children invited to discuss a text they've read together may resist adult attempts to restrict turn-taking to one speaker at a time. In some cases Native Hawaiian students may perceive such an activity setting in terms of a culturally familiar participation pattern in which over-lapping speech and co-constructed text interpretations are not only permitted but preferred (Tharp & Gallimore, 1988). The setting is the same as a conventional reading comprehension lesson: one adult, a small group of children, a common instructional test, and an invitation to discuss the text. But the "meaning" of the setting—what interaction and participation patterns are called for—is very different depending on what cultural lens is employed. The "reality" to which participants react is partly in their heads and partly the objective features of the setting. Where do the "objective" facts end, and "subjective" beliefs or socially constructed of meanings begin?

This complex mix of objective and subjective elements is one reason why intervention programs must take account of the cultural schema and practices of the hosts of interventions. The importance of such account-taking is vividly illustrated by Roberts (this volume). When Roberts and his colleagues began working with Native Hawaiian parents to develop preschool programs, they began with a "do to/for" strategy which "attended marginally if at all to the principle that programs should be developed in partnership with constituents." Although professionals routinely talked to Native Hawaiians families, during program development the families served only as sources of information not as active co-developers. As a result, an otherwise effective program failed to survive for long once the developmental scaffolds were taken down, in marked contrast to subsequent efforts which employed a "do with" approach. Roberts makes this point with a powerful anecdote: A Native Hawaiian father commented, in amicable but direct terms, that he would fire Roberts as a program developer if he had the power to do so. To this father, Roberts was just another missionary to Hawai'i who had come "to do good and did well." It didn't matter if Roberts' theory yielded a "correct, objective" analysis of necessary program components if parents were treated merely as sources of information. The cultural schemata of Native Hawaiians are a part of the fabric of the activity settings in which a program is to be delivered. There were some settings in which Roberts and his colleagues could participate and some contributions they make, and there were some settings in which their role was altogether different, and properly so if viewed through the cultural lenses of the Native Hawaiians. From a researcher's perspective unpacking these complexities is a compelling challenge; for the program developer and implementer, respecting them is an enduring obligation. Treating them as immaterial subjective perceptions is a mistake. Cultural schemata are part of a setting, even if not everyone can see them.

A complicating observation regarding culture is introduced by Yamauchi (this volume)—culture is not a static "thing" that remains unchanging. Cultures frequently change, from the micro-interactional to macro influences, for instance the influence of ecological changes illustrated in Maynard's (this volume) discussion of changes in traditional subsistence activities among the Maya. This adds another level of complexity to cultural effects on activity settings. Yamauchi's examples show that professionals seeking culturally compatible programs must avoid stereotyping based on a child's ethnic or cultural label because of individual variations in how quickly schema and practices change within a supposedly homogenous cultural community. Where different communities share the same ecology, it is expectable all gravitate toward the same adaptive solutions. All things equal, parents in all cultural communities adopt schemata and practices which they perceive to be in the adaptive best interests of their families and their children. To treat all the same based on ethnic label or some other social address is to overlook the adaptive potential of culture. Stereotyping based on ethnic labels is as potentially damaging to the best interests of children and adults as insensitivity to cultural differences.

Personal Factors

Individual characteristics and values include a wide range of factors which affect what settings are created and sustained. For example, stress research suggests no routine is sustainable if it takes too great a toll on any single individual, or exceeds emotional or behavior capacity to cope (Beresford, 1994b). There are many accounts of mothers taken to the breaking point trying to sustain a routine that might optimize developmental gains for a child with disabilities (Featherstone, 1981; Kaufman, 1988). No matter how much is gained in a child's development and safety, in domains of family functioning, or the instantiation of values into everyday life, if the emotional or social costs are too great for the participants a setting cannot be sustained.

Individual values operating can also enable or constrain what settings can be constructed or sustained. While the U.S. social norms include a relatively broad range from which to choose, individuals vary in what schemata they appropriate and shape to fit their purposes. An individual may choose among what appear to be contradictory cultural schemas, applying one to justify behavior in one setting, while appearing to follow a different model of behavior in another setting. For instance, many Americans believe both that one should take risks to achieve upward economic mobility and that one should avoid risks to protect the family's subsistence base; such diversity of cultural schemata may provide for adaptive responses that prepare individuals for changing circumstances, such as economic and employment cycles (Strauss, 1992). For another example, where psychologists see benefits of contingent positive reinforcement to reduce problem behavior of a child, parents might resist what they perceive to be a violation of personal values—if they believe good behavior should be a moral obligation and its own reward (Tharp & Wetzel, 1969).

A Summary Thus Far

Barker, Mischel, and others questioned the assumption that interventions could ignore settings and focus on the individual in isolation. Once examination of settings began in earnest, the complications were evident. Because settings are a combination of the objective and socially constructed, it takes a while to get comfortable with the implications (O'Donnell & Tharp, 1990). A task or activity is not just an objective sequence of behaviors; it is partly socially constructed in the heads of the participants. As a result a setting is not only just the ecological constraints and enablers, it is also partly how it is perceived. Ignoring this mix of objective and subjective features of settings puts an intervention at risk. One solution to the "objective/subjective" problem attempted to integrate ideas from ecological/cultural theory and socio-historical/activity theory (Tharp & Gallimore, 1988; Weisner & Gallimore, 1985) and from community psychology (O'Donnell, 1980; O'Donnell, 1984; O'Donnell & Tharp, 1990). To describe this integration, the term "activity setting" was adopted to reflect contributions from various theoretical traditions.

As a unit of analysis, the concept of the "activity setting" subsumes previously proposed ideas and adds a more inclusive analysis: It incorporates objective reality and subjective experience, and an account of their interaction with individual characteristics and development. The result provides for a dynamical analysis of behavior in context and a guide for planning behavior change (O'Donnell & Tharp, 1990).

Activity Settings

> Activity settings are as homely and familiar as old shoes and the front porch. They are the social furniture of our family, community, and work lives. They are the events and people of our work and relating to one another—they are the who, what, when, where and whys, the small recurrent dramas of everyday life, played on the stages of home, school, community, and workplace. (Tharp & Gallimore, 1988, p. 72)

But why do settings of everyday life arise, what causes them to be constructed and maintained, and provide opportunities for interaction and behavior influence? Ecological/cultural (or ecocultural) theory hypothesizes that constructing and sustaining the activity settings of a daily routine is a universal adaptive problem (LeVine, 1977; Super & Harkness, 1986; Weisner, 1984, 1989; Whiting & Edwards, 1988).

> The settings one frequents are in turn related to the…activities that occupy males and females of various ages in the normal course of daily living, activities that are determined by economic pursuits, the division of labor, and the organization of people in space. (Whiting & Edwards, 1988, p. 4)

In socio-historical theory, activity refers to individual(s) engaged in goal-directed behavior within a framework of implicit cultural assumptions and expectations within which actions and operations are carried out (Cole, 1985).

Putting ideas together from socio-historical and ecocultural theories suggests the *activity setting* unit of analysis. Activity settings have these four features: personnel present and available (who), the tasks being enacted (what), and the goals and purposes of activity (why), and the nature of the resulting interactions (how). For example, two tasks might seem equivalent at the level of *what* (the structure of external activity), but not necessarily at the level of *why* (at the level of motive, or the cultural and personal schemata through which the task is viewed). For instance, adults interacting with children can regard a task as a teaching/learning opportunity, or as job to be efficiently finished, e.g., setting the table for a large family party can be a chore, or a chance to teach and practice some simple arithmetic. The task requirements may be objectively similar, but the purpose or the "why" in the head of the adult will affect "how" the activity unfolds.

Consider a variation on the same example of setting the table. Imagine a parent changes employment, and comes in contact with new social influences, through which new knowledge is learned about the teaching/learning opportunities available in everyday routines. Over time that parent, because of an ecological change, might start using chores to teach children arithmetic. With the new information, the parent no longer "sees" table-setting as a routine task. This mundane example illustrates how variation in one feature of an activity setting can affect one or more others.

This is the point, in brief. The four features are a useful lens for analyzing activity settings to assess their possible effects on behavior, and the potential ways a setting might be changed in order to change behavior. It's not hard to see the appeal of revamping, tweaking, or even creating activity settings to achieve behavior change. Change the setting in the just the right way, and behavior changes. Compelling examples of which are provided by Maynard (this volume).

For instance, Maynard summarizes studies of Zinacatecan Mayan weavers which documents how a change in the local ecology produced changes in traditional activity settings which altered behavior in dramatic ways. As recently as 1970, older expert-weavers apprenticed young girls using a teaching script that was directive and highly scaffolded; with resources scarce and the cost of weaving errors high, the purpose of the expert in this traditional activity setting was to minimize errors. As the local economy changed and opened more opportunities for selling to tourists, the traditional activity setting for apprentices also changed. Younger experts were allowed to teach apprentices; the teaching script was loosened up to allow for more independent, trial-and-error learning. Rather than learning to weave as a subsistence adaptation, it became an opportunity to participate in a local market-driven economy in which what was once traditional women's work became an industry and an opportunity to earn income. Sensitive as all activity settings are to the ecology, the behaviors in and around weaving apprenticeship changed.

Another example. The *how* of interaction is a complicated function of other activity setting factors. For example, in everyday activity settings, humans influence one another through conversation that arises in work on jointly defined tasks or in the solution of mutually identified problems. As Wells and Haneda (this volume) note, conversation is a medium for coordinating and reflecting on actions (joint and otherwise), describing and explaining actions, and exercising control over the material and social world of human beings. It can also be a powerful means of influencing behavior. For instance, in joint productive activity more expert participants may rely on probing questions and other conversational devices to guide and thereby influence the behavior of less capable individuals. The conversations may on the surface appear equitable and responsiveness, but more careful analysis may reveal social and behavioral influence being wielded perhaps without the awareness of its targets. Young students might, for example, think a map reading task involved locating their own houses on a map, when another lens reveals they are being "taught" by an agenda-guided adult to understand and use topographic and geographic representations and vocabulary in two-dimensional space.

For the students it is an engaging, free-flowing activity in which they are free to initiate conversation; for the teacher it is using the arrangement of the who, what, and why of the setting to achieve an instructional agenda through the *how* that is seldom fully recognized by young apprentices. Contrast this combination of instruction and conversation with the default teaching script in wide use in American classrooms. It is highly teacher-directed with a focus on getting students to give answers the teacher expects, rather the development of student understanding and ideas. Rarely are students permitted opportunities for responsive interactions (conversations) that might scaffold development of deeper text analysis and comprehension. However, if the activity setting is arranged so that teacher does not know the "correct answer" and must use conversational devices to discover what students know, the quality of the interaction changes—from a stilted, directive model to a conversational mode that opens up unexpected learning opportunities (Tharp & Gallimore, 1988). Wells and Haneda offer multiple examples in which teachers arrange classroom activities that can produce a very different kind of learning opportunity than is afforded by the default teaching script. Change the setting and behavior may change.

Why Settings Are Hard to Change and Why People Like Them That Way

Tharp and Wetzel's analysis of resistances foreshadowed that settings are not easy to change, a quality that makes behavior hard to change. This puts a spotlight on Barker's conclusion that there was more variance across than within the settings he investigated. One way to look at these issues is to examine some of the reasons activity settings are resistant to change, and by inference, so is human behavior.

Settings do change, often when environmental changes impact daily routines (Edgerton, 1992), though this is accomplished through what might seem a paradoxical means. Namely, in response to environmental perturbations, people make as few changes as possible to get their daily routines back as close as possible to what they were before the perturbation. When a perturbation occurs, the strategy of most individuals and groups is to cautiously adapt through small experiments on the margins of cultural practice (Chibnik, 1981; Johnson, 1972). For example, hybrid corn varieties were slow to be adopted by small-scale farmers who chose to plant only a small percent of their fields with new seed until a season or two showed yields superior to varieties previously used (Chibnik, 1981).

In general, if change involves re-negotiating many hard-won solutions to competing pressures, people prefer to stick with the worked-out daily routine they already have. Perhaps it is not optimal, but it works just well enough to make it preferable to the conflict and disruption that negotiating a new one might entail. For example, public schools are stable institutions with a long history and a well developed set of stable activity settings and daily routines (Lortie, 1975; Sarason, 1971). These stable patterns create a virtually impenetrable barrier to change (Goldenberg, 2004; Saunders & Goldenberg, this volume). Is the problem the resistant behavior of individual teachers or an expectable consequence of the everyday settings multiply determined and reinforced by history, culture, and ecology? These mundane settings sustain behavior and make it difficult to change because that is their purpose, and that's why people like them. Teachers don't resist change because they object to innovation. Resistance stems from the fact that existing daily routines evolved for good reasons, and changing them can be risky.

Existing activity settings evolved and endured because they are a compromise between the possible and the desirable. They bring predictability, coherence, and a sense of agency or control to everyday life at home and work. Like everyone else, teachers defend their daily settings and routines because they are working well enough, and initiating change may lead to disruption, uncertainty, and potential conflict. Activities and settings are modified just enough to make things work—humans are satisficers rather than maximizers to use Herbert Simon's (1957) terms, seldom seeking the ideal solution when an existing one is working just-good-enough to get by (Edgerton, 1992). Better it seems to accept the limitations of our durable if imperfect settings than to open up our lives to the multiple pressures and constraints that gave rise to daily routines in the first place.

Ecological constraints are another reason settings resist change. Ecological presses may simply prohibit changes. Changing personnel available in an ecological niche, for example, is often difficult. For example, Datnow, Stringfield, and Castellano (this volume) describe the inability of a well-regarded educational reform program to implement its model in a particular circumstance. State regulations required that all English learners be instructed by ESL-certified teachers. Because too few were available, it was not possible to place primary grade students in classrooms according to reading level (a key component of the reform program). Local administrators were not permitted to alter *personnel available* to a key instructional setting. In this case changing policy had to precede changing the instructional setting. Other examples could be provided, for instance where certain activities are prescribed or proscribed, so that whatever change in behavior was sought had to focus on other levers of change. This restates another quality of activity settings: They are a compromise among many competing features of the ecology, culture, and individual characteristics.

However, innovation and change do occur, including changes in personnel available, and they can have profound effects on behavior and distal constraints which in turn affect what settings can be constructed and sustained. A history of family research (Skolnick, 1993), for example, reveals that over time household settings (and interactions and behavior embedded in them) do show significant alteration. For instance the increase in number of women in paid employment have had profound impact across many settings, domestic settings and workplaces alike.

Ecology and culture are powerful influences, but there is evidence that in every generation some families deliberately innovate, and manage to alter developmentally significant settings. For example, Weisner, Bausano, and Kornfein (1983) studied experimenting American families determined to implement household settings that supported what they considered to be innovative patterns of child rearing. A subsequent follow-up study—when the experimenting parents were middle-aged—suggested that they had experienced some success in constructing and implementing their goals, e.g., voluntary poverty to insulate children from competitive pressures and "consumerism," maintaining non-gendered social roles or very devout religious lifestyles, communal households. In addition, the parents had experienced some limited success achieving the kinds of child outcomes they sought. But some of their desired innovations were too hard to sustain, in part because they were at odds with U. S. cultural norms and ecological constraints. For some, the greatest pressures to revert to cultural norms were experienced when their children reached school age. At that point, many parents, like so many other Americans, began to worry about off-springs' economic futures which they saw as dependent on educational attainment. The American ecological/cultural system—at the level of income base and domestic arrangements—pressed some innovating families to gradually abandon or alter efforts to create innovative settings in their daily routines (Weisner & Bernheimer, 1998). Thus, even in a society that valorizes individualism and innovation and permits a wide latitude in lifestyle, the ecological/cultural surround mitigates against many innovations and changes no matter how hard individuals and groups try. The same consequences can await efforts to achieve behavior change in the natural environment.

Schools are also pressed by the surrounding ecological and cultural system back to traditional practices even after improved achievement has been secured through implementing reforms. Goldenberg (2004) described a 5-year prospective study of a single elementary school as it attempted a major change in its instructional program. An explicit focus of this effort was creating a few new settings and the revamping of existing school settings, e.g., faculty and grade-level meetings. As a result of this theory-guided intervention, student achievement rose from lowest in the district to the highest after six years. However, within a year after the project ended, these significant gains were diminishing. One reason was the settings which had proved so critical to implementing changes had gradually begun to revert to functioning as they had before the project, and closer to what is typical in American elementary schools. A similar outcome was reported for a long operating laboratory school (Tharp & Gallimore, 1988), again seemingly illustrating the regression to the mean effects of ecology and culture.

Why are settings so resistant to change? To be sustainable, settings are a compromise among ecological constraints, cultural and personal values, and the characteristics of the participating individuals. Sustaining the settings of daily routines to reconcile potentially competing ecological, cultural, and individual factors is an enduring human project, at home, work, and all other contexts. Changing a setting may mean re-opening conflicting issues, and initiating a long, possibly stressful search for a sustainable alternative that accommodates competing interests and re-distributes limited resources.

For example, families adapting to children with developmental problems illustrated how sustaining a daily routine depends on balancing multiple factors. Ninety-three families were followed over more than ten years; they were recruited into the study because each had a 3-year old who had been diagnosed with non-specific developmental delays in cognition, speech, behavior, and/or physical domains (Gallimore, Keogh, & Bernheimer, 1999). Repeated assessments and interviews suggested the emotional costs were not the pre-eminent factor driving parents' choices and efforts. The sustainability of their daily routine was often the focus of their efforts, which included balancing work hours, transportation to appointments for the child, household chores, childcare, and so forth. From preschool to late childhood, families reported a statistically significant increase in the number of daily routine accommodations made. However, the amount of effort families put into making daily routine accommodations showed little change over the same period. The discrepancy between increased frequency and stable effort levels suggested that by late childhood families were spreading their adaptive efforts and energies across more domains.

While the daily routines they managed to sustain were usually not described as perfect or optimized for every individual, they were "good enough" and, most importantly, they could be sustained. Many mentioned what kind of routine they would "like it to be" but quickly added that what they were sustaining was as close as they were likely to get to their ideal—give or take a few adjustments here and there. This possibility of making "a few adjustments" to daily routines is what makes *settings* a workshop for changing behavior. Change settings, and behavior will change.

Changing Settings: A Few Propositions

The features of activity settings represent levers for behavior change, including: What personnel are available and participating? What activities are undertaken? What are the goals, motives, and purposes of the setting? What are the embedded activities and interactions? Finally, what are the rules of interaction, participation structures, dialogic styles, and so forth. Focusing on these levers to conceptualize and plan behavior change is very different from a focus on the individuals for whom change has been requested, invited, or intended. O'Donnell and Tharp (1990) captured this different focus with this insight about grasping the levers of settings to secure change: the client is the social context that produced the problem(s) which an intervention is to resolve. The first task is, therefore, to analyze the dynamics of the activity settings that produce and sustain problems and to locate the levers of influence that bring about some reorganization. Unless the sustaining context of activity settings are changed, no permanent behavior change is likely.

So, of the levers in an existing activity setting the question is which ones offer the prospects for being revised to achieve behavior change? A comprehensive examination of this question was presented earlier in O'Donnell and Tharp (1990). What follows are a few propositions for consideration.

A Proposition

All things considered, a key lever for changing settings (in order to change behavior) is setting and sharing common goals. In activity setting terms, this means participants in a joint activity alter somehow the "why" of activities in a given setting. When the "why" in an activity changes, the way people interact changes, and the perception of the task activities change as well. This proposition rests on findings from a variety of fields from sociolinguistics to developmental psychology to school reform to improving health practices (e.g., Fishbein et al., 1992;

Gallimore & Goldenberg, 1993; Ochs, 1982; Rogoff, 2003; Wertsch, Minick, & Arns, 1985).

The idea that goals, motives, and intentions influence behavior is an old one (Murray, 1938; Rotter, 1954). Intentions and motives (goals) have the most impact on behavior according to an NIMH sponsored consensus panel (Fishbein et al., 1992), environment and skills permitting. However, changing settings to change behavior leads to a different strategy from changing the goals and intentions of each individual. It focuses instead on participants in stable settings setting and sharing common goals and purposes around a *joint productive activity*.

> [W]hen people work together toward a common objective or to produce something together, two rare conditions emerge that have the most profound consequences....First, common motives are created, at least within the bounds of the shared activity and its settings....
>
> The second rare condition of joint productive activity is that it creates [mutual empathy among the participants]. Because participants want the same thing, it becomes possible...to feel together the pleasures of progress and the disappointments of setbacks....
>
> Thus working together for a common objective is not one among an infinite and casual variety of social arrangements, but rather an existential condition with unique powers for human transformation. (Tharp, Estrada, Dalton, & Yamauchi, 2000, pp. 57–58)

Where goals are shared, the possibility of joint productive activity arises. Where there are no shared goals, or conflicting goals, joint activity is likely to be abandoned and productive outcomes placed out of reach (O'Donnell & Tharp, 1990). To share goals they must share some common view of the world, their situation, and what they want or need to achieve as individuals or as a group. Common views, understandings, and meanings—inter-subjectivity—do not arise in a vacuum. They are a product of often intense dialogue and interaction over time. The most likely context of such exchanges are joint productive activities, which of course they cannot sustain because they do not have the inter-subjectivity to develop shared goals. This is one way to describe the situations in which the professional behavior changer is invited to assist. If participants troubled by their failure to be jointly productive could develop shared goals, perhaps their troubles would dissolve in the glow of productive outcomes.

An example of this fundamental dynamic for changing behavior was presented by Saunders and Goldenberg (this volume). Working in under-performing elementary schools, they began their intervention by organizing existing settings (grade level groups) to engage in the setting and sharing of joint goals for student achievement. Although, similarly to most schools, the faculties had general goals (raise test scores), there were no explicit goals shared at each grade level that organized joint efforts to improve student learning. As a result most grade level meetings seldom dealt with instructional practices or how teachers could plan and assist each other in ways to increase student learning. Another example is successful programs that address anti-social behavior in schools, for which there is no substantial evidence of effectiveness (Walker, Ramsey, & Gresham, 2003/2004). Rather than focusing only on especially troublesome cases, after an exhaustive review, Walker et al. conclude it is more effective to begin by implementing a consistently enforced school-wide behavior code that is jointly developed by all stakeholders—administrators, teachers, staff, students, and parents. After everyone learns about the code, including students, success depends on the code and consequences being applied across multiple settings, e.g., classrooms, hallways, playgrounds, and so forth.

For shared goals to have an effect, monitoring of progress is mandatory. Without knowing whether there is progress toward goals, there is no basis on which to adjust behavior. When performance is monitored, individuals compare their behavior against the standards defined by shared goals. When there is a modest or moderate discrepancy, individuals make efforts to change their behavior to be more in line with the shared goal. If the discrepancy is too large or perceived to be too difficult to reduce, they may spurn the situation, attempt to discount the goal, or engage in some other avoidant behavior (Carver & Scheier, 1981).

Shared goals focus participants' attention on the same criteria against which to compare individual and group performance. There is robust evidence that goals and indicators function in this way, and that indicators alone (knowledge of results or feedback) have much less effect in the absence of goals (Locke, Cartledge, & Koeppel, 1968). By focusing on goals and indicators shared within enduring settings of the everyday routine, the odds of sustaining behavior change might be increased substantially over individual-focused interventions.

Although there are some compelling demonstrations of these ideas working well in some natural environment interventions, the evidence base is hardly substantial. One reason is that tendency in recent decades for researchers and practitioners to work in so many different areas of human problems. Coupled with a quarter-century disinterest in more generalized theory, the power of shared goals and indicators to produce behavior change might be a profitable area for investigation. This idea is taken up again in the final section of this chapter.

Another Proposition

Another lever for change in activity settings is the "what," or the specific behavioral change that is sought. What are some principles for gauging the likelihood a given behavior is a suitable candidate for change?

One lens for examining behavior (and activities) for change potential was ground and polished by research on the innovation diffusion. Changes in behavior are a form of innovation, whatever the locus of initiation—the individual, a social group, or a professional change agent. A group engaged in joint productive activity may not perceive individual behavior change/innovation as a purpose, but whether or not it is, it is often a by-product of goal attainment.

So what are some of the factors that affect this function of a social group working in a stable setting? Rogers (1995), after a survey of innovation diffusion in many fields, e.g., agricultural, medicine, public health, technology, etc., concluded that there is a recurrent pattern of adoption. Innovations spread slowly at first, often through the work of change agents. Adoption accelerates as more people accept it, and then slows as all who will adopt have done so.

The degree to which an innovation is adopted, and the speed of its adoption, partly depends on five qualities of a new activity or behavior:

1. *Relative advantage*: The degree to which a changed activity or behavior is perceived as better or whether it offers some advantage relative to the status quo;
2. *Compatibility*: The degree to which a change is perceived as compatible with existing values, past experiences, and current needs;
3. *Complexity*: The degree of difficulty to implement, use, and sustain a change;
4. *Trailability*: The degree to which a change can be tried out before adoption, or to what extent it can be modified once it is adopted;
5. *Observability*: The degree to which the benefits and costs of a change are visible to others.

Rogers' five qualities might be useful lenses for assessing the likelihood of specific behaviors being adopted into a given setting and determining in what order they might be sought. If a change endures, and/or is adopted by others who observe its consequences, this exemplifies implementation as evolution through diffusion of innovation according to Majone and Wildavsky (1979). Their case studies suggest untidy details intervene in even the best planned programs, so that most constraints and other untidy details are not discovered until intervention begins, and thus hardly anyone ever literally follows the original plan. In addition, even when feasibility of a setting as a host for intervention is determined in advance, feasibility conditions keep changing over time—feasibility is never a permanent condition. An intervention is perhaps better seen as a dynamic interaction, one that evolves over time, rather than as an invariant input. As a consequence, interventions usually turn out to be, Majone and Wildavsky suggest, something different from what was intended. Sometimes it takes this form: "'This particular problem may not be solvable…how about substituting one that can be solved.' In other words, if problems are best understood through solutions, then implementation includes not only finding answers, but also framing questions" (p. 189).

These extensions from other areas have, for the most part, not been taken up by behavior change researchers and practitioners as possible outcome criteria. Perhaps using these ideas might improve the precision of behavior change planning, and increase the likelihood that a behavior or practice would be sustained. Sustainability of behavior changes across time within settings is an indicator of social validity (Kennedy, 2002). If a change is adopted by others observing its consequences, this might represent the most robust indicator of durability and social validity. This might be another interesting line worthy of future investigators' attention.

A Final Proposition

Better appreciated since Tharp and Wetzel (1969) is the idea that constrained as they are by ecology and culture, humans are not passive. They have their own ideas and plans about what ought to be, albeit socially constructed through their activity settings, and the means by which to achieve it, as Roberts (this volume) and his colleagues have learned. In every context individuals and groups are already engaging in behavior control and change of some kind, and to some degree. A key to improving behavioral interventions is learn what kinds of attempts are already going on, and how are people already trying to alter their daily routines so that they support the kinds of activities and behaviors they deem desirable.

The control people have over their daily routines (and the embedded activity settings) is one way active agency is exercised, limited as it might be by ecology and culture. Through many means, they adjust and tweak the routines and settings in which joint activity takes place in order to move them closer to what they desire, e.g., the ongoing and increasing number of daily routine accommodations reported by families adapting to children with developmental delays (Gallimore, Keogh, & Bernheimer, 1999). The levers of change in an activity setting are available to individuals, and they use them.

Most of the attention in this essay has been on individuals and groups that are sufficiently adaptive, with or without professional guidance, to be able to use the levers of change outlined here. As Evans (this volume) notes, people differ in opportunity and ability to manipulate their local environments, and in the plasticity of their environments. The inability to construct new or adapt their everyday routines to achieve change might distinguish those who are so distressed that they seek clinical help. For the severely troubled, it often falls to the behavior therapist to arrange opportunities to participate in settings which promote new learning and (hopefully) the weakening of troubling behaviors. However, there is evidence that some clinically distressed individuals can learn to manage troubling behavior through self-directed manipulation of social contexts—an idea to which Tharp and his colleagues made early and important contributions (e.g., Watson & Tharp, 1977).

Learning more about the ubiquitous efforts that humans make to manage their daily routines, however mundane and ordinary that they might appear, is an important avenue for behavior change research and practice (Gallimore, Bernheimer, & Weisner, 1999).

Conclusions and a Challenge

A search of the PsycINFO database (1840–Current) for articles with "behavior change" in the title produced 777 items. Admittedly a crude measure, what's most striking is the number of different foci of intervention in everyday settings. These range from drug and alcohol rehabilitation, homelessness, community, medical and mental health, HIV/AIDS prevention, early childhood intervention, school reform, and family formation and maintenance, to name a few. Compared to 1969, in the 21st century, many sub-disciplines work in many settings toward many ends, ranging from the remediation of "troubled behavior" to the promotion of pro-social adaptation and resilience to early education and school reform. The age of practice specialization has produced no general theoretical or knowledge base for behavior change practice.

Despite the substantial evidence and experience that has accumulated, a distinguished evaluation researcher recently observed there has been little movement toward identifying common factors and principles of behavior change (Lee Sechrest, personal communication, December 8, 2003). Indeed, a search of PsychINFO and the Web turned up little indication of interest in a general theory of behavior change. However, even a cursory review suggests that evidence from a variety of fields—clinical and community psychology, public health, drug and alcohol addiction, and education—suggests it is possible that a general model of behavior change might be constructed from the past half-century of research and experience. Indeed, Evans (this volume) suggests "if one can step back…it becomes obvious…we are talking about a relatively small number of universal principles." Much of the research in behavior therapy is segmented by the syndromes and problem categories on which investigators focus. Although a cursory review of these knowledge bases suggest common principles may have been identified, there has so far been little effort to codify these into a more general set of principles. Perhaps sometime in this century, interest in a general theories of behavior change will be re-kindled.

Roland Tharp has often argued that such a theory is possible, and necessary, for improving the practice of behavior change in the helping professions. The challenge, as his own scholarship and career trajectory have illustrated, is to combine concepts and findings from all the social and behavioral sciences. His goal has been to retain the power of a psychological analysis, but develop units of analysis that take culture and social context into account (Hoshmand, this volume).

The outlines of such a theory are beginning to be seen in the work of Tharp and his colleagues. For example, he proposed that there is a limited number (seven at this counting) of basic, universal means of behavior influence and change (Tharp & Gallimore, 1988; Tharp et al., 2000), e.g, modeling, feeding-back, contingency managing, and cognitive restructuring. The seven means of influence are universal, and their workings can be seen in all the "ings," and in all the settings that the "ings" are practiced: Parenting, teaching, pastoring, coaching, training, mentoring, and all the other "ings."

Although the means of influence may be limited to a few familiar processes, they are employed in an infinite variety of activity settings because these are a joint product of ecology, culture, and human agency. Such variety complicates practice, and the principles for taking advantage of activity settings for behavior change are less well understood than the means of influence. One way to tackle the complications that culture and context present is the evolutionary knowledge generation strategy that Tharp employed throughout his research and practice career, an approach which might be likened to what has been called Pasteur's Quadrant (Stokes, 1996).

Stokes argues that research cannot always be neatly divided into "basic and applied." He envisions "pure" research as a vertical axis of research space, while strictly "applied" research is visualized as a horizontal axis. One of the resulting quadrants is "Pasteur's Quadrant," so labeled because his work exemplifies investigations that concatenate features of both basic and applied research. In Pasteur's Quadrant, research is often applied, practical, and basic at the same time and frequently use-inspired. While it might borrow from theory and previous research, the focus is the solving of specific, practical problems, such as marital conflicts, or the promotion of pro-social behaviors, and the reduction of delinquent behaviors. Another goal is to teach under-achieving children to read on grade level or to change resistant teaching practices rooted in resilient school culture and to increase excellence, fairness, inclusion, and harmony in public school classrooms. Another goal is to mentor students and colleagues toward new ways of thinking and investigating.

> When many academic researchers have turned to theoretical knowledge as the starting point of inquiry, [Tharp] and his associates have continued to engage in research that begins with problems identified outside of the academy. This mode of knowledge generation that often involves stakeholders and researchers from multiple disciplines in collaborative problem-solving will perhaps pave the way to a new sociology of knowledge. It goes beyond both basic research and the types of applied research that have characterized academic knowledge production. Contrary to a discipline-based form of scholarship and the exclusive use of a dominant research approach, Tharp was able to demonstrate the utility of pluralistic research methods for diverse setting analyses (of home, school and community). His interest in other fields of knowledge has allowed him to achieve a more comprehensive understanding of the chosen substantive domains, using the language and inquiry methods of different disciplines. (Hoshman, this volume, p. 244)

This approach has taken us a long way and can take us further toward developing a robust general theory and practice of behavior change in the natural environment.

References

Bandura, A. (1969). *Principles of behavior modification*. New York: Holt, Rinehart, & Winston.

Barker, R. G., & Wright, H. F. (1951). *One boy's day*. New York: Harper & Row.

Beresford, B. A. (1994a). Resources and strategies: How parents cope with the care of a disabled child. *Journal of Child Psychology and Psychiatry, 35*, 171–209.

Beresford, B. A. (1994b). Easing the strain: assessing the impact of a Family Fund grant on mothers caring for a severely disabled child. *Child: Care, Health, and Development, 19*, 369–378.

Bernheimer, L. P., & Keogh, B. K. (1995). Weaving interventions into the fabric of everyday life: an approach to family assessment. *Topics in Early Childhood Special Education, 15* (4), 415–433.

Carver, C. S., & Scheier, M. F. (1981). *Attention and self-regulation: A control-theory approach to human behavior.* New York: Springer Verlag.

Chibnik, M. (1981). The evolution of cultural rules. *Journal of Anthropological Research, 37*, (3), 256–268.

Cole, M. (1985). The zone of proximal development: Where culture and cognition create each other. In J. V. Wertsch (Ed.), *Culture, communication, and cognition: Vygotskian perspectives* (pp. 146–161). Cambridge: Cambridge University Press.

Edgerton, R. B. (1992). S*ick societies: Challenging the myth of primitive harmony.* New York: Free Press.

Featherstone, H. (1981). *A difference in the family.* London: Penguin Books.

Fishbein, M., Bandura, A., Triandis, H. C., Kanfer, F. H., Becker, M. H., Middlestadt, E. E., & Hitchcock, P. J. (1992). *Factors influencing behavior and behavior change: Final Report-Theorist's Workshop.* Rockville, MD: National Institute of Mental Health.

Gallimore, R., Bernheimer, L., & Weisner, T. (1999). Family life is more than managing crisis: Broadening the agenda of research on families adapting to childhood disability. In R. Gallimore et al. (Eds.), *Developmental Perspectives on High Incidence Handicapping Conditions Papers in Honor of Barbara K. Keogh* (pp. 55–80). Mahwah, NJ: Erlbaum & Associates.

Gallimore, R., & Goldenberg, C. N. (1993). Activity settings of early literacy: Home and school factors in children's emergent literacy. In.E. Forman, N. Minick, and C. A. Stone (Eds.), *Contexts for learning: Sociocultural dynamics in children's development* (pp. 315–335). Oxford, UK: Oxford University Press.

Gallimore, R., Goldenberg, C. N., & Weisner, T. S. (1993). The social construction and subjective reality of activity settings: Implications for community psychology. *American Journal of Community Psychology, 21* (4), 537–559.

Gallimore, R., Keogh, B. K., & Bernheimer, C. (1999). The nature and long-term implications of early developmental delays: A summary of evidence from two longitudinal studies. *International Review of Research in Mental Retardation, 22*, 105–135.

Goldenberg, C. N. (2004). *Successful school change: Creating settings to improve teaching and learning.* New York: Teachers College Press.

Johnson, A. (1972). Individuality and experimentation in traditional agriculture. *Human Ecology, 1*, 145–159.

Kaufman, S. (1988). *Retarded isn't stupid, mom!* Baltimore: Paul H. Brookes Publishing.

Kennedy, C. H. (2002). The maintenance of behavior change as an indicator of social validity. *Behavior Modification, 26* (5), 594–604.

LeVine, R. (1977). Child rearing as cultural adaptation. In P. Leiderman, S. Tulkin, & A. Rosenfeld (Eds.), *Culture and infancy* (pp. 15–27). New York: Academic Press.

Locke, E. A., Cartledge, N., & Koeppel, J. (1968). Motivational effects of knowledge of results: A goal-setting phenomenon? *Psychological Bulletin, 70* (6, Pt. 1), 474–485.

Lortie, D. (1975). *School teacher: A sociological study.* Chicago: University of Chicago Press.

MacDonald, S. Gallimore, R., & MacDonald, G. (1970). Contingency counseling by school personnel: An economical model of intervention. *Journal of Applied Behavior Analysis, 3,* 175–182.

Majone, G., & Wildavsky, A. (1979). Implementation as evolution. In J. L. Pressman & A. Wildavsky (Eds.), *Implementation* (2nd Ed.) (pp. 163–189). Oakland, CA: Oakland Project.

McCord, J. (1978). A thirty-year follow-up of treatment effects. *American Psychologist, 33*(3), 284–289.

Merritt, D. M., Greene, G. J., Jopp, D. A., & Kelly, J. G. (1998). A history of division 27 (Society for Community Research and Action). In D. A. Dewsbury (Ed.), *Unification through division: Histories of the American Psychological Association,* Vol. 3 (pp. 73–99). Washington, DC: American Psychological Association.

Mischel, W. (1968). *Personality and assessment.* New York: Wiley.

Murray, H. A. (1938). *Explorations in personality: A clinical and experimental study of fifty men of college age.* New York: Oxford University Press.

Ochs, E. (1982). Talking to children in Western Samoa. *Language in Society, 11,* 77–104.

O'Donnell, C. R. (1980). Environmental design and the prevention of psychological problems. In M. P. Feldman & J. R. Orford (Eds.), *The social psychology of psychological problems* (pp. 279–309). New York: Wiley.

O'Donnell, C. R. (1984). Behavioral community psychology and the natural environment. In C. M. Franks & C. Diament (Eds.), *New developments in practical behavior therapy: From research to clinical application* (pp. 495–524). New York: Haworth Press.

O'Donnell, C. R., & Tharp, R. G. (1990). Community intervention guided by theoretical development. In A. S. Bellack, M. Hersen, & A. E. Kazdin (Eds.), *International handbook of behavior modification and therapy* (2nd ed.) (pp. 251–266). New York: Plenum Press.

Powers, E., & Witmer, H. (1951). *An experiment in the prevention of delinquency: the Cambridge-Somerville Youth Study.* New York: Columbia University Press.

Rogers, E. M. (1995). *The diffusion of innovations* (5th ed.). New York: The Free Press.

Rogoff, B. (2003). *The cultural nature of human development.* Oxford, UK: Oxford University Press.

Rotter, J. B. (1954). *Social learning and clinical psychology.* New York: Prentice-Hall.

Sarason, S. (1971). *The culture of the school and the problem of change.* Boston: Allyn & Bacon.

Sarason, S. (1972). *The creation of settings and the future societies.* San Francisco: Jossey-Bass.

Simon, H. (1957). *Administrative behavior* (2nd ed.). New York: Macmillan.

Skolnick, A. (1993). Changes of heart: Family dynamics in historical perspective. In P. A. Cowan, D. Field, D. A. Hansen, A. Skolnick, & G. E. Swanson (Eds.), *Family, self, and society: Toward a new agenda for family research* (pp. 43–68). Hillsdale, NJ: Lawrence Erlbaum.

Staats, A. W. (1968). *Learning, language, and cognition.* New York: Holt, Reinhart, & Winston.

Stokes, D. E. (1996). *Pasteur's quadrant: Basic science and technological innovation.* Washington, DC: The Brookings Institution Press.

Strauss, C. (1992). What makes Tony run? Schemas as motives reconsidered. In R. D'Andrade & C. Strauss (Eds.), *Human motives and cultural models* (pp. 197–224). Cambridge, UK: Cambridge University Press.

Super, C., & Harkness, S. (1986). The developmental niche: A conceptualization at the interface of child and culture. *International Journal of Behavior Development, 9,* 1–25.

Tharp, R. G., Estrada, P., Dalton, S. S., & Yamauchi, L. A. (2000). *Teaching transformed: Achieving excellence, fairness, inclusion, and harmony.* Boulder, CO: Westview.

Tharp, R. G., & Gallimore, R. (1988). *Rousing minds to life: Teaching, learning, and schooling in social context.* Cambridge, UK: Cambridge University Press.

Tharp, R. G., & Wetzel, R. (1969). *Behavior modification in the natural environment.* New York: Academic Press.

Thompson, E. P. (1966). *The making of the English working class.* New York: Vintage Books.

Walker, H. M., Ramsey, E., & Gresham, F. M. (2003/2004). Heading off disruptive behavior how early intervention can reduce defiant behavior—and win back teaching time. *American Educator, 27,* 4, 6–15, 18–21, 45–46.

Watson, D. L., & Tharp, R. G. (1977). *Self-directed behavior: Self-modification for personal adjustment* (2nd ed.). Monterey, CA: Brooks/Cole.

Weisner, T. S. (1984). Ecocultural niches of middle childhood: A cross-cultural perspective. In W. A. Collins (Ed.), *Development during middle childhood: The years from six to twelve* (pp. 335–369). Washington, D.C: National Academy of Sciences Press.

Weisner, T. S. (1998). Human development, child well-being, and the cultural project of development. In D. Sharma & K. Fischer (Eds.). Socio-emotional development across cultures *New directions in child development, No. 81* (pp. 69–85). San Francisco: Jossey-Bass.

Weisner, T. S., & Bernheimer, L. P. (1998). Children of the 1960s at midlife: Generational identity and the Family Adaptive Project. In R. A. Shweder (Ed.), *Welcome to middle age! (And other cultural fictions)* (pp. 211–257). Chicago: University of Chicago Press.

Weisner, T. S., Bausano, M., & Kornfein, M. (1983). Putting family ideals into practice: Pronaturalism in conventional and nonconventional California families. *Ethos, 11*(4), 278–304.

Wertsch, J. V., Minick, N., & Arns, F. A. (1984). The creation of context in joint problem-solving. In B. Rogoff & J. Lave (Eds.), *Everyday cognition: Its development in social contexts* (pp. 151–171). Cambridge, MA: Harvard University Press.

Whiting, B., & Edwards, C. (1988). *Children of different worlds: The formation of social behavior.* Cambridge, UK: Harvard University Press.

Wishart, M. C., Bidder, R. T., & Gray, O. P. (1981). Parents' report of family life with a developmentally delayed child. *Child: Care, Health, and Development, 7,* 267–279.

CHAPTER 11

Man of Knowledge and Conviction: Biographical Tribute to Roland G. Tharp

Lisa Tsoi Hoshmand

When the editors asked me to write the biographical chapter for this book, my immediate response was that it would be an honor and a pleasure to accept their invitation. Upon further consideration, I became aware of the inherent challenges of this assignment, the fact that I was charged with accomplishing this as part of a surprise dedication to Roland Tharp. How could one capture nearly half a century of a living man's professional career without consulting him? It is hardly good manners for a biographer. My hope is that he will be amused and forgiving when he finally reads these pages.

I was Roland Tharp's student in the doctoral clinical psychology program at the University of Hawai'i more than thirty years ago. As is often the case with mentoring relationships, we became colleagues and friends over time by staying in touch with each other's lives. In 1997 I had the opportunity to do a project based on the professional careers of psychologists who have made uncommon contributions, interviewing them about issues of knowledge and moral commitment, and asking each to write an autobiographical chapter. The book, *Creativity and Moral Vision in Psychology*, includes a chapter by Tharp (1998). Tharp's own account served as a foundation for writing the present chapter. Additional information was gathered to provide a more complete professional history than was given previously. I consulted with the editors Clifford O'Donnell and Lois Yamauchi, and his long-time collaborator and friend Ronald Gallimore to be certain that I have included the significant aspects of his professional career. I also contacted Tharp's wife Stephanie Stoll Dalton who has been involved in many key aspects of the work in education that they co-led. Sam Stringfield, Principal Research Scientist of the Center for Social Organization of Schools at Johns Hopkins University offered additional information as a participant in the network of researchers with whom Tharp has collaborated. I am grateful for everyone's input.

Like the previous autobiographical account, however, this biographical chapter will not give a complete story. It is not possible to do justice with a short essay on a man with such vision and talent, who was at once a psychologist, educator, reformer, poet, and artist. Tharp is listed in directories of people of scientific achievement and distinction in America and internationally, in the *Outstanding Educators of America* and *Who's Who in American Education*, and in *Poets of America* and the *International Who's Who in Poetry* and *Poets' Encyclopaedia*. I see the purpose of this biographical sketch as being largely descriptive. Although I hope to offer an appraisal of the significance of his work, the final reflections on his career should come from Tharp himself when he writes his memoir.

The Road to Life in Psychology

If one were to search for early threads with which to weave a story of youthful precursors to a life in psychology, one might fall short of a convincing tale here. Writing was Tharp's early sense of vocation, which could have meant journalism or a career in the language arts. He worked in his teens as a copyboy and part-time journalist for a Texas newspaper, and subsequently enrolled at the University of Texas in the hope of becoming a writer. But perhaps an interest in observing the human drama that unfolds in daily life was finding expression in his propensity to write. By his own account (Tharp, 1998), his fascination with other peoples and cultures can be traced to his childhood. Tharp grew up during the 1930s in La Marque, Texas, a town where Black Americans and migrants from Mexico coexisted with White Americans in spite of separate neighborhoods. His early encounters with "otherness" were clearly a significant formative force. And then there was his grandmother of Cherokee descent whom Tharp described in his autobiographical account. Her colorful persona and ability to inspire imaginative play were likely ingredients for a richly textured life.

Tharp had mentioned to colleagues how he also benefited from his loquacious mother whose talkativeness he believes to be a necessary component in a child's development. He further credited his own blossoming as a young writer to the experience of challenge and support from what was otherwise an ordinary high school. The impact of an effective teacher and a high-participation school environment in encouraging talented young people like himself, probably gave Tharp the first notions of successful schooling. He believes that when resources are limited and there is ample opportunity for everyone to fill the roles, young people can flourish under caring adults who encourage their full participation.

Tharp attended college in the 1950s. After a halting start, he returned home to work for his father's lumber business. His hunger for knowledge, however, led him to resume his studies within three years. Like many who are less privileged for whom his subsequent career would be an inspiration, he attended night classes as a commuting student. Tharp was in his element with the creative arts, but he also was drawn to psychology as a promising new field, and thus settled for a dual major in psychology and literature.

After graduating cum laude in 1957 from the University of Houston, Tharp continued with studies in psychology. Graduate school at the University of Michigan–Ann Arbor provided him with the intellectual and political socialization in debating ideas and social convictions. He appeared to have been granted tremendous latitude in independent inquiry and free expression, including challenging the psychoanalytic teachings in vogue at the time with phenomenological-existential ideas. His own reasoning was that psychoanalysis was too removed from the live world as given in experience. He further took a minor in cultural anthropology, which placed him in the social and community context of cultural realities, a perspective that would inform his study of clinical/social psychology as an area of specialization.

Although he could not continue with the dual concentration in psychology and English as a graduate student, Tharp's prized writing (Tharp, 1956–57) won him the opportunity to study at Middlebury College's Bread Loaf School of English. These Vermont summers in the company of major poets of his generation, including an audience with Robert Frost, must have nurtured and expanded his capacity for comprehending the human condition. Yet the seemingly welcome tensions of a dual pursuit gave way eventually to the practical. In realizing the constraints of divided attention and incomplete affiliation with either scholarly community, Tharp had to make a choice. The broader horizons of working as a psychologist held a greater appeal at the time than the world of literary criticism. Literary writing would continue as an avocation, more for personal development than as a professional goal.

Tharp completed his doctorate at Michigan after applying Lowell Kelly's role theory to the study of marital relationships. His dissertation and related work that resulted in a number of articles on marital roles and family interventions (Tharp, 1963a, 1963b, 1964, 1965) involved framing interactions with the sociological concepts of Talcott Parsons and Theodore Newcomb. Contrary to intrapsychic approaches to human experience, this research demonstrated that patterns of social interaction have observable regularities more informative than personality traits (Crago & Tharp, 1968). This work solidified the position that he would continue to hold regarding the theory and practice of psychology. As he recalled, "I moved permanently toward analyses of individuals in social interaction settings…as a more authentic and inclusive frame for understanding behavior and experience" (Tharp, 1998, p. 153). Tharp's interest in relationship patterns was reinforced by his pre-doctoral internship at the Palo Alto Veterans

Administration Hospital where he was exposed to the communication theory of Gregory Bateson and the family therapist Don Jackson as well as the community psychiatry of George, Fairweather. The revolutionary thinking of this group also included the new behaviorism of Len Ullman and Len Krasner. It was the action potentials of behaviorism that would serve him later.

Culture and Community in an Era of Behaviorism

In 1961 Tharp opted for a half-time academic appointment at the University of Arizona that allowed him to work half-time as a practicing psychologist. He started a Psychological Clinic for the University, and subsequently held a clinical position at the first Model Community Mental Health Center funded by the National Institutes of Mental Health where he became the Assistant Director for Program in 1967. The Center was staffed by a multidisciplinary team that included an anthropologist named Bill Holland. Tharp was drawn to Holland because of his growing interest in the cultural patterns of clients from the Mexican American and Native American communities. The two studied folk medicine and native healing practices (Holland & Tharp, 1964), and journeyed to Mexico and the Mayan country of Guatemala. This immersion in "otherness" was memorialized in the death of Holland at Tikal, a fateful turn with meanings that the reader should only glean from Tharp's own account (Tharp, 1998, p. 156). In the years to come, he never seemed to have lost his sense of awe for what is timeless and mystical.

Tharp's continuing research was aimed as much at theory building as the evaluation of therapeutic interventions. He was joined by Ralph Wetzel and Montrose Wolf who brought applied behaviorism from the University of Washington to Arizona. Together, they developed an applied research and intervention program targeting at-risk youth in school and home settings, a praxis that he would grow and model over a significant part of his career. He and Wetzel published their work under the title *Behavior Modification in the Natural Environment* (Tharp & Wetzel, 1969). Their triadic model of behavioral consultation reached beyond what had been attempted in applied treatment settings. It was one of the first books on behavior modification in everyday social settings, subsequently translated into German in 1975.

Tharp had been pondering on human change processes from the days of his involvement in psychotherapy and role-based marital interventions. By the late 1960s he was ready for a change in career and location where he would be able to follow this interest. His pioneering work with behavioral psychology and interest in cultural aspects of clinical psychology landed him the role of Clinical Director at the University of Hawai'i where he served as the founding director of the doctoral program in Clinical Studies from 1968 to 1972.

Hawai'i was an ideal setting for students of culture, offering not only its own exotic mix, but also a community of scholars representing many other cultural and ethnic groups. The University of Hawai'i had a partnership with the State Department funded East-West Center that is still housed today on its Mānoa campus. The mission of the Center at the time was international exchange and the advancement of intercultural understanding. In a climate warmed with aloha and the openness of sixties liberalism, the possibilities were endless. Faculty and students like myself could take advantage of talks by East-West Center Fellows, enjoy the arts from Pacific Rim countries, and benefit from the day-to-day ethnography of campus life. The intellectual climate was just as rich as the cultural. As an example, Tharp sent me one day to consult with Gregory Bateson who was then a Center Fellow, on the double bind theory that I was considering for my master's thesis. I left Bateson's office with his generous draft copy of the manuscript for what was to be *Steps to an Ecology of Mind* (Bateson, 1972).

It was in Hawai'i that Tharp brought cultural theory and community research and action into synergy with the powers of behaviorism. His direction was not simply to follow the Zeitgeist of behaviorism. Students in the program were to learn about the role of culture in human behavior and how to apply behavioral principles in community settings such as schools and mental health agencies. Tharp also was creating a community of learners among students and faculty. As an academic leader, if one were to apply Campbell's (1979) tribal model of social system vehicle for knowledge creation and dissemination, he was undoubtedly a most effective and charismatic tribal chief. One could feel the magic in Gartley Hall, home of the Psychology Department at UH. The original team of social-personality cultural theorists and community-behavioral researchers—Ronald Gallimore, Anthony Marsella, Scott MacDonald, Arthur Staats, and David Watson—were joined by talented young faculty Michael Diamond, Ian Evans, and Clifford O'Donnell. The Clinical Studies program with its diverse strengths received full accreditation by the American Psychological Association in its initial founding period that ended in 1972.

Many publications resulted from this time, including the book *Self-directed Behavior: Self Modification for Personal Adjustment*, co-authored with David Watson (Watson & Tharp, 1972). This book, now in its seventh edition, was translated into the German language in 1974. To quote from a description provided by Cliff O'Donnell, "Over its many iterations, the text has evolved to reflect a shift in the field of psychology to emphasize social and cultural contexts, as the current edition includes application of neo-Vygotskian theory." Tharp's philosophical attraction to Vygotsky is not surprising, for he was engaged in sustaining a community of learning and practice in a Vygotskian sense. Tharp's leadership continued in a different setting after he resigned as Clinical Director in 1972 for a project that would engage him for the next two decades.

From KEEP (1969–1986) to CREDE (1996–2003)

The Kamehameha Schools, funded by the estate of Princess Bernice Pauhi Bishop to educate Hawaiian and part-Hawaiian children, was struggling with the poor performance of its students. In 1969–1970, Jack Darvill, President of the Kamehameha Schools, sought help from Ronald Gallimore who had been conducting ethnographic research in the Hawaiian community. Tharp was asked to join efforts with Gallimore in finding answers to why the students were reading below national norms, and what could be done to improve their learning achievement. Tharp became the principal investigator and chief executive officer of the Kamehameha Early Education Program (KEEP) for the next sixteen years. Tharp and Gallimore worked with anthropologists, including Tharp's former wife Cathie Jordan, teachers, linguists, and those interested in early education in developing a program of research and intervention.

The undertaking was unprecedented. Two elementary schools built for Hawaiian children with a population that grew to 600 students served as the laboratory. Using a multimethod approach and painstakingly thorough observation and systematic evaluation, learning settings were analyzed and components of intervention programs tested. Over the years, with gradually demonstrated results and gains in credibility, ten public elementary schools on three islands serving 5,000 students a year were incorporated as field sites. At the height of activity, KEEP employed more than 200 staff, with five research departments and 42 active researchers and research assistants. The continuing commitment of funding by the Bishop estate and other grants enabled the project to operate at an average annual budget of five million dollars. Students in the KEEP program eventually achieved at or above national norms on standardized reading tests while comparison groups continued to score well below average. The program effects were found in the KEEP research school and in public school classrooms.

The success story of the KEEP project could hardly be explained by any factor alone, though the fact that it did not have to be subject to whimsical changes in politically driven agendas (as is often the case with external funding) was a key factor. It took unusual leadership and organizational skills to create an R & D center from scratch. The vision and drive of Tharp, his exceptional ability to work with a multidisciplinary team, and to value the input of front-line teachers and workers were reflected in the ethos of the program and the dedication of those involved. Gallimore also deserves much of the credit, as he remained involved the entire time after moving to California for a professorship at UCLA. The two collaborators mentored many research projects on the cultural patterns of Hawaiian students, and on teaching and learning, behavioral training and consultation, and evaluation technology. The most complete report on the work associated with KEEP is found in their book *Rousing Minds to Life: Teaching, Learning and Schooling in Social Context* (Tharp & Gallimore, 1988).

It would be misleading to give the impression of smooth sailing over such an extended period of time. The initial plan of educational innovation was based on five years of previous work associated with the Hawaiian Community Research Project (HCRP). In the first two years of implementation, many of the approaches failed or had negligible effects. Extrapolating from research to classroom practice required a laboratory-school setting where the interventions could be fine-tuned, and where the characteristics of public school classrooms were replicated to a credible degree (R. Gallimore, personal communication, 2003). Hence began the KEEP research and development school in 1972. It took another five years for the team to develop an effective reading program. When progress was slow in the early years, Tharp and Gallimore had to stay on course by resisting pressures to follow other directions. Gallimore recalls one high power national figure recommending to the president of Kamehameha Schools to abandon the field-based research and development for a theory-based approach. "Roland's ability to handle these challenges in his deft and articulate manner won the day" (Gallimore, personal communication, 2003). Impatience of another kind came from the desire to accelerate the outreach of KEEP to the public schools. It would not have been wise, however, to proceed with large scale replication before the program was sufficiently tested in the laboratory-school. There was a continuing need to communicate the process and outcome of the project to different constituencies. Again, Gallimore credits Tharp for his ability to capture the essence of KEEP activities, thereby producing useful road maps for others.

The intellectual and professional yields of the KEEP period, as with its social significance, are immeasurable. A model of cultural accommodation had emerged to inform education and community-based psychosocial intervention (Tharp, 1989a, 1991, 1992). Hundreds of scholarly and professional reports were disseminated in the twenty-year period between 1969 and 1989. Some of the technical reports were published by the Center for Studies of Multicultural Higher Education that Tharp directed at the University of Hawai'i from 1987 to 1989. The College of Education at the University of Hawai'i had also recognized the importance of preparing teachers by collaborating with KEEP in developing the PreService Education for Teachers of Minorities Program (PETOM). Co-founded by Tharp with Stephanie Stoll Dalton, this program was the precursor of similar cohort programs in teachers' education. A generation of teachers and researchers were trained on this model that resulted from their collaborative participation in the project, an experience that was itself an invaluable lesson in the communal search for problem solutions. For Tharp, "it represented a confirmation…that the adequate plane of analysis for human service delivery (whether educational or clinical) is not the individual considered as an isolated unit, but the individual in the context of social interaction" (Tharp, 1998, p. 162).

After the successful run with the KEEP project, the Kamehmeha Schools decided to shift its priorities by the mid-1980s. More resources and attention were to be given to the high performing students who would have a better chance of pursuing a college education. For Tharp, it was time to move on. Tharp's article on psychocultural variables and constants (Tharp, 1989b) punctuated his work on teaching and learning in schools up to this point. He furthered his interest in the sociocultural perspective by looking to the cultural-historical activity theory of Vygotsky (1978) for an inclusive developmental framework that could account for the historical, psychological, interpersonal, and the communal. He and his collaborators saw applications of Vygotskian ideas in cognitive development, mentoring, and schooling (Gallimore & Tharp, 1990; Gallimore, Tharp, & John-Steiner, 1994; Tharp & Gallimore, 1991).

Following his resignation from KEEP, Tharp took early retirement from the University of Hawai'i. He applied his leadership skills to academic administration at the United States International University based in San Diego. The desire to continue his life's work in education, however, brought him soon to the University of California, Santa Cruz in 1991 as Professor of Education and Psychology and Chair of the Board of Studies in Education. There, he co-directed with Eugene Garcia and Barry McLaughlin the National Center for Research on Cultural Diversity and Second Language Learning (NCRCDSLL), one of the national centers for research and development funded with a $6 million cooperative agreement by the U.S. Department of Education.

In this research and development consortium he continued his earlier efforts by focussing on Native American, Latino, Asian immigrant, and diverse ethnic and cultural groups. The research and program development involved an ethnogenetic analysis of socialization and cognition, and application of the principles of cultural accommodation (Tharp, 1994a; Tharp, Dalton, & Yamauchi, 1994; Yamauchi & Tharp, 1995). The cumulative research work conducted at the University of Hawai'i, University of California, Santa Cruz, and in field settings that extended beyond Hawai'i, California, and New Mexico to Haitian, Appalachian, and rural Alaskan native communities reflected an emphasis on school-community relationships as they impact on at-risk students. The general principles derived from the KEEP years seemed to apply—to change activity in context requires sustained work in changing the context, including both school and community.

Tharp had always been interested in community development as a necessary measure in working with educationally and socially at-risk youth (O'Donnell & Tharp, 1982; Tharp, Cutts, & Burkholder, 1970). An example was the Zuni project on community programs for youth development for which he was the principal investigator (Tharp & O'Donnell, 1994). He understood the importance of involving the community, in this case tribal leaders, families, juvenile police, and alcohol and drug programs, in implementing culturally appropriate ecological interventions. The Zuni project reflects current understanding about the need to build resiliency and protective factors with integrative school-based and community-based services. By collaborating with community psychologists, Tharp contributed to community development in both theory and practice (O'Donnell & Tharp, 1990; O'Donnell, Tharp & Wilson, 1993; O'Donnell, Wilson & Tharp, 2001; Tharp, 2003; Wilson, O'Donnell, & Tharp, 1994).

Since 1986 Tharp has been a member of the Board of Directors for Intermountain Centers for Human Development based in Tucson, Arizona, and Santa Fe, New Mexico. The Intermountain Centers provide community-based residential and support services to at-risk Native American youth and persons with disabilities. Tharp provides training and intellectual leadership in addressing issues related to the development of at-risk youth. For many years he also served on the National Evaluation Advisory Panel of Early Intervention Systems for Navajo children and families. He was in a position to comment on the social, institutional and policy issues in educational practice and reform (Tharp, 1993, 1994b).

The early 1990s, however, were much more recalcitrant to innovation and change than the 1960s and the 1970s. Communities in California and nationwide did not seem to have cohesive pro-education values such as those shared by stakeholders of the KEEP project. It required Tharp to assemble nationally a diverse team of collaborators who were involved in applied educational research that addressed underserved populations, and to seek funding for a large-scale R & D center. In 1996 he became the director of the Center for Research on Education, Diversity, and Excellence (CREDE). Created with U.S. Department of Education support of $20 million funding in a five-year cooperative agreement, the mission of CREDE was to promote excellence by targeting at-risk students especially from linguistically and culturally diverse communities. With a network of about a hundred colleagues, it created and evaluated programs in educational development at psychological, social, and community levels. Many of the collaborators were neo-Vygotskians who believe in the value of mentoring and assisted learning by communities of practice in activity settings.

During the height of its operation, the Center coordinated 31 projects nationwide that gathered data and tested curriculum models with diverse student populations in wide-ranging settings. As described on the CREDE Web site (http://www.crede.org), its philosophy includes challenging students with high standards, regarding bilingual proficiency as desirable for all students, and cultural diversity as assets for teaching and learning, as well as emphasizing social and learning skills as ways of mitigating risk factors. The approach was informed by both a general theory of developmental, teaching and schooling processes and a model of individual and cultural accommodation. Some of the work associated with CREDE can be found in Tharp (1997) and the interactive video package *Teaching Alive! Effective Pedagogy for Diverse Classrooms*. Based on the synthesis of research in the field, five standards for the educational development of at-risk students were articulated. These standards for effective pedagogy presented in *Teaching Transformed: Achieving Excellence, Fairness, Inclusion and Harmony* (Tharp, Estrada, Dalton, & Yamauchi, 2000), aim at the development of cognitive complexity and competency in language and literacy across the curriculum. The approach Tharp and his associates advocated involves teachers and students co-constructing meanings through dialog and joint productive activity. As the title of the book suggests, educational transformation is viewed as a path to social equity and a just society. The authors proposed to offer end goals for policy makers, new hope for burned-out educators, and a liberation pedagogy for critical theorists who have pointed to structural inequalities in society.

During 2000–2003 seven synthesis teams were constituted by CREDE with researchers, practitioners, and policymakers in education. Each team was charged with extracting the major findings from the field and focusing on a specific area of language learning and academic achievement, professional development, or pre-service teacher education for diversity, and school, family, and community. These teams have continued to produce state-of-the-art knowledge on diversity education and recommendations for future research, policy, and practice. As an example of the productivity of those involved, from one project alone at the Center for Social Organization of Schools of Johns Hopkins University, a book (Datnow, Hubbard, & Mehan, 2002), an article (Datnow, Borman, Stringfield et al., 2003), half of one of three most successful volumes in the last decade for the National Society for the Study of Education (Stringfield & Land, 2002), three special issues (Cooper & Gandara, 2001; Datnow, 1999) of the *Journal of Education for Students Placed at Risk* (JESPAR), and a fourth in the planning resulted from this period (Stringfield, 2003).

Legacy of a Theorist, Researcher, and Educator

As a theorist, Tharp has shown that it is possible to capture the complexities of human learning and interaction with units of analysis that take culture and social context into account. What he accomplished in spite of the reductionistic bias of psychology as a behavioral science is further supported by the usefulness of his inclusive conceptual frame. The programs created during the KEEP years have been modeled by others throughout the United States, and in Australia, New Zealand, Canada, Europe, and Latin America. Tharp and his collaborators have developed a theory of teaching and schooling that includes both the personal and the social plane. He taught us that conceptual work does not have to parallel methodological reductionism. His theoretical synthesis of behavioral principles and neo-Vygotskian perspectives on human development found widespread application in educational settings and other venues for fostering human change.

The research praxis that Tharp has developed over time illustrates the utility of methodological pluralism as well as a reflective understanding of one's research practice. The metamethodology of evaluation practice and research and development, described by Tharp (1981) and Tharp and Gallimore (1979, 1982), represents yet another contribution from Tharp as a methodologist and evaluation practitioner. The seral model of evaluation succession was hailed as an admirable innovation in the history of program evaluation (Sechrest & Figueredo, 1993). By articulating the meta-reasoning involved in the inquiry process, his work with Gallimore provides R & D practitioners with an invaluable resource. Unlike the sterile and often decontextualized presentation of research designs and methods, this modeling of experienced research practice can better serve students of research and evaluation.

As a man of knowledge, Tharp's lived philosophy was in the best of the pragmatist tradition, with action being the sphere of knowledge generation and evaluation. When many academic researchers have turned to theoretical knowledge as the starting point of inquiry, he and his associates have continued to engage in research that begins with problems identified outside of the academy. This mode of knowledge generation that often involves stakeholders and researchers from multiple disciplines in collaborative problem-solving will perhaps pave the way to a new sociology of knowledge. It goes beyond both basic research and the types of applied research that have characterized academic knowledge production. Contrary to a discipline-based form of scholarship and the exclusive use of a dominant research approach, Tharp was able to demonstrate the utility of pluralistic research methods for diverse setting analyses (of home, school, and community). His interest in other fields of knowledge has allowed him to achieve a more comprehensive understanding of the chosen substantive domains, using the language and inquiry methods of different disciplines. Few psychologists have the breadth of interdisciplinary scholarship as Tharp.

Although Tharp seldom refers to his own work as action research, he was interested in engaging others in a joint process of articulating the goals and values that inform their inquiry in addition to fine-tuning their programs of research and development. The CREDE project offered the opportunity for representatives from multiple R & D sites across the country to convene and discuss their activities. Tharp worked hard at using his leadership to build intersubjectivity among the diverse researchers from these different sites. As described by Lois Yamauchi (personal communication, 2003), "to be part of that team was an incredible experience." This was echoed by Sam Stringfield (personal communication, 2003) who reported that the meetings "were unlike anything I'd experienced in my professional career—and better." Tharp provided a wide range of interactions between teams from diverse projects, "all in a strikingly accepting atmosphere."

Over time, Tharp attempted to facilitate discussions among the project leaders and to help them derive shared principles such as those eventually summarized in Tharp et al. (2000). Whether all project leaders have embraced these principles with a sense of collective ownership is hard to determine. As Lois Yamauchi and I both surmised, in an academic culture of individualism it is difficult sometimes to resocialize researchers in the ideology and practice of participatory action research. Nonetheless, his great mind, tenacity, and heart seem to have inspired others to improve the education of disadvantaged youth. Stringfield (personal communication, 2003) probably speaks for many of Tharp's collaborators when he stated "For his big dreams, hard work, and warm friendship, we all owe Roland our deepest gratitude."

Tharp and Gallimore received the prestigious Grawemeyer Award in Education in 1993 for their book *Rousing Minds to Life: Teaching, Learning and Schooling in Social Context* (Tharp & Gallimore, 1988) and related work. Not only did they provide insights into the relationship between language, thought, and literacy, but they also redefined school as only meaning a place where all can learn. This vision of schooling is clearly held by Tharp who views education as a personalized experience whereby the student can fully participate by bringing his or her cultural being into learning activities that result in co-constructed understanding. Yet, the relationship between culture and education is intricate and increasingly politicized. Culture affects not only the social organization of schools and whether a student would fit into a given classroom environment; it also brings with it the history of social power and control. The baggage for the politically disempowered and those who have failed them presents further barriers to transforming the nature of schooling in American society. For Tharp, who proffers hopes of a just society through inclusion, excellence, and harmony, these realistic challenges must limit the fulfillment of a vision that some might regard as utopian. He has no illusions about the viability of reform or the sustainability of hard-earned changes.

As an educator, Tharp has been advocating for school reform that implies social reform. Sarason (1990) had predicted the failure of educational reform even before the National Education Goals were codified for implementation. Those who have followed education reform movements in the past few decades (e.g., Tharinger et al., 1996) saw the need for integrating education, health, and social reform initiatives. Multi-pronged systemic approaches such as proposed by Tharp and his associates would need to be supported by a sea change in public understanding and political leadership. Meanwhile, the legacy of KEEP and CREDE is best appreciated for the rare combination of idealistic vision and immense practicality. The same could be said of Tharp's life-time contribution as a man of knowledge and conviction. With values not unlike that of critical theorists and those who espouse a liberation pedagogy, Tharp has moved beyond ideology and rhetoric to generative theory and effective action that yielded unmistakable social good.

Sunset on Santa Cruz Mountains

Tharp retired in December 2004. His writing calendar however extends well beyond this date, with contracts for yet another book and a collection of poems. He plans to write a memoir of his professional life that will shed light on the human struggles and triumphs involved in the problem solving efforts he has undertaken with diverse cultures and communities. He had published literary works between 1956 and 1984 (see Appendix). For about an interim of sixteen years, it appears that he devoted his time and energy to the research and education projects that have defined his career. A few years ago, he resumed poetry writing, and he is poised to produce more creative writing at this point. This man of many talents had also been a film-maker while living in Hawai'i. During the years he dedicated to educational work, he completed various media productions (see Appendix). It is only fitting to characterize Tharp as a wizard of words and an artist in a double life. In his autobiographical chapter (Tharp, 1998) he offers a creative short piece that could be a poem or play or film. Titled "Containing the Lie," it reflects his fascination with language and the framing of human experience. For one fiercely committed to truth-telling in both art and science, he seems to have retained a certain philosophical fortitude toward the subject.

Tharp has lived a full life, with four children, Donald, Tom, Michael, and Julie, step-daughter Jessica, and three grandchildren, James, Carissa, and Avery. There is much to look forward to in retirement. As he looks out at the skyline of his Santa Cruz residence, I imagine him picturing himself by the ocean writing poetry, or having a quiet afternoon painting in his studio. Or perhaps he might travel the globe and share his knowledge and creativity in other venues? The last summer when I saw him, he had just finished teaching a course for graduate students in Education at the University of Hawai'i. According to Lois Yamauchi, these students reported that Tharp's course was the best learning experience they have ever had. There is no doubt that the teaching must go on and the story has to be told again for the next generation.

Appendix
Career Summary of Roland Tharp

Roland Tharp was born 1930 in La Marque, Texas. He is the author or co-author of five books, twenty-one book chapters, more than seventy journal articles, and over a hundred conference papers and technical reports in psychology and education. A Diplomate of the American Board of Examiners in Professional Psychology, he has maintained a multifaceted career, with contributions to psychology, education, literature, and the arts. He was the recipient of the Grawemeyer Award in Education in 1993, and has received other honors for scholarly achievement and excellence in teaching. His literary contributions include a book of poems and forty-seven poems, short fiction, and essays. He was the recipient of a number of literary awards, including the Grand Prize in the *Atlantic Monthly* National Contest for Essay in 1956, the Robert Frost Fellowship in Poetry in 1960, and the *Arizona Quarterly* Prize for Fiction in 1964. He has also been the producer, writer, and director of several films, video, and photography-poetry and poetry-drama. He received the Silver Monitor Award from the International Television Association in 1985, and the American Film Magazine Award in the Hawai'i International Film Festival in 1990. His academic and professional history follows.

1957	B.A., Cum Laude (Literature & Psychology), University of Houston.
1958	M.A. (Psychology, Minor, Anthropology), University of Michigan.
1961	Ph.D. (Clinical/Social Psychology), University of Michigan.
1961–68	Assistant Professor to Associate Professor, University of Arizona.
1964–66	Field Selection Officer, Peace Corps, Washington, D.C.
1964–68	Founding Executive Director, The Psychological Clinic, University of Arizona.
1967–68	Assistant Director for Program, Southern Arizona Mental Health Center.
1968	Diplomate, American Board of Examiners in Professional Psychology.
1968–89	Associate Professor to Professor, University of Hawai'i; Founding Director of Clinical Studies Program, 1968–72.
1968, 69, 74	Visiting Psychologist, American Psychological Association.
1969–86	Founder, Chief Executive Officer, and Principle Investigator, Kamehameha Early Education Program (KEEP), Center for Development of Education, Honolulu.

1971–72	President, Hawai'i Psychological Association.
1975	Visiting Professor, California State University at Long Beach.
1978	President, Hawai'i Literary Arts Council.
1985	Co-Founder, Preservice Education for Teachers of Minorities (PETOM) Program, College of Education, University of Hawai'i.
1986–present	Board of Directors, Intermountain Center for Human Development, Santa Fe, New Mexico, and Tucson, Arizona.
1987–89	Founding Director, Center for the Study of Multicultural Higher Education, University of Hawai'i.
1989–present	Professor Emeritus of Psychology, University of Hawai'i.
1989–90	Dean, School of Human Behavior; Provost and Vice-President for Academic Affairs, United States International University.
1991–present	National Evaluation Advisory Panel, Early Intervention Systems for Navajo Children and Families.
1991–present	Professor of Education and Psychology, University of California, Santa Cruz; Chair of Board of Studies in Education, 1991–95.
1995–96	Co-Director, Center for Research on Cultural Diversity and Second Language Learning, OERI-USDOE and University of California at Santa Cruz.
1996	Director, Center for Research on Education, Diversity and Excellence (CREDE), OERI-USDOE and University of California at Santa Cruz.

Professional Awards

The Grawemeyer Award in Education, 1993.

Shunzo Sakamaki Extraordinary Lecturer, University of Hawai'i, 1992. "Life on the border: Between two cultures."

Significant Professional Contribution Award, Hawai'i Psychological Association, 1987.

Regents Medal for Excellence in Teaching, University of Hawai'i, 1970.

Literary and Artistic Awards

Runner-up, Impact Poetry Book Award, 1979.

Sou'wester Prize in Poetry, Winter, 1974, for "Last Things."

Arizona Quarterly Prize for fiction, 1964, for "Bald She Walks Among the Peacocks."

Ida and Charles Freeman Short Story Award, 1964, Voices, Wayne State University, for "Cat-House."

Avert Hopwood Award, Major, in Poetry, 1961, University of Michigan, for "Poems."

Robert Frost Fellowship in Poetry, 1960, Middlebury College.

Grand Prize, *Atlantic Monthly* National Contest (Essay), 1956, for "Romanesque Sculpture: A Study in the Hideous."

Claire Raymer Greenwood Award, Poetry, 1954, 1955, 1956, University of Houston.

American Film Magazine Award, Best Hawai'i Production, Hawai'i International Film Festival, 1990.

Silver Monitor Award (for Information Video Documentary of KEEP), International Television Association, Honolulu, 1985.

Selected Publications in Psychology and Education

Crago, M., & Tharp, R. G. (1968). Psychopathology and marital role disturbance: A test of the Tharp-Otis descriptive hypothesis. *Journal of Consulting and Clinical Psychology, 32*, 338–341.

Cunningham, T. R., & Tharp, R. G. (1981). The influence of settings on accuracy and reliability of behavioral observation. *Behavioral Assessment, 3*, 67–78.

Day, R., Boggs, S., Tharp, R. G., Speidel, G. E., & Gallimore, R. (1974). A standard English performance measure for young children: The Standard English Repetition Test (SERT). *Working Papers in Linguistics, 6*.

Gallimore, R., & Tharp, R. G. (1990). Teaching mind and society: A theory of education and schooling. In L. Moll (Ed.), *Vygotsky and education: Instructional implications and applications of sociohistorical psychology* (pp. 175–205). Cambridge: Cambridge University Press.

Gallimore, R., Tharp, R. G., & Speidel, G. E. (1978). The relationship of sibling caretaking and attentiveness to a peer tutor. *American Educational Research Journal, 15*, 267–273.

Gallimore, R., Tharp, R. G., & John-Steiner, V. (1994). The developmental and socio-historical foundations of mentoring. In C. Herrrington (Ed.). *Mentoring.* New York: Columbia University Institute for Urban Minority Education.

Holland, W. R., & Tharp, R. G. (1964). Highland Maya psychotherapy. *American Anthropologist, 66*, 41–53.

Marsella, A. J., Tharp, R. G., & Ciborowski, T. (Eds.). (1979). *Perspectives in cross-cultural psychology.* New York: Academic Press.

O'Donnell, C. R., & Tharp, R. G. (1982). Community intervention and the use of multi-disciplinary knowledge. In A. S. Bellack, M. Hersen, & A. E. Kazdin (Eds.), *International handbook of behavior modification and therapy* (pp. 291–318). New York: Plenum Press.

O'Donnell, C. R., & Tharp, R. G. (1990). Community intervention guided by theoretical development. In A. S. Bellack, M. Hersen, & A. E. Kazdin (Eds.), *International handbook of behavior modification and therapy* (pp. 251–266). 2nd ed. New York: Plenum Press.

O'Donnell, C. R., Tharp, R. G., & Wilson, K. (1993). Activity setting as the unit of analysis: A theoretical basis for community intervention and development. *American Journal of Community Psychology, 21*, 501–520.

O'Donnell, C. R., Wilson, K., & Tharp, R. G. (2001). The cross-cultural context: What can be learned from community development projects. In G. B. Melton, R. A. Thompson, & M. A. Small (Eds.), *Toward a child-centered neighborhood-based child protection system* (pp. 104–114). Westport, CT: Praeger.

Roberts, R. N., & Tharp, R. G. (1980). Naturalistic study of children's self-directed speech in academic problem-solving. *Cognitive Research and Therapy, 4*, 341–352.

Speidel, G. R., Tharp, R. G., & Kobayashi, L. (1985). Is there a comprehension problem for children who speak nonstandard English? A study of children with Hawaiian English backgrounds. *Applied Psycholinguistics, 6*, 83–96.

Tanaka-Matsumi, J., & Tharp, R. G. (1977). Teaching the teachers of Hawaiian children: Training and consultation strategies. *Topics in Culture Learning, 5*, 92–106.

Tharp, R. G. (1963a). Dimensions of marriage roles. *Journal of Marriage and Family Living, 25*, 389–404. Reprinted in S. T. Habel (Ed.). (1969). *Readings in marriage and family.* New York: MSS Educational Publishing Co.

Tharp, R. G. (1963b). Psychological patterning in marriage. *Psychological Bulletin, 60*, 97–117. Reprinted in several sources.

Tharp, R. G. (1964). Marriage roles: Structure, function, and effects on child development. *American Journal of Orthopsychiatry, 34* (2), 303–304.

Tharp, R. G. (1965). Marriage roles, child development, and family treatment. *American Journal of Orthopsychiatry, 25*, 531–538.

Tharp, R. G. (1981). The metamethodology of research and development. *Educational Perspectives, 20* (1), 42–48.

Tharp, R. G. (1982). The effective instruction of comprehension: Results and description of the Kamehameha Early Education Program. *Reading Research Quarterly, 17*, 503–527.

Tharp, R. G. (1989a). Culturally compatible education: A formula for designing effective classrooms. In H. T. Trueba, G. Spindler, & L. Spindler (Eds.), *What do anthropologists have to say about dropouts?* (pp. 51–66). New York: The Falmer Press.

Tharp, R. G. (1989b). Psychocultural variables and constants: Effects on teaching and learning in schools. *American Psychologist, 44*, 349–359.

Tharp, R. G. (1991). Cultural diversity and treatment of children. *Journal of Consulting and Clinical Psychology, 59*, 799–812.

Tharp, R. G. (1992). Cultural compatibility and diversity: Implications for the urban classroom. *Teaching Thinking and Problem Solving, 14* (6), 1–9.

Tharp, R. G. (1993). The institutional and social context of educational practice and reform. In E. A. Forman, N. Minick, & C. A. Stone (Eds.), *Contexts for learning: Sociocultural dynamics in children's development* (pp. 269–282). Cambridge: Cambridge University Press.

Tharp, R. G. (1994a). Intergroup differences among Native Americans in socialization and child cognition: An ethnogenetic analysis. In P. Greenfield

& R. Cocking (Eds.), *Cross-cultural roots of minority child development* (pp. 87–105). Hillsdale, NJ: Lawrence Erlbaum.

Tharp, R. G. (1994b). Research knowledge and policy issues in cultural diversity and education. In B. McLeod (Ed.), *Language and learning: Educating linguistically diverse students* (pp. 129–167). Albany, NY: State University of New York Press. Reprinted in R. J. Anson (Ed.), *Systemic reform: Perspectives on personalizing education* (pp. 169–200). Washington, DC: Office of Educational Research and Improvement, U.S. Department of Education.

Tharp, R. G. (1997). *From at-risk to excellence: Research, theory and principles for practice.* Research Report No. 1. Washington, DC: Center for Applied Linguistics and Center for Research on Education, Diversity and Excellence.

Tharp, R. G. (1998). Send in the angel. In L. T. Hoshmand (Ed.), *Creativity and moral vision in psychology: Narratives of identity and commitment in a postmodern age* (pp.144–172). Thousand Oaks, CA: Sage Publications.

Tharp, R. G. (2003). Juvenile delinquency: Culture and community, person and society, theory and research. In C. R. O'Donnell (Ed.), *Culture, peers, and delinquency* (pp.1–11). New York: Haworth Press.

Tharp, R. G., Cutts, R. I., & Burkholder, R. (1970). The community mental health center and the schools: A model for collaboration through demonstration. *Community Mental Health Journal, 6,* 126–135. Reprinted in J. Fischer (Ed.). (1973). *Interpersonal helping: Emerging approaches for social work practice.* Springfield, IL: C. C. Thomas.

Tharp, R. G., Dalton, S., & Yamauchi, L. A. (1994). Principles for culturally compatible Native American education. *Journal of Navajo Education, 11* (3), 21–27.

Tharp, R. G., & Gallimore, R. (1979). The ecology of program research and development: A model of evaluation succession. In L. B. Sechrest (Ed.), *Evaluation studies review annual.* Vol. 4. Beverly Hills: Sage Publications.

Tharp, R. G., & Gallimore, R. (1982). Inquiry process in program development. *Journal of Community Psychology, 10,* 103–118.

Tharp, R. G., & Gallimore, R. (1985). The logical status of metacognitive training. *Journal of Abnormal Child Psychology, 13,* 455–466.

Tharp, R. G., & Gallimore, R. (1988). *Rousing minds to life: Teaching, learning and Schooling in social context.* New York: Cambridge University Press.

Tharp, R. G., & Gallimore, R. (1991). A theory of teaching as assisted performance. In P. Light, S. Sheldon, & M. Woodhead (Eds.), *Learning to think: Child development in social context* (pp. 42–61). Vol. 2. London: Routledge.

Tharp, R. G., P. Estrada, S. Dalton, & L. Yamauchi (2000). *Teaching transformed: Achieving excellence, fairness, inclusion and harmony.* Boulder, CO: Westview Press.

Tharp, R. G., & Meadow, A. (1973). Differential change in folk disease concepts. *Interamerican Journal of Psychology, 7* (1–2), 55-63.

Tharp, R. G., Meadow, A., Lennhoff, S., & Satterfield, D. (1968). Changes in marriage roles accompanying the acculturation of the Mexican-American wife. *Journal of Marriage and the Family, 30,* 404–412. Reprinted in S. W. Webster (Ed.). (1971). *Knowing and understanding the disadvantaged.* Scranton, PA: International Textbook Co.

Tharp, R. G., & Note, M. (1988). The triadic model of consultation: New developments. In F. West (Ed.). *School consultation: Interdisciplinary perspectives on theory, research, training, and practice* (pp. 35–51). Austin, TX: Research and Training Project on School Consultation, The University of Texas at Austin and The Association of Educational and Psychological Consultants, Austin, Texas.

Tharp, R. G., & O'Donnell, C. R. (1994). *Native American Education Demonstration Project: Youth issues.* Santa Cruz, CA: University of California at Santa Cruz Native American Education Project.

Tharp, R. G., & Otis, D. (1966). Toward a theory for therapeutic intervention in families. *Journal of Consulting Psychology, 30,* 426–434. Reprinted in L. N. Glasser & P. H. Glasser (Eds.). (1970). *Families in crisis.* New York: Harper and Row.

Tharp, R. G., & Wetzel, R. J. (1969). *Behavior modification in the natural environment.* New York: Academic Press.

Thorne, G. L., Tharp, R. G., & Wetzel, R. J. (1967). Behavior modification techniques: New tools for probation officers. *Federal Probation, 31,* 21–27. Reprinted in W. C. Becker (Ed.), (1971), *An empirical basis for change in education.* Science Research Associates; and in W. C. Trow & E. E. Haddan (Eds.), (1974). *Technology and teaching: A textbook in educational psychology.* Educational Technology Publications.

Vogt, L. A., Jordan, C., & Tharp, R. G. (1992). Explaining school failure, producing school success: Two cases. *Anthropology and Education Quarterly, 18,* 276–286. Reprinted in E. Jacob & C. Jordan (Eds.). (1992). *Minority education: Anthropological perspectives* (pp. 53-66). Norwood, NJ: Ablex.

Watson, D. R., & Tharp, R. G. (1972, 1977, 1981, 1985, 1988, 1992, 1996). *Self-directed behavior.* CA: Brooks/Cole.

Wilson, K., O'Donnell, C. R., & Tharp, R. G. (1994). *Six principles of practice in community and neighborhood development viewed from an asset perspective.* Center for Youth Research Publication No. 364. Honolulu: University of Hawai'i at Mānoa.

Yamauchi, L. A., & Tharp, R. G. (1995). Culturally compatible conversations in Native American classrooms. *Linguistics and Education, 7,* 349–367.

Selected Literary Publications

When we kill the world. *The Atlantic Prize Papers,* 1953–54.

Old mad woman. *The Atlantic Prize Papers,* 1954–55.

Romanesque sculpture: A study in the hideous; and the cosmogony of Dylan Thomas, *The Atlantic Prize Papers,* 1956–57.

Cat-house (short fiction), *Voices,* Summer 1963.

Bald she walks among the peacocks (short fiction), *Arizona Quarterly,* Summer 1964.

A girl is fresh stormed snow; For my wife in February, *Prairie Schooner,* Spring 1974.

Last things; Railroad yard, *Prairie Schooner,* Winter 1973–74.

Colding nights; Because; Essay on the evolution of social influence, *Prairie Schooner,* Winter 1974–75.

From the woods, *Shenandoah,* Summer 1975, vol. 26, no. 4.

Fright tale for an adolescent daughter, *Shenandoah,* vol. 10, Summer 1976.

Kyrie Eleison; Ogive; Tremor Harmonic, *Quixote,* 1976, vol. 9, no. 9.

Along the road to the ruins, *Prairie Schooner,* Summer 1978.

Highland Station: Poems by Roland Tharp, Poetry Texas Press, 1977. Second Printing, 1978.

The aged apostles. *Christianity and Literature*, vol. 27 (2), Winter 1978.

The Piero poems, II: The baptism; The Piero poems, III: The nativity, *Christianity and Literature,* Spring 1978 & Winter 1979.

Cabin at Bread Loaf Mountain; Stony Littleton, *Poetry Now*, 1979, vol. 5, no. 1 (25).

Carpenters, waterfall, stream, sea; The ageing friends; Sack-of-bones; Two incantations of ill will, *Prairie Schooner*, Spring 1980.

Before the storm in Progresso, *Hawai'i Review*, 1984, no. 16.

Multimedia Productions for Education

Teaching alive! Effective pedagogy for diverse classrooms. Interactive CD-ROM, videotape, text, transcripts, activities. CREDE, University of California, Santa Cruz, 95064.

Ka na'i pono: Striving for excellence (KEEP). (A documentary overview of the essential components of the Kamehameha Early Education Reading Program.) Videocassette. Honolulu: The Kamehameha Schools, 1982.

Coming home to school. (Cross-cultural psychology and education). Film and videocassette. Honolulu: The Kamehameha Schools, 1981.

Catch them being good. (Classroom management techniques). Videocassette. Honolulu: The Kamehameha Schools, 1974.

Visual and Performing Arts Productions

In celebration of eros, Poetry/Drama, Mānoa Valley Theater, Honolulu, May 1978.

Scenes from the life. Athens International Video Festival, 1982.

My Aunt May. American Film Magazine Award, Hawai'i International Film Festival, 1990.

Note

All references to Tharp's psychology and education publications are listed in Selected Publications in Psychology and Education.

References

Bateson, G. (1972). *Steps to an ecology of mind*. San Francisco: Chandler Press.

Campbell, D. T. (1979). A tribal model of social system vehicle carrying scientific knowledge. *Knowledge: Creation, Diffusion, Utilization, 1*, 181–201.

Cooper, C., & Gandara, P. (Eds). (2001). When diversity works: Bridging families, peers, schools and communities at CREDE. *Journal of Education for Students Placed At Risk, 6* (1 & 2).

Datnow, A. (1999). The integrated reform projects of CREDE. *Journal of Education for Students Placed at Risk, 4* (1), 1–3.

Datnow, A., Borman, G., Stringfield, S., Rachuba, L., & Castellano, M. (2003). Comprehensive school reform in culturally and linguistically diverse contexts: Implementation and outcomes from a four-year study. *Educational Evaluation and Policy Analysis, 25* (2), 143–170.

Datnow, A., Hubbard, L., & Mehan, H. (2002). *Extending educational reform from one school to many*. London: RoutledgeFalmer.

Sarason, S. (1990). *The predictable failure of education reform*. San Francisco: Jossey-Bass.

Sechrest, L., & Figueredo, A. J. (1993). Program evaluation. *Annual Review of Psychology, 44*, 645–674.

Stringfield, S., & Land, D. (Eds.). (2002). *Educating At-Risk Students*. Chicago: National Society for the Study of Education.

Tharinger, D. J., Lambert, N. M., Bricklin, P. M., Feshbach, N., Johnson, N. F., Oakland, T. D., Paster, V. S., & Sanchez, W. (1996). Education reform: Challenges for psychology and psychologists. *Professional Psychology: Research and Practice, 27*, 24–33.

Vygotsky, L. S. (1978). *Mind in society: The development of higher psychological processes*. (Eds. and Trans. by M. Cole, V. John-Steiner, S. Scribner, & E. Souberman). Cambridge, MA: Harvard University Press.

Contributors

Marisa Castellano, *Associate Research Scientist*, Center for Social Organization of Schools, Johns Hopkins University, Baltimore, MD.

Amanda Datnow, *Associate Professor of Education*, USC Rossier School of Education, Los Angeles, CA.

Ian M. Evans, *Professor and Head,* School of Psychology—Te Kura Hinengaro Tangata, Massey University, Palmerston North, New Zealand.

Ronald Gallimore, *Professor of Psychology and Psychological Studies in Education*, University of California, Los Angeles, CA.

Claude N. Goldenberg, *Professor of Teacher Education and Associate Dean,* College of Education, California State University, Long Beach, CA.

Mari Haneda, *Assistant Professor,* Graduate Program of Language, Literacy and Culture in the College of Education, Ohio State University, Columbus, OH.

Lisa Tsoi Hoshmand, *Director of Counseling and Psychology,* Lesley University, Cambridge, MA.

Ashley E. Maynard, *Assistant Professor of Psychology,* University of Hawai'i at Mānoa. Honolulu, HI.

Clifford R. O'Donnell, *Professor of Psychology,* University of Hawai'i at Mānoa, Honolulu, HI.

Richard N. Roberts, *Director,* Early Intervention Research Institute, Utah State University, Logan, UT.

William M. Saunders, *Research Psychologist,* California State University, Long Beach, CA and *Director,* Getting Results Network.

Samuel C. Stringfield, *Professor and Co-Director,* Nystrand Center for Excellence in Education, University of Louisville, Louisville, KT.

Gordon Wells, *Professor of Education,* University of California, Santa Cruz, CA.

Lois A. Yamauchi, *Associate Professor of Education,* University of Hawai'i at Mānoa, Honolulu, HI.

Author Index

Abbot, D. A. *91, 93*
Abrams, S. B. *38*
Adams, G. R. *95*
Agnew, R. *87, 93*
Akers, A. L. *72, 75, 84*
Aladjem, D. *203*
Alessandri, M. *90, 96*
American Academy of Pediatrics *82*
Anderson, J. L. *182, 203*
Andrade, R. *114, 122*
Andrews, A. D. *87, 96*
Anson, R. J. *252*
Ariely, D. *28, 36*
Arnold, M. E. *87, 93*
Arns, F. A. *222, 232*
Au, K. H. *44, 46, 57, 60, 107, 108, 111, 122*
Aviezer, O. *43, 60*
Ayllon, T. *14, 36*

Baer, D. M. *15, 36*
Baker-Sennett, J. *42, 60*
Bakhtin, M. M. *150, 151, 152, 153, 175*
Bandura, A. *24, 36, 207, 209, 228, 229*
Banks, C. A. *122, 123*
Banks, J. A. *104, 122, 123, 181, 190, 197, 202*
Barker, R. G. *93, 94, 210, 211, 214, 217, 228*
Barnes, D. *164, 177*
Bascia, N. *187, 202*
Basu, A. M. *57*
Bateson, G. *236, 237, 256*
Battin-Pearson, S. *88, 96*
Bausano, M. *219, 231*
Beaman, J. *88, 99*
Becker, M. H. *229*
Becker, W. C. *253*
Bedinger, S. *203*
Behl, D. D. *72, 75, 84*

Bellack, A. S. *59, 83, 98, 123, 230, 250*
Bell, E. E. *78, 82*
Belle, D. *61*
Bereiter, C. *154, 155, 156, 168, 171, 177, 178*
Beresford, B. A. *211, 213, 228*
Bernheimer, L. P. *42, 61, 211, 219, 220, 225, 226, 228, 229, 231*
Bernstein, D. J. *36*
Berry, J. W. *58*
Berryman, J. S. *33, 37*
Bidder, R. T. *211, 232*
Bierman, K. *89, 94*
Big Brothers/Sisters *90, 94*
Billig, S. H. *118, 124*
Bingenheimer, J. B. *88, 100*
Binkoff, J. A. *38*
Blechman, E. A. *92, 94*
Blount, W. R. *88, 99*
Boggs, J. W. *44, 57, 107, 122, 249*
Borman, G. *180, 202, 243, 256*
Bornstein, M. H. *122*
Borvin, G. J. *88, 96*
Bouton, M. E. *18, 37*
Bradbury, H. *74, 78, 82, 83, 84*
Braukman, C. J. *98*
Bricklin, P. M. *256*
Brigham, N. *203*
Brislin, R. *104, 122*
Brofenbrenner, U. B. *93, 94*
Brown, A. L. *60, 98*
Brown, C. H. *88, 94*
Brown, F. *19, 37*
Brown, M. E. *98*
Brown, S. *180, 202*
Bruner, J. S. *41, 58, 59*
Buchard, J. *85, 94*
Buecker, B. *92, 94*
Burgess, R. *124*

Busfield, J. *122*
Bulter, S. *90, 94*
Buriel, R. *52, 59*
Burkholder, R. *241, 252*
Butts, R. *127, 149*

Cabot, R. C. *209*
Cacioppo, J. T. *25, 37*
Calkins, R. P. *44, 60*
Campbell, D. T. *237, 256*
Caplinger, T. E. *89, 95*
Carrington, B. *112, 124*
Carroll, J. H. *113, 119, 125*
Cartledge, N. *223, 230*
Carton, A. S. *178*
Carver, C. S. *223, 229*
Castellano, M. *7, 121, 218, 256*
Cazden, C. *123*
Ceppi, A. K. *109, 125*
Chasin, G. *148, 149*
Chattergy, V. *124*
Chavajay, P. *49, 57*
Chesney-Lind, M. *86, 98*
Chibnik, M. *217, 228*
Childs, C. P. *42, 51, 57, 58*
Christensen, A. *15, 37*
Christian, D. *125*
Chung, I. *88, 96*
Ciborowski, T. *250*
Civil, M. *114, 122*
Clark, C. *148, 149*
Claxton, G. *177, 178*
Cleland, J. *49, 57*
Cocking, R.R. *41, 58, 60, 252*
Coie, J. D. *87, 90, 94, 96*
Colby, A. *61*
Colby, S. M. *38*
Cole, M. *41, 56, 57, 84, 93, 94, 100, 104, 105, 124, 178, 215, 228*
Collier, V. P. *111, 122*
Collins, W. A. *231*
Conger, R. D. *88, 99*
Connolly, P. *114, 124*
Cooper, C. *243, 256*

Cooper, H. *91, 95*
Corbin, J. *184, 203*
Cosaro, W. A. *91, 94*
Cowan, P. A. *231*
Crago, M. *235, 249*
Cuban, L. *69, 82*
Cullingford, C. *87, 94*
Cummins, J. *111, 122, 181, 184, 187, 188, 190, 202*
Cunnigham, T. R. *249*
Curtis, T. *90, 94*
Cutts, R. I. *241, 252*

Dalton, S. S. *4, 9, 64, 84, 93, 103, 176, 172, 177, 204, 231, 233, 240, 241, 242, 252, 253*
Damon, W. *59*
D'Amoto, J. *67*
D'Andrade, R. G. *104, 114, 122, 231*
Darvill, J. *238*
Dasen, P. R. *41, 57*
Datnow, A. *7, 121, 182, 186, 198, 202, 203, 286, 243, 256*
D'Augelli, A. R. *9, 71, 82, 83, 84*
Davey, G. C. L. *17, 37*
Davis, E. *91, 93*
Day, R. *249*
Dembo, R. *88, 94*
DeRosier, M. E. *86, 96*
Derzon, J. H. *87, 97*
Dewey, J. *175, 177*
Dewsbury, D. A. *230*
Diament, C. *230*
Diamond, M. *237*
Diaz, T. *88, 96*
DiClemente, C. C. *28, 38*
Dimidjian, S. *24, 37*
Dishion, T. J. *87, 88, 89, 94, 95, 98*
Doherty, R. W. *119, 122*
Donnell, F. *43, 60*
DuBois, D. L. *91, 95, 98*
Duquette, G. *122*
Dyson, A. H. *106, 122*

Earls, F. *88, 98*
Eccles, J. S. *29, 37*
Eddy, J. M. *90, 95*
Edgerton, R. B. *217, 218, 228*
Edwards, C. P. *41, 43, 61, 211, 215, 232*
Eggins, S. *154, 177*
Eisenberg, N. *59*
Elliott, D. S. *87, 95*
Elmore, R. E. *180, 202*
Emler, N. *87, 95, 180, 202*
Endo, R. *124*
Ensher, E. A. *92, 95*
Erickson, F. *104, 105, 122*
Erickson, M. L. *87, 95*
Estrada, P. *4, 9, 64, 84, 93, 99, 103, 181, 204, 231, 253*
Estrada, S. *242*
Evans, I. M. *3, 4, 5, 13, 14, 16, 18, 19, 29, 31, 32, 33, 37, 38, 39, 207, 226, 228*
Eysenck, H. J. *23, 37*

Fairweather, G. *236*
Farley, C. *92, 95*
Farnworth, M. *87, 88, 99*
Farrington, D. P. *87, 94, 96, 97, 99, 100*
Farver, J. A. M. *42, 43, 57*
Fashola, O. *180, 203*
Featherstone, H. *213, 228*
Feldman, M. P. *230*
Feldman, R. A. *89, 95, 97*
Feshbach, N. *256*
Fetterman, D. M. *74, 78, 82*
Field, D. *231*
Figeira-McDonough, J. *88, 95*
Figueredo, A. J. *243, 256*
Fillmore, L. W. *181, 203*
Fink, D. *180, 203*
Fischer, J. *252*
Fischer, K. *61, 231*
Fishbein, M. *221, 222, 229*
Fo, W. S. O. *85, 86, 90, 95, 97*
Forman, D. *113, 125*
Forman, E. A. *229, 251*
Foster, M. *106, 111, 122*

Foster, S. *90, 96*
Fox, M. *91, 99*
Franklin, U. *154, 177*
Franks, C. M. *230*
Fredrickson, B. L. *25, 37*
French, S. E. *9, 71, 82, 83, 84*
Fullan, M. *129, 148, 149, 180, 202, 203*

Gallimore, R. *4, 7, 8, 9, 42, 43, 44, 56, 57, 60, 61, 64, 66, 69, 84, 93, 95, 99, 107, 116, 117, 120, 121, 122, 128, 140, 150, 151, 152, 156, 176, 178, 179, 196, 198, 204, 207, 208, 211, 212, 214, 215, 217, 220, 222, 225, 226, 227, 229, 231, 232, 233, 237, 238, 239, 240, 243, 245, 249, 250, 252*
Galyer, K. T. *31, 37*
Gamse, B. *203*
Gandara, P. *243, 256*
Garcia, E. *240*
Gardner, W. L. *25, 37*
Gaskins, S. *54, 57*
Gauvain, M. *52, 55, 58*
Gay, J. *41, 57*
Gayler, K. T. *31, 37*
Geertz, C. *105*
Genesee, F. *125*
Genessee, F. *187, 203*
Genishi, C. *106, 122*
George, W. H. *27, 38*
Glasser, L. N. *253*
Glasser, P. H. *253*
Glick, J. *41, 57*
Gold, M. *87, 95*
Goldenberg, C. *6, 7, 42, 57, 121, 128, 129, 130, 149, 150, 151, 177, 212, 218, 220, 222, 229*
Goldsmith, D. *42, 60*
Goncu, A. *54, 57, 58*
Gonzalez, N. *114, 123*
Gottfredson, D. C. *88, 96*
Gottfredson, G. D. *88, 96*
Gottlieb, D. J. *91, 96*
Grant, C. *181, 203*

Gray, O. P. *211, 232*
Greene, G. J. *79, 209, 230*
Greenfield, P. M. *41, 46, 47, 50, 51, 52, 53, 56, 57, 58, 59, 60, 61, 251*
Gresham, F. M. *222, 231*
Gribskov, L. S. *90, 95*
Griffin, K. *88, 96*
Grossman, J. B. *91, 96, 98, 100*
Guerra, N. G. *89, 100*
Gulliver, S. B. *38*
Gullotta, T. P. *95*
Guthrie, E. R. *26*
Guthrie, G. P. *57, 122*
Gutierrez, K. D. *115, 120, 122*

Habel, S. T. *251*
Haddan, E. E. *253*
Haertig, E. W. *110, 124*
Hagen, J. W. *57*
Halford, W. K. *39*
Hall, J. A. *87, 97*
Halliday, M. A. K. *152, 153, 156, 177, 178*
Haneda, M. *7, 216, 217*
Hannon, A. E. *14, 39*
Hanson-Schwoebel, K. *90, 94*
Hargreaves, A. *59, 180, 202, 203*
Harkness, S. *55, 58, 59, 61, 211, 215, 231*
Hansen, D. A. *231*
Harwood, R. L. *55, 59*
Hasan, H. *156, 178*
Hasenstab, K. *130, 150*
Hauser, R. M. *49, 59*
Hawkins, J. D. *88, 95, 96*
Hayashi, Y. *91, 96*
Hayes, S. C. *32, 37*
Heath, R. W. *67, 82, 106*
Heath, S. B. *106, 123*
Heckman, P. *148, 149*
Heide, K. M. *88, 99*
Henggeler, S. W. *87, 97*
Herman, R. *180, 203*
Heron, J. *66, 82*
Hersen, M. *59, 83, 98, 123, 230, 250*
Herrenkohl, T. L. *88, 96*

Herrington, C. *95, 250*
Herskovitz, M. J. *104, 122*
Hewes, G. *180, 202*
Heyman, R. E. *15, 39*
Hilberg, R. S. *119, 122*
Hilbert, S. M. *91, 99*
Hill, K. G. *88, 96*
Hirshfeld, L. A. *42, 59*
Hitchcock, P. J. *229*
Hofschire, L. *118, 124*
Hofstede, G. *109, 110, 123*
Hoge, D. R. *87, 96*
Holland, W. R. *236, 250*
Holloway, B. E. *91, 95*
Hopkins, D. *202*
Hosaka, C. J. *68, 82*
Hoshmand, L. T. *8, 227, 228, 252*
Howell, J. C. *3, 9, 90, 96*
Hubbard, L. *243, 256*
Huberman, M. *184, 203*
Hughes, D. L. *9, 82, 83, 84*
Hughes, J. N. *87, 93*
Hymes, D. *123*

Innocenti, M. S. *74, 82*

Jacka, N. *187, 202*
Jackson, A. P. *104, 122*
Jackson, D. *236*
Jackson, Y. *91, 96*
Jacob, E. *254*
Jacobson, N. S. *15, 24, 37*
Jang, S. J. *87, 88, 99*
Jeffery, R. *57*
Jejeebhoy, S. *49, 57*
Jensen, G. F. *87, 95*
Jessor, R. *61*
Johnson, A. *88, 217, 229*
Johnson, C. *99*
Johnson, N. F. *256*
John, V. *123*
John-Steiner, V. *84, 93, 95, 100, 124, 154, 178, 240, 250*
Jones, M. *198, 203*

Author Index

Jones, M. R. *94*
Jopp, D. A. *209, 230*
Jordan, C. *44, 46, 57, 60, 61, 66, 84, 107, 108, 109, 111, 116, 122, 124, 238, 254*

Kaftarian, S. J. *82*
Kagitscibaci, C. *56*
Kail, R. V. *57*
Kaloi, L. *113, 125*
Kanfer, F. H. *229*
Kaomea, J. *114, 123*
Kaufman, S. *213, 229*
Kavanagh, K. A. *88, 94*
Kazdin, A. E. *59, 83, 94, 98, 123, 230, 250*
Kearns, D. I. *203*
Keating, L. M. *90, 96*
Keller, H. *56, 59*
Kelley, L. *235*
Kelley-Baker, T. *90, 97*
Kelly, J. G. *209, 230, 235*
Kelly-Vance, L. *91, 99*
Kennan, K. *87, 96*
Kennedy, C. H. *225, 229*
Keogh, B. K. *69, 82, 211, 220, 225, 228, 229*
Kim, H. S. *18, 38*
Klein, M. W. *89, 96*
Klein, T. W. *44, 60*
Kluckhom, C. *104, 123*
Kobayashi, L. *250*
Koeppel, J. *223, 230*
Kohn, A. *19, 37*
Konrad, E. L. *75, 83*
Kornfein, M. *219, 231*
Kowal, M. *157, 178*
Krasner, L. *236*
Kroeber, A. L. *104, 123*
Krohn, M. D. *87, 88, 99*
Kuhn, T. S. *63, 83*
Kupersmidt, J. B. *86, 90, 96*
Kurose, M. *113, 125*

Lacasa, P. *42, 60*
LaGrange, R. L. *87, 100*
Lamb, M. E. *60, 122*

Lambert, N. M. *258*
Lambert, W. E. *111, 123*
Lamon, M. *171, 178*
Land, D. *243, 256*
Lange, J. *90, 97*
Lau-Smith, J. *109, 125*
Lave, J. *51, 58, 232*
Leadbeater, B. J. *96*
Lee, C. A. *110, 124, 178*
Lahey, B. B. *94*
Leiderman, P. *229*
Lennhoff, S. *253*
Leont'ev, A. N. *93, 97*
Leschied, W. A. *87, 96*
Levin, H. *148, 149*
LeVine, R. A. *49, 50, 59, 60, 211, 215, 229*
LeVine, S. E. *49, 50, 59*
Levis, D. J. *17, 18, 22, 37, 39*
Liabo, K. *91, 98*
Lieberman, A. *148, 149, 202*
Light, P. *253*
Linehan, M. M. *31, 38*
Lipsey, M. W. *87, 97*
Livert, D. *9, 82, 83, 84*
Lizotte, A. J. *87, 88, 99*
Locke, E. A. *223, 230*
Loeber, R. *87, 88, 94, 96, 97, 99*
Lortie, D. *218, 229*
LoSciuto, L. *91, 97, 99*
Lucas, P. *91, 98*
Lucca Irizarry, N. *55, 59*
Lydgate, T. *86, 97*
Lyon, E. *122*
Lyon, J. M. *87, 97*

MacDonald, G. *207, 230*
MacDonald, S. *207, 230, 237*
Madden, N. *180, 203*
Magrab, P. R. *75, 82, 83, 84*
Maguin, E. *88, 97*
Mahn, H. *154, 178*
Majone, G. *224, 225, 230*
Malave, L. *122*
Malloy, P. F. *17, 22, 37*

Manos, M. J. *86, 98*
Marcelletti, D. *130, 150*
Markman, H. *39*
Marlatt, G. A. *27, 38*
Marquart, J. M. *83*
Marsella, A. *237, 250*
Martell, C. R. *24, 37*
Martini, M. *125*
Maton, K. L. *96*
Masem, E. *203*
Matheson, C. *42, 61*
Maurice, A. *92, 94*
Maxfield, M. G. *88, 97*
Maynard, A. E. *4, 5, 42, 46, 50, 51, 53, 55, 58, 59, 61, 125, 213, 216*
Mayseless, O. *43, 60*
McCord, J. *87, 94, 97, 209, 230*
McDougall, D. *129, 130, 149*
McFadden, A. S. *16, 38*
McGee-Banks, C. A. *202*
McGilley, K. *178*
McGrath, J. E. *63, 83*
McLaughlin, B. *240*
McLeod, B. *252*
McMahon, P. *203*
McNeil, R. J. *88, 96*
McPartland, J. M. *91, 97*
Meadow, A. *253*
Meadows, F. B. *104, 123*
Mehan, H. *117, 123, 243, 256*
Mehra, B. *113, 123*
Melton, G. B. *250*
Menard, S. *87, 95*
Merchant, B. *123*
Meredith, W. H. *91, 93*
Merritt, D. M. *209, 230*
Mertinko, E. *90, 97*
Metcalf, J. *25, 38*
Meyer, L. H. *33, 37*
Meyer, L. M. *181, 203*
Meyer, S. *118, 124*
Michael, J. *14, 36*
Michener, J. A. *80*
Middlestadt, E. E. *229*

Miles, M. *184, 203*
Miller, J. *55, 59*
Miller, L. *148, 149*
Miller, N. E. *21, 38, 88, 96*
Miller, P. M. *49, 60*
Miller-Johnson, S. *87, 94*
Millsap, M. *203*
Minick, N. *178, 222, 229, 232, 251*
Mischel, W. *25, 38, 207, 209, 210, 214, 230*
Moll, L. C. *114, 122, 123, 249*
Montemayor, R. *95*
Monti, P. M. *38*
Morris, E. K. *98*
Morrison, J. *87, 94*
Mosenthal, P. *150*
Moss, M. *203*
Mowrer, O. H. *21, 38*
Moylan, T. *52, 60*
Mulligan, I. *203*
Murphy, S. E. *92, 95*
Murray, H. A. *222, 230*

National Commission on Excellence in Education *127, 150*
Nelson, R. O. *29, 38*
Nesselrodt, P. *203*
Nettles, S. M. *91, 97*
Neville, H. A. *91, 95*
Newcomb, T. *235*
Notaro, P. C. *88, 100*
Note, M. *253*
Novotney, L. C. *90, 92, 97*
Nucci, L. P. *58*

Oakes, J. *149, 180, 198, 203, 207*
Oakland, T. *256*
O'Brien, G. *130, 150*
Ochs, E. *222, 230*
O'Donnell, C. R. *6, 9, 42, 43, 56, 59, 70, 71, 83, 85, 86, 87, 89, 90, 91, 93, 95, 96, 97, 98, 99, 116, 120, 123, 210, 214, 221, 222, 230, 233, 237, 241, 250, 252, 253, 254*
Olson, D. R. *177*
Olver, R. R. *41, 59*

Author Index

O'Malley, A. *203*
Orford, J. R. *97, 230*
Osgood, W. *98*
Otis, D. *253*
Ottewill, R. *178*
Overman, L. *180, 202*
Owen, V. *19, 37*

Palmer, D. J. *91, 99*
Pandina, R. J. *87, 100*
Pandy, J. *58*
Parke, R. D. *52, 59*
Parra, G. R. *91, 95*
Parsons, T. *235*
Paster, V. S. *256*
Patterson, C. J. *86, 96*
Patterson, G. R. *20, 38, 87, 88, 89, 94, 95, 98*
Pavlov, I. *17*
Peet, D. Y. *68, 83*
Pellrgrini, A. D. *60*
Phillips E. L. *85, 98*
Philips, S. U. *106, 109, 123*
Piaget, J. *4, 9, 42, 54, 59*
Pinal, A. *119, 122*
Plett, J. D. *67, 82*
Poole, E. D. *87, 89, 98*
Poortinga, Y. *58*
Poulin, F. *87, 94*
Powers, E. *208, 230*
Pressman, J. L. *230*
Prochaska, J. O. *28, 38*
Pugh-Lilly, A. O. *91, 95*
Pukui, M. K. *110, 124*

Quartz, H. *149*
Quinones, S. *203*
Quiroz, B. *46, 47, 59, 60, 61*

Rachman, S. *24, 38*
Rachuba, L. *256*
Raeff, C. *47, 59*
Rajala, A. K. *91, 97*
Ramsey, E. *223, 231*
Rappaport, J. *63, 83*

Raudenbush, S. W. *88, 98*
Reason, P. *66, 74, 78, 82, 83, 84*
Reeve, A. *203*
Reich, L. C. *41, 59*
Reicher, S. *87, 95*
Resch, N. L. *91, 98, 100*
Rescorla, R. A. *17, 38*
Revenson, T. A. *3, 9, 64, 82, 83, 84*
Rhodes, J. E. *91, 95, 96, 98*
Richman, A. L. *49, 60*
Rieber, R. W. *178*
Rigoli, R. M. *87, 89, 98*
RMC Research Corp. *118, 124*
Roberts, H. *91, 98*
Roberts, R. N. *5, 6, 64, 66, 67, 68, 69, 72, 74, 75, 82, 83, 84, 209, 212, 213, 225, 250*
Rogers, C. R. *13, 14, 38*
Rogers, E. M. *224, 230*
Rogoff, B. *4, 9, 41, 43, 51, 55, 57, 58, 60, 93, 98, 113, 115, 120, 123, 124, 211, 222, 230, 232*
Rohner, R. P. *104, 124*
Rosenfeld, A. *229*
Rohsenow, D. J. *27, 30, 38*
Ross, A. *87, 95*
Ross, S. *180, 182, 203, 204*
Rothstein-Fisch, C. *46, 60*
Rotter, J. B. *222, 230*
Rourke, P. *18, 39*
Royse, D. *91, 98*
Rubonis, A. V. *38*

Sagi, A. *43, 60*
Saldivar, E. *130, 150*
Salkovskis, P. M. *23, 24, 38*
Sampson, R. J. *88, 98*
Sanchez, W. *256*
Sarason, S. B. *80, 81, 84, 127, 128, 148, 150, 218, 230, 245, 256*
Satterfield, D. *253*
Saunders, W. M. *6, 7, 121, 129, 130, 149, 150, 218, 222*
Saxe, G. B. *52, 58, 60*
Scardamalia, M. *171, 177, 178*

Schaffer, E. *203*
Scharmer, O. *78, 79, 84*
Schegloff, E. *138, 160*
Scheier, M. F. *88, 96, 223, 229*
Schellenbach, C. J. *96*
Scherer, M. M. *128, 150*
Schmeidler, J. *88, 94*
Schmidt, P. *150*
Schnell, B. *50, 59*
Schwendinger, H. *87, 88, 99*
Schwendinger, J. *87, 88, 99*
Scribner, S. *41, 57, 84, 100, 124, 178*
Scudder, R. G. *88, 99*
Sechrest, L. B. *226, 243, 252, 256*
Seidman, E. *9, 82, 83, 84*
Selinger, M. *178*
Self-Kelly, R. *91, 93*
Senge, P. *64, 74, 78, 79, 84*
Sharma, D. *61, 231*
Shannon, L. W. *88, 99*
Sharp, J. *41, 57*
Sheldon, S. *253*
Sheldon, T. *91, 98*
Sherman, D. K. *18, 38*
Shinn, M. *9, 65, 82, 83, 84*
Shweder, R. A. *61, 233*
Silverman, I. J. *88, 99*
Simon, H. *218, 231*
Simons, R. L. *88, 99*
Singer, J. L. *54, 60*
Skinner, B. F. *13, 14, 20, 38*
Skinner, M. L. *89, 95*
Skolnick, A. *219, 231*
Slade, D. *154, 177*
Slavin, R. E. *180, 203*
Sleeter, C. *181, 203*
Slicker, E. K. *91, 99*
Sloat, K. C. M. *44, 60*
Smagorinsky, P. *178*
Small, M. A. *250*
Smith, L. *182, 203, 204*
Snively, F. *182, 203*
Snow, C.E. *111, 124*
Solarz, A. L. *96*
Sonkowsky, M. *91, 99*

Souberman, E. *84, 100, 124, 178*
Speidel, G. E. *44, 57, 60, 249, 250*
Spencer-Oately, H. *110, 124*
Spindler, G. *251*
Spindler, L. *251*
Staats, A. W. *18, 20, 25, 31, 38, 209, 231, 237*
Steinberg, L. *87, 88, 99*
Steiner, J. *240*
Stevenson, H. *58*
Stokes, D. E. *227, 231*
Stone, C. A. *229, 251*
Stoolmiller, M. *89, 95*
Stouthamer-Loeber, M. *87, 96*
Strauss, A. *184, 203*
Strauss, C. *214, 231*
Stringfeild, S. *7, 121, 180, 182, 203, 204, 218, 233, 243, 244, 245, 256*
Strosahl, K. D. *32, 37*
Stuart, R. B. *15, 39*
Sullivan, J. *129, 149*
Super, C. *58, 59, 61, 211, 215, 231*
Swanson, G. E. *231*
Szasz, T. *14*

Tamura, E. *124*
Tanaka-Matsumi, J. *251*
Tapia Uribe, M. F. *49, 50, 60*
Taylor, A. S. *90, 91, 97, 99*
Ten Houten, W. *91, 96*
Tharinger, D. J. *245, 256*
Tharp, R. G. *3, 4, 5, 6, 7, 8, 9, 13, 14, 36, 39, 42, 43, 44, 45, 56, 57, 59, 60, 61, 63, 64, 66, 69, 70, 71, 80, 83, 84, 85, 86, 87, 90, 93, 95, 98, 99, 100, 103, 104, 105, 108, 109, 111, 112, 114, 116, 117, 119, 120, 121, 122, 123, 124, 125, 128, 129, 140, 149, 150, 151, 152, 156, 157, 176, 177, 178, 179, 180, 181, 182, 184, 188, 196, 197, 198, 204, 207, 208, 209, 210, 212, 214, 215, 217, 220, 221, 222, 225, 226, 227, 228, 230, 231, 233, 234, 235, 236, 237, 238, 239, 240, 241, 242, 243, 244, 245, 246, 249, 250, 251, 252, 253, 254*
Thompson, E. P. *208, 231*

Thompson, L. A. *91, 99*
Thompson, R. A. *250*
Thornberry, T. P. *87, 88, 99*
Thorndike, E. L. *26*
Thorne, G. L. *85, 100, 253*
Tierney, J. P. *91, 92, 100*
Tolan, P. H. *89, 100*
Tomishima, M. A. *90, 96*
Tonry, M. *97*
Townsend, T. N. *91, 97*
Torrance, N. *177*
Triandis, H. C. *229*
Troyna, B. *112, 124*
Trueba, H. T. *57, 122, 251*
Tremblay, R. *94, 97*
Trow, W. C. *252*
Trumbull, E. *46, 60, 61*
Tulkin, S. *229*
Turiel, E. *58*
Tyler, V. *85, 94*

U.S. Department of Education *149, 204*
Ullman, L. *236*
Unger, W. *18, 39*
UNICEF *49, 50, 61*

Valentine, J. C. *91, 95*
Van Ijzendoorn, M. H. *43, 60*
Van Kammen, W. B. *87, 96*
Van Patton, D. E. *91, 100*
Voeltz, L. M. *19, 29, 39*
Vogt, E. Z. *43, 61*
Vogt, L. A. *123, 254*
Von der Lippe, A. L. *50, 61, 63*
Vygotsky, L. S. *41, 65, 78, 93, 105, 124, 151, 152, 154, 155, 157, 175, 180, 238, 240, 249, 256*

Wagner, D. *58*
Wagner, T. *148, 150*
Walker, H. M. *223, 231*
Wandersman, A. *79, 80, 82, 84*
Warr, M. *87, 88, 100*
Warren, N. *57*

Washington State Institute for Public Policy *100*
Wasik, B. H. *75, 84*
Watson, D. L. *13, 36, 39, 226, 231, 237, 254*
Webster, S. W. *253*
Weed, K. A. *19, 37*
Weisner, T. S. *41, 42, 43, 44, 54, 55, 57, 61, 66, 84, 116, 124, 211, 212, 214, 215, 219, 226, 229, 231, 232*
Weiss, R. L. *15, 39*
Wells, G. *7, 155, 157, 174, 178, 198, 203, 216, 217*
Wertenbroch, K. *28, 36, 177*
Wertsch, J. V. *94, 100, 178, 222, 229, 232*
West, D. J. *87, 100*
West, F. *253*
Wetzel, R. J. *8, 9, 14, 39, 85, 90, 99, 100, 207, 208, 209, 210, 214, 217, 225, 231, 236, 253*
Whitbeck, L. B. *88, 99*
White, H. R. *87, 100*
Whiting, B. B. *41, 43, 61, 62, 93, 100, 211, 215, 232*
Whiting, J. M. *41, 62*
Widom, C. S. *88, 97, 100*
Wigfield, A. *29, 37*
Wildavsky, A. *224, 225, 230*
Wilhelm, P. *109, 113, 125*
Williams, L. *88, 94*
Willis, A. *123*
Wilson, G. T. *14, 39*
Wilson, H. *87, 88, 100*
Wilson, K. G. *32, 37, 42, 59, 70, 83, 93, 98, 241, 250, 254*
Winitz, H. *123*
Winkler, R. C. *16, 28, 39*
Wishart, M. C. *211, 231*
Witmer, H. *208, 230*
Wodarski, J. S. *89, 95*
Wolf, M. M. *15, 39, 236*
Wong, R. S. K. *49, 59*
Wood, D. *4, 9*
Woodhead, M. *253*
Woodruff, D. *203*

Wothke, W. *88, 94*
Wright, C. *124, 228*
Wright, H. F. *113, 210*
Wyatt, T. *119, 125*
Wynn, J. *178*

Yamauchi, L. A. *4, 6, 9, 64, 84, 93, 99, 103, 109, 112, 113, 115, 117, 118, 119, 124, 125, 181, 204, 212, 213, 231, 233, 241, 242, 244, 246, 252, 253, 254*

Yin, R. *184, 204*
Yoder, N. *203*
Yoerger, K. *87, 88, 98*
Yoshikawa, H. *9, 65, 82, 83, 84*

Zambrano, I. *58*
Zhaang, Q. *87, 96*
Zimmerman *88, 100*
Zukow, P. G. *49, 62*

Subject Index

Academic achievement 5, 6, 7, 47, 85, 105, 117, 126, 128, 129, 130, 132, 135, 146, 147, 148, 180, 243
Academic Achievement Leadership Teams (AALT) 130, 135, 136, 137, 138, 139, 140, 141, 142, 143, 144
Acceptance and commitment therapy 15, 32
Action plan 72, 73, 74
Active avoidance paradigm 21
Activity setting theory 5, 42, 43, 46, 48, 49, 52, 54, 56, 86, 93, 240
Activity settings 5, 7, 42, 43, 44, 45, 46, 47, 48, 49, 51, 52, 53, 54, 55, 56, 70, 71, 86, 87, 89, 93, 116, 117, 118, 120, 121, 128, 207, 208, 210, 211, 213, 214, 215, 216, 217, 218, 219, 220, 220, 222, 223, 224, 225, 227, 242, 250
Adolescents 19, 87, 254
Analysis of resistance 215
Artifacts 104, 105, 114, 174
At-risk peers/students/youth 27, 67, 86, 87, 88, 89, 90, 91, 92, 117, 182, 202, 214, 236, 241, 242
Audrey Cohen College System of Education 182, 183, 188, 189, 190, 194, 199
Autonomy 13, 29, 30, 32, 33, 36
Avoidance behavior 21, 23, 24, 27, 28, 29, 31, 32

Behavior change interventions 3, 4, 7, 89, 128, 219, 221, 223, 224, 225, 226, 227
Behavior therapy 3, 4, 5, 13, 14, 15, 16, 17, 19, 21, 24, 26, 28, 29, 31, 32, 33, 34, 35, 227, 250
Behavioral assessment 19
Behavioral modification 3, 4, 5, 8, 14, 20, 48, 63, 85, 86, 103, 120, 121, 208, 209, 210, 214, 221, 222, 225, 226, 227, 236, 250, 253

Big Brothers Big Sisters 90
Bilingual schools 111, 115, 186, 187, 188, 197
Bridging Cultures study 5, 46, 47
Buddy System 85, 86, 90

Center for Research on Education, Diversity, & Excellence (CREDE) 103, 181, 242, 244, 245, 248, 252
Child development 41, 42, 43, 55, 56, 63, 67, 69, 251, 252, 253
Classical conditioning 4, 16, 17, 18, 19, 21, 24, 36
Clinical psychology 4, 26, 35, 63, 209, 235, 237, 242, 247, 254
Coalition of Essential Schools 182, 183, 184, 186, 198, 190
Co-construction of meaning 167, 168, 242, 245
Cognition 4, 5, 23, 24, 54, 63, 70, 87, 114, 220, 240, 241, 251
Cognitive behavior therapy 13, 250
Collaborative knowledge 154, 156, 159, 171, 175
Comer School Development Program 180, 182, 185, 192, 195
Community & research tools 105, 112, 115, 119, 243
Community development 64, 70, 72, 73, 74, 75, 76, 77, 78, 113, 158, 164, 168, 171, 174, 175
Community involvement 3, 55, 70, 72, 73, 75, 76, 77, 78, 117, 118, 119, 158
Community of learners 5, 63, 64, 65, 78, 79, 81, 82, 237
Community partnerships 70, 72, 73, 75, 76, 77, 114, 115, 116, 130
Community-Peer Model 89, 90
Community psychology 3, 4, 5, 6, 8, 64, 65, 209, 214, 226, 252

Community research 5, 6, 65, 67, 69, 70, 73, 74, 75, 76, 77, 79, 112, 164, 237
Community self-assessment 74
Community service mapping 74
Community settings 63, 66, 67, 68, 69
Computer Supported Intentional Learning Environment (CSILE) 171, 177
Conditioned response (CR) 17, 21
Conditioned stimulus (CS) 17, 21
Connecting across settings 129, 138, 139, 140, 141, 142
Contingency management 14, 19, 36
Conversation 7, 48, 49, 76, 80, 92, 107, 108, 115, 119, 144, 150, 152, 154, 155, 156, 157, 164, 170, 173, 174, 175, 176, 177, 216, 217, 254
Coping 22, 24, 28, 30
Core knowledge sequence 182, 186
Cultural context 3, 4, 5, 7, 8, 34, 41, 43, 52, 55, 56, 119, 120, 186
Cultural historical activity theory 93, 105, 151, 182, 240, 249, 250, 251
Culture 4, 5, 6, 15, 16, 33, 52, 53, 54, 55, 56, 65, 67, 70, 71, 80, 104, 105, 106, 108, 109, 110, 112, 114, 115, 116, 118, 119, 120, 143, 144, 148, 152, 153, 180, 181, 185, 187, 191, 192, 193, 195, 197, 209, 210, 211, 213, 214, 217, 218, 219, 220, 225, 227, 228, 237, 244, 245, 248, 251, 252, 254

Daily routines 19, 207, 217, 218, 219, 220, 221, 225, 226
Decontextualized talk 50, 243
Developmental psychology 3, 4, 5, 8, 41, 52, 54, 56, 64, 221
Deviant behavior 87, 207, 209, 228
Dialogue 31, 111, 119, 140, 152, 153, 155, 171, 174, 176, 182, 222, 242
Discourse 7, 23, 63, 151, 152, 154, 155, 156, 168, 170, 198
Distributed leadership 171
District ESL policies 185, 186, 187, 188, 189, 190

Early Intervention Research Institute 65
Ecocultural theory 42, 66, 67, 215
Education 3, 4, 5, 6, 7, 8, 42, 44, 49, 50, 55, 64, 66, 67, 68, 69, 70, 71, 77, 119, 120, 151, 153, 157, 175, 177, 179, 180, 181, 182, 185, 186, 187, 188, 191, 193, 194, 195, 196, 197, 198, 199, 201, 209, 218, 219, 226, 227, 239, 240, 242, 245, 246, 247, 248, 249, 251, 252, 255
Effective classroom instruction 4, 7, 44, 107, 114, 117, 118, 119, 121, 142, 148, 151, 156, 158, 159, 162, 168, 170, 171, 174, 175, 179, 181, 182, 190
Emotion regulation 31
Empowerment evaluation 77, 78
English Language Learners (ELL) 6, 115, 131, 163, 186, 187, 180, 197
English as a Second Language (ESL) 179, 185, 186, 187, 189, 190, 192, 218
Establishing settings 129, 134, 135, 136, 137, 138
Evaluation 64, 65, 66, 69, 70, 71, 73, 77, 78, 79, 90, 92, 118, 130, 132, 182, 226, 238, 243, 244, 252
Extinction 17, 19, 21, 22, 27, 29, 30

Faculty meetings 7, 128, 133, 134, 135, 139, 143
Families 3, 6, 8, 46, 47, 48, 50, 52, 54, 64, 65, 66, 67, 68, 69, 70, 71, 72, 73, 74, 75, 76, 77, 79, 80, 87, 88, 89, 90, 93, 103, 109, 113, 129, 163, 191, 195, 196, 208, 209, 210, 211, 212, 213, 219, 220, 225, 243, 251, 253
Five Standards for Effective Pedagogy 118, 119, 123, 181, 184, 196, 198, 242

Getting Results Model 129, 130, 135, 136, 138, 140, 146, 147
Goals 29, 44, 70, 73, 75, 76, 81, 107, 113, 128, 129, 130, 132, 133, 136, 141, 143, 147, 148, 154, 156, 176, 181, 193, 197, 198, 199, 211, 215, 219, 221, 222, 223

Subject Index

Grade level team meeting *128, 133, 135, 136, 137, 139, 140, 141, 142, 146, 147, 148, 220, 222, 223, 228*
Guatemalan Maya *49, 236*

Hands-on tactile activity *163, 164, 167, 170, 175*
Hawai'i Community Research Project (HCRP) *239*
Hawaiian Creole English *107, 108, 250*
Hawaiian Studies Program (HSP) *117, 118*
Heterogeneous classrooms *6, 112, 116, 117, 118, 189*
High-risk peers *89*
Home language instruction *108, 111, 158, 186, 187, 188, 189, 190, 191, 202*
Home-school match *44, 45, 46, 47, 48, 103, 105, 106, 107, 108, 109, 111, 114, 115, 119, 121, 157, 196, 197, 212*
Human agency *227*

Immigrants *16, 111, 179, 185, 240*
Improvable objects *156, 157, 170, 173, 174, 176*
Inclusion *73, 104, 188, 192, 193, 228*
Indicators of success *129, 130, 180*
Individualism vs. collectivism *46, 48, 108, 119, 120, 219*
Innovative settings *50, 158, 185, 219, 224, 241, 244*
Insider/outsider issues *6, 112, 113, 114, 120*
Instructional conversation *7, 8, 119, 151, 152, 154, 155, 156, 157, 164, 170, 173, 174, 175, 176*
Intellectual development *175*
Intentions *28, 29, 154, 222*
Intersubjectivity (see also shared meaning) *6, 71, 76, 78, 79, 86, 87, 105, 106, 244*
Intervention implementation *7, 15, 16, 31, 46, 47, 66, 67, 68, 73, 74, 75, 76, 79, 80, 81, 85, 90, 91, 92, 93, 211, 212, 214, 225, 226*

Intervention programs/methods *13, 15, 66, 67, 68, 69, 70, 71, 72, 73, 85, 79, 90, 91, 92, 93, 109, 191, 192, 208, 209, 210, 222, 235, 236, 238, 239, 241, 250*

Joint productive activity *5, 47, 48, 70, 78, 105, 107, 108, 116, 118, 119, 137, 141, 151, 152, 153, 154, 155, 157, 174, 175, 176, 182, 188, 207, 216, 221, 222, 224, 225, 242*
Juvenile delinquency *3, 6, 8, 85, 88, 89, 90, 91, 252*
Juvenile Mentoring Program (JUMP) *90, 91, 92, 93*

Kamehameha Early Education Program (KEEP) *6, 44, 67, 103, 108, 109, 238, 239, 240, 241, 242, 243, 245, 247, 249, 251, 255*
Knowledge construction *152, 153, 154, 155, 164, 169, 170, 171, 174, 175*

Language development *119, 189, 190*
Latino *5, 46, 48, 129, 131, 183, 240*
Leadership *129, 132, 133, 138, 140, 143, 144, 145, 148, 176, 185, 186, 198, 199*
Leadership team model *133, 136, 139, 140, 141, 142, 143, 185*
Learning settings *127*
Levers of settings *221, 225*
Limited English Proficient (LEP) students *163, 186, 188, 189, 190, 197*
Literacy *68, 111, 134, 182, 186, 211, 242, 245*

Maternal schooling *5, 49*
Mechanisms of change *16, 17, 26, 29, 32, 36, 41, 55*
Mentors *85, 88, 91, 92, 93, 151*
Mentoring *7, 85, 86, 90, 91, 92, 93, 207, 227, 240, 250*
Mentor-youth relationship *91, 92*
Modern Red Schoolhouse *182, 183, 190, 191, 199*

Motivation *19, 26, 28, 29, 34, 35, 41, 43, 44, 47, 49, 52, 53, 54, 105, 108, 111, 116, 117*
Multicultural curriculum *187, 193*
Multilingual schools *7*

Native Hawaiians *5, 6, 45, 110, 112, 114, 116, 212, 213, 238, 239, 250, 251*
Natural environment *8, 14, 16, 19, 53, 85, 86, 207, 208, 209, 210, 219, 223, 226, 228, 236, 253*
Natural mentors *6, 85, 88*
Navajo *5, 44, 45, 47, 109, 241, 248, 252*
Neighborhoods *3, 130, 185, 209, 211, 250, 254*
New American Schools *182, 199, 185*

Office of Juvenile Justice and Delinquency Prevention (OJJDP) *90*
Opening Doors into Rural Communities (ODRC) *66, 71, 72, 73, 74, 75, 76, 77, 79, 80, 81*
Operant conditioning *4, 16, 18, 19, 21, 36*
Organizational change *7, 121, 127, 128, 135, 196, 197, 198*
Otherness *152, 234, 236*

Parent-teacher conference *47, 48*
Participant involvement *73, 154, 155, 156, 157, 171, 173*
Participation structures *175*
Participatory action research (PAR) *71, 72, 73, 74, 75, 76, 78*
Pedagogy *7, 114, 118, 158, 159, 162, 163, 181, 184, 190, 196, 198, 242, 244, 255*
Peer network effect *86, 87*
Peer networks *6, 68, 86, 87, 89, 90, 91, 210*
Peers *4, 14, 31, 33, 44, 45, 55, 87, 88, 89, 93, 107, 108, 117, 118, 176, 250, 252*
Personal factors *128, 213, 214*
Personnel *43, 45, 46, 47, 48, 49, 51, 52, 56, 103, 215, 218, 219, 221*
Pine Elementary School *6, 7, 127, 128, 130, 131, 132, 133, 134, 135, 136, 137, 139, 141, 143, 144, 145, 146, 147, 148*

Pluralistic research methods *105, 120, 181, 184, 228, 243, 244*
Power *14, 18, 19, 29, 65, 66, 67, 77, 78, 108, 110, 112, 120, 127, 135, 181, 207, 212, 222, 223, 227, 245*
Prekindergarden Education Program (PREP) *66, 67, 69, 70, 71, 77, 78, 80*
Professional development *4, 5, 127, 128, 134, 145, 148, 164, 175, 243*
Prevention programs *85, 86, 89, 90, 93, 180, 181, 207, 210, 226*
Program assessment *86, 89*
Progressive discourse *154, 155, 156, 168, 170*
Pro-social behavior *85, 87, 89*
Psychology *7, 55, 65, 70, 235, 238, 243, 246, 247, 248, 250, 251, 253, 255*

Reciprocal influence *15, 16*
Reform adaptations *180, 188*
Reinforcement contingencies *18, 19, 20, 21, 24, 25, 27, 34, 85, 167, 208, 214*
Relapse prevention *27, 29*
Responsive interactions (conversations) *151, 155, 176, 217*
Role expectations *33, 52, 109*
Role theory *235*

School change *48, 180*
School improvement research *179, 180*
School reform *181, 183, 185, 186, 196, 198, 199, 201, 221, 226*
School settings *4, 128, 129, 197, 220*
Schooling *4, 42, 48, 49, 50, 51, 56, 68, 105, 151, 153, 179, 181, 197, 211, 234, 239, 240, 242, 243, 245, 249, 252*
Schools *3, 6, 7, 68, 69, 86, 87, 88, 89, 103, 105, 107, 109, 110, 111, 113, 114, 117, 119, 121, 127, 128, 130, 131, 132, 133, 134, 136, 138, 143, 144, 147, 148, 149, 157, 171, 180, 181, 182, 183, 184, 185, 186, 188, 189, 190, 191, 192, 193, 194, 195, 197, 198, 199, 190, 201, 207, 218, 220, 222, 223, 234, 236, 237, 238, 240, 241, 244, 251, 254*

Subject Index

Science inquiry *163, 164, 168*
Scripts *43, 45, 47, 49, 51, 52, 53, 55, 56*
Self regulation *4, 13, 26, 27, 28, 29, 30*
Self-determination *14, 32, 33*
Self-directed change *13, 30, 35, 254*
Semiotic mediation *152*
Shared meaning (see also intersubjectivity) *6, 152, 153, 155*
Sibling schooling *5, 49, 50*
Social constructs *63, 64, 66, 78, 193, 194, 197, 198, 214, 225*
Social/cultural context *3, 4, 5, 8, 14, 15, 27, 31, 33, 34, 36, 41, 42, 43, 55, 56, 115, 116, 139, 148, 179, 180, 181, 185, 193, 196, 207, 209, 225, 226, 227, 235, 238, 239, 240, 241, 245, 251, 252, 253*
Social networks *6, 34, 68, 86, 87, 93*
Society for Organizational Learning (SOL) *79*
Standard achievement *105, 130, 136, 143, 144*
Stereotyping *7, 112, 114, 115, 116, 120, 195, 213*
Strange situation procedure *54*
Success For All/Roots and Wings *180, 182, 183, 184, 189, 193, 196, 190*
Sustaining settings *128, 129, 134, 137, 138, 143, 144, 145, 146, 147, 148*
Systems integration *76*

Tasks *24, 28, 29, 41, 43, 45, 47, 49, 51, 52, 53, 71, 76, 105, 142, 215, 216*
Teacher focus group *133, 135, 136, 137, 138, 139, 140, 141, 143, 145, 146*
Teaching *4, 22, 24, 27, 30, 33, 35, 44, 45, 47, 51, 103, 111, 118, 119, 127, 129, 131, 136, 137, 140, 141, 142, 145, 148, 149, 174, 175, 179, 181, 182, 187, 188, 193, 195, 197, 211, 215, 215, 225, 226, 237, 238, 240, 241, 243, 245, 246, 247, 249, 252, 253*
Theory of change *4, 13, 24, 34*
Ties that bind *5, 63, 76, 81*
Triadic model *85, 140, 253*
Two-factor theory *21*

Unconditioned response (UCR) *17, 21*
Unconditioned stimulus (UCS) *17, 21, 22*
Utterances *152, 153, 154, 155*

Weaving apprenticeship *41, 50, 51, 52, 56*

Youth culture *91, 107, 109, 110, 118*
Youth gang *87*
Yucatec Maya *54*

Zinacantec Maya *43, 50, 51, 52, 53, 213, 216*
Zuni *103, 112, 115, 116, 241*

Joseph L. DeVitis & Linda Irwin-DeVitis
GENERAL EDITORS

As schools struggle to redefine and restructure themselves, they need to be cognizant of the new realities of adolescents. Thus, this series of monographs and textbooks is committed to depicting the variety of adolescent cultures that exist in today's post-industrial societies. It is intended to be a primarily qualitative research, practice, and policy series devoted to contextual interpretation and analysis that encompasses a broad range of interdisciplinary critique. In addition, this series will seek to provide a pragmatic, pro-active response to the current backlash of conservatism that continues to dominate political discourse, practice, and policy. This series seeks to address issues of curriculum theory and practice; multicultural education; aggression and violence; the media and arts; school dropouts; homeless and runaway youth; alienated youth; at-risk adolescent populations; family structures and parental involvement; and race, ethnicity, class, and gender studies.

Send proposals and manuscripts to the general editors at:
> Joseph L. DeVitis & Linda Irwin-DeVitis
> College of Education and Human Development
> University of Louisville
> Louisville, KY 40292-0001

To order other books in this series, please contact our Customer Service Department at:
> (800) 770-LANG (within the U.S.)
> (212) 647-7706 (outside the U.S.)
> (212) 647-7707 FAX

or browse online by series at:
> WWW.PETERLANGUSA.COM